Health Benefits

Soy Boys and Snowflake Myths

Bo-Jack Terry

ISBN: 978-1-77961-465-0
Imprint: Holy Fuck Shut The Fuck Up
Copyright © 2024 Bo-Jack Terry.
All Rights Reserved.

Contents

Introduction   1
The Rise of Soy Boys and Snowflakes   1

Understanding Health Benefits   9
Importance of Health and Wellness   9
Role of Diet in Overall Health   25
Different Perspectives on Health Benefits   40

Debunking Soy Boy Myths   57
Dispelling Misconceptions about Soy   57
Unraveling Soy Boy Stereotypes   67

Exploring the Snowflake Phenomenon   81
Understanding the Snowflake Generation   81
Debunking Snowflake Myths   96

Health Benefits of Soy Consumption   111
Nutritional Profile of Soy   111
Cardiovascular Health   116
Bone Health   125
Cancer Prevention   136
Hormonal Balance   148

Promoting a Balanced Approach   157
The Importance of Diversity in Diet   157
Educating About Nutrition   171
Supporting Mental Health   181

Conclusion   195

Recap of Key Points 195
Embracing Diversity and Wellness 204
Moving Forward 211

Index 223

Introduction

The Rise of Soy Boys and Snowflakes

Definition of Soy Boys

In recent years, the term "soy boy" has gained popularity in online discussions and social media. It is often used as a derogatory term to describe men who are perceived as weak or effeminate. However, the term itself is steeped in misconceptions and stereotypes. In this section, we will explore the definition of soy boys, shedding light on its origins and debunking the myths associated with it.

The term "soy boy" typically refers to a man who is seen as lacking strength, assertiveness, or traditional masculinity. It is often used to belittle individuals who are deemed sensitive, politically correct, or supporting ideals considered outside the mainstream. The term gained traction particularly within certain online communities and the alt-right movement.

However, it is important to note that the concept of a "soy boy" is primarily based on stereotypes and is not backed by scientific evidence. The connection between consuming soy products and being perceived as weak or effeminate is entirely unfounded. In fact, soy products are a staple in many traditional Asian diets and have been consumed by both men and women for centuries without any negative effects on their masculinity.

Soy is a versatile legume that provides a range of essential nutrients and can be consumed in various forms, including tofu, tempeh, soy milk, and edamame. It is a rich source of protein, fiber, vitamins, minerals, and beneficial plant compounds. Soy products have been shown to have numerous health benefits when included as part of a balanced diet.

It is essential to debunk the myths surrounding soy and its perceived effects on masculinity. One common misconception is that soy contains high levels of estrogen, a female hormone, and consuming it can lead to hormonal imbalances in men. However, the estrogen-like compounds in soy, known as phytoestrogens, are structurally different from human estrogen and have different effects on the body. Research indicates that moderate soy consumption does not have adverse effects on testosterone levels or male reproductive health.

Moreover, the fear that consuming soy products can lead to the development of feminine characteristics is unfounded. Soy foods do not contain enough phytoestrogens to cause such changes in the body. In fact, research suggests that incorporating soy into the diet may have various health benefits, including reduced risks of cardiovascular diseases and certain types of cancers.

It is crucial to recognize that masculinity is a complex construct and cannot be defined by the foods one chooses to consume. Rather than perpetuating stereotypes and spreading misinformation, it is important to promote a balanced and open-minded approach to healthy eating. By debunking the myths surrounding soy boys, we can foster a more inclusive and educated conversation about nutrition and masculinity.

In summary, the term "soy boy" is a derogatory term used to belittle individuals who are perceived as weak or effeminate. However, the connection between consuming soy products and these characteristics is unfounded. Soy is a nutrient-rich food that can be enjoyed as part of a balanced diet, and it does not have adverse effects on masculinity or hormone levels. By challenging stereotypes and debunking myths, we can promote a healthier understanding of soy and its benefits.

Definition of Snowflakes

In today's society, the term "snowflake" has become a popular label used to describe a certain group of individuals. However, the term itself is often used in a derogatory manner, creating a negative connotation. To truly understand the concept of snowflakes, it is important to delve into its definition and the factors that contribute to its emergence.

In the context of this book, a "snowflake" refers to a person who is seen as overly sensitive, easily offended, and lacking resilience in the face of adversity. This term is often used to describe individuals who are perceived as fragile and unable to cope with challenges or differing opinions. However, it is crucial to approach this definition with empathy and open-mindedness, as using labels like "snowflake" can perpetuate stereotypes and hinder understanding.

The term "snowflake" has its origins in the idea that each snowflake is unique and delicate, easily melted with even the slightest touch. This metaphorical comparison highlights the perceived vulnerability and fragility that is associated with being a snowflake.

It is important to recognize that the snowflake phenomenon is not confined to a specific generation or age group. The term is often used to describe individuals from the millennial and Gen Z generations. However, it is essential to understand that not all individuals from these generations fit the snowflake stereotype. The snowflake phenomenon is a complex sociocultural issue that is influenced by various factors.

Factors influencing the snowflake phenomenon include changes in parenting styles, increased exposure to technology and social media, and shifts in societal values and expectations. These factors have led to a generation that may have different perspectives on topics such as mental health, self-expression, and inclusivity.

The emergence of social media platforms has played a significant role in shaping the snowflake phenomenon. Social media allows for the rapid spread of ideas, making it easier for individuals to connect and share their thoughts and experiences. This increased connectivity has provided a platform for individuals to amplify their voices and advocate for causes they believe in. However, it has also created an environment where differing opinions can lead to intense debates and heightened emotions.

Mental health concerns are also intertwined with the snowflake phenomenon. The increased prevalence of mental health issues among younger generations has contributed to a greater emphasis on self-care, emotional well-being, and the need for safe spaces. It is important to recognize that these concerns are valid and should not be dismissed as mere sensitivity.

It is crucial to debunk the myths and stereotypes surrounding the snowflake phenomenon. One common misconception is that snowflakes lack resilience. However, resilience is a complex and multifaceted trait that cannot be universally applied to an entire group of people. It is essential to consider the unique experiences, backgrounds, and circumstances that individuals face before making broad generalizations.

Addressing the concerns of the snowflake generation requires open dialogue, empathy, and understanding. It is important to foster an environment that promotes conversation, empathy, and personal growth. Encouraging self-discipline, mental well-being, and critical thinking skills can help individuals navigate the challenges they encounter in today's society.

In conclusion, the term "snowflake" is often used to describe individuals who are perceived as overly sensitive or lacking resilience. However, it is crucial to approach this term with empathy and understanding, recognizing the complex factors that contribute to the snowflake phenomenon. By fostering conversations and promoting personal growth, we can create a more inclusive society that values diverse perspectives and nurtures resilient individuals.

Origins of the Terms

The terms "Soy Boys" and "Snowflakes" have gained popularity in recent years, especially in online communities and social media. These terms are often used in a derogatory manner to describe individuals who are perceived as weak, overly sensitive, or lacking in resilience. However, it is important to understand the origins of these terms and the context in which they are used.

The term "Soy Boy" originated from the association between soy consumption and perceived femininity. Soy is a plant-based source of protein that has been widely consumed in many cultures for centuries. However, in certain online communities, there is a belief that consuming soy products can lead to higher levels of estrogen, the primary female sex hormone, and therefore result in decreased masculinity.

This association between soy and femininity has led to the stereotype of the "Soy Boy." The term is often used to mock or belittle men who are perceived as weak or lacking in traditional masculine traits. It is important to note that these stereotypes are not based on scientific evidence and are often used as a form of derogatory labeling.

Similarly, the term "Snowflake" has its origins in the idea of fragility and sensitivity. The term gained popularity in the context of discussing millennials and younger generations who are often perceived as sensitive or easily offended. This term is used to describe individuals who are seen as overly emotional, easily triggered, or requiring special treatment or accommodations.

The term "Snowflake" is often used to criticize or dismiss the concerns and experiences of these individuals, implying that their emotions and perspectives are fragile or delicate. However, it is crucial to recognize that everyone has unique experiences and that dismissing someone's concerns based on the perception of their sensitivity can be harmful and perpetuate a lack of understanding and empathy.

It is important to approach these terms critically and question the stereotypes and misconceptions associated with them. Using such language to categorize and label individuals can perpetuate harmful stereotypes and hinder meaningful conversations about diverse experiences and perspectives.

As we delve further into the book, we will explore the origins and implications of these terms, challenging common misconceptions and promoting a more empathetic and understanding approach. It is essential to move beyond these derogatory labels and foster an inclusive and accepting society that values diversity and different perspectives.

Stereotypes and Misconceptions

Stereotypes and misconceptions surrounding the terms "soy boys" and "snowflakes" have become prevalent in contemporary discourse. These stereotypes often stem from a lack of understanding and perpetuate harmful misconceptions about individuals who may identify with these labels. In this section, we will delve into the origins of these terms and debunk the stereotypes associated with them.

The term "soy boys" emerged in popular culture to mock men who were perceived as weak or effeminate. It is often used to stereotype individuals who consume soy products, as well as those who adhere to plant-based diets. However, this stereotype is based on misinformation and a limited understanding of the science behind soy consumption.

One common misconception associated with soy consumption is the belief that it can negatively impact hormone levels, particularly estrogen and testosterone. However, research has consistently shown that soy does not have feminizing effects or reduce testosterone levels in men. In fact, soy contains isoflavones, which are phytoestrogens that have a similar structure to estrogen but have much weaker hormonal activity. These phytoestrogens do not have the same effect on the body as human estrogen and do not disrupt hormonal balance.

Another misconception surrounding soy consumption is the belief that it can lead to a decrease in muscle mass and strength. This stereotype has been particularly prevalent in athletic and bodybuilding communities. However, numerous studies have demonstrated that soy protein can have comparable effects to animal-based protein in promoting muscle protein synthesis and enhancing muscle recovery.

Stereotypes associated with the term "snowflakes" often refer to young individuals who are perceived as overly sensitive or easily offended. This term has gained traction in recent years, largely due to the influence of social media and the amplification of certain voices on these platforms. However, it is important to recognize that this stereotype oversimplifies the complex nature of mental health and emotional well-being.

One misconception surrounding the "snowflake" phenomenon is the belief that individuals identifying as such lack resilience and are unable to cope with adversity. However, it is crucial to understand that mental health challenges affect people of all generations, and dismissing the concerns of younger individuals as mere sensitivity is both unfair and unhelpful. Moreover, by invalidating their experiences, we run the risk of exacerbating mental health issues and perpetuating stigma.

Addressing stereotypes and misconceptions requires open-mindedness, empathy, and a willingness to challenge our own preconceptions. It is essential to recognize that these labels are often used to demean and undermine certain groups of people, and engaging in these stereotypes can contribute to a culture of exclusion and discrimination.

As we navigate discussions around soy consumption and generational differences, it is important to prioritize accurate information, scientific evidence, and open dialogue. By dispelling these stereotypes and misconceptions, we can create a more inclusive and understanding society where individuals are not judged based on narrow stereotypes, but rather on their unique qualities and contributions to the world.

Purpose of the Book

The purpose of this book is to provide a comprehensive exploration of the health benefits of soy consumption, while also debunking the myths and stereotypes surrounding soy boys and snowflakes. By examining the scientific evidence, cultural influences, and societal perspectives, readers will gain a balanced understanding of the potential advantages of incorporating soy into their diets.

The book aims to address common misconceptions about soy, such as its alleged negative impact on masculinity and testosterone levels. Through an in-depth analysis of the research, readers will gain a better understanding of the science behind soy, its nutritional profile, and its potential role in optimizing health and wellness.

In addition, the book will dig deeper into the snowflake phenomenon, exploring the factors that contribute to this generational mindset. By examining the impact of social media and cultural shifts on the snowflake generation, readers will gain valuable insights into the mental health concerns that this group faces. The goal is to foster empathy and understanding, while debunking the stereotypes and prejudices often associated with the snowflake generation.

The holistic approach of the book incorporates different perspectives on health and wellness, including Western medicine, traditional medicine, and holistic approaches. By considering these diverse viewpoints, readers will be empowered to make informed decisions about their own health and well-being.

The book also emphasizes the importance of a balanced approach to nutrition, acknowledging that soy should be just one component of a diverse and varied diet. It encourages readers to explore different cultural diets and ways of eating, as well as to consider sustainability and ethical considerations in their food choices.

Furthermore, the book highlights the need for critical thinking skills and nutrition education in order to navigate the abundance of food myths and fads that pervade modern society. It provides practical tools and guidance to understand food labels, plan balanced meals, and optimize mental well-being through mindfulness and self-care practices.

Ultimately, the book seeks to promote educated discussions, challenge prejudice and bias, and foster a culture of inclusivity. By creating a safe and informative space, it strives to support personal and societal growth, and to encourage acceptance and empathy.

Through a combination of scientific research, cultural exploration, and practical guidance, this book aims to equip readers with the knowledge and understanding necessary to make informed decisions about their health, while debunking the myths and stereotypes associated with soy boys and snowflakes. It is our hope that this book will inspire readers to embrace a balanced approach to health and wellness, and to strive for personal growth in an ever-changing world.

Understanding Health Benefits

Importance of Health and Wellness

Physical Health

Physical health is an essential aspect of overall well-being. It refers to the state of our body and its ability to function optimally. A healthy body allows us to perform daily activities efficiently and enjoy a high quality of life. In this section, we will explore the importance of physical health, the key components that contribute to it, and strategies to improve and maintain it.

The Importance of Physical Health

Physical health plays a crucial role in our lives as it affects various aspects of our well-being. It is strongly linked to our ability to engage in physical activities, prevents the onset of chronic diseases, and enhances our overall quality of life. Here are some of the reasons why physical health is important:

- **Energy and Vitality:** When we are physically healthy, we have more energy and vitality to carry out our daily tasks. Regular exercise and proper nutrition boost our energy levels, allowing us to be more productive and engaged in our daily activities.

- **Disease Prevention:** Maintaining physical health significantly reduces the risk of developing chronic diseases such as heart disease, diabetes, and certain types of cancer. Engaging in regular physical activity and adopting a balanced diet are crucial in preventing such conditions.

- **Weight Management:** Physical health is closely tied to weight management. Regular exercise helps burn calories and maintain a healthy weight, reducing the risk of obesity and related health issues.

- **Improved Mental Health:** Physical activity releases endorphins, which are known as "feel-good" hormones. These hormones contribute to a positive mood and reduced stress levels. Engaging in regular exercise also improves sleep quality and enhances cognitive function.

- **Enhanced Longevity:** Taking care of our physical health promotes longevity. By adopting a healthy lifestyle, we increase our chances of living a longer, disease-free life.

Understanding the significance of physical health motivates us to prioritize activities that promote its well-being.

Components of Physical Health

Physical health comprises various components that work together to maintain a healthy body. These components include:

1. **Cardiorespiratory Endurance:** This component relates to the ability of the heart, lungs, and blood vessels to deliver oxygen and nutrients to the body's tissues. It is developed through activities that increase heart rate and breathing rate, such as aerobic exercises like running, swimming, or cycling.

2. **Muscular Strength and Endurance:** Muscular strength refers to the ability of muscles to exert force, while muscular endurance is the ability to sustain that force over time. Strength training exercises, such as weightlifting or resistance training, help build and maintain strong muscles.

3. **Flexibility:** Flexibility refers to the range of motion around a joint. It is essential for performing daily activities and preventing injuries. Stretching exercises, yoga, and Pilates are effective in improving flexibility.

4. **Body Composition:** Body composition refers to the proportion of fat, muscle, bone, and other tissues in the body. Maintaining a healthy body composition, including a healthy percentage of body fat, is important for overall health and well-being.

5. **Balance and Coordination:** Balance and coordination are essential for maintaining stability and preventing falls or injuries. Activities such as yoga, Tai Chi, or specific balance exercises help improve balance and coordination.

A well-rounded physical fitness program should address all these components to ensure overall physical health and prevent imbalances or weaknesses in any specific area.

Strategies for Improving Physical Health

Improving physical health requires adopting healthy habits and making deliberate lifestyle choices. Here are some strategies to enhance physical health:

1. **Regular Exercise:** Engage in at least 150 minutes of moderate-intensity aerobic exercise or 75 minutes of vigorous-intensity aerobic exercise per week. Additionally, incorporate strength training exercises at least twice a week to build and maintain muscle strength.

2. **Balanced Diet:** Follow a balanced diet that includes a variety of nutrients, including carbohydrates, proteins, healthy fats, vitamins, and minerals. Focus on consuming whole foods, such as fruits, vegetables, lean proteins, whole grains, and healthy fats, while limiting processed and sugary foods.

3. **Adequate Hydration:** Drink sufficient water throughout the day to maintain proper hydration. Water plays a vital role in numerous bodily functions, including digestion, circulation, and temperature regulation.

4. **Sufficient Rest and Sleep:** Aim for 7-9 hours of quality sleep each night. Sleep is crucial for physical and mental restoration, supporting overall health and well-being.

5. **Stress Management:** Develop effective stress management techniques, such as regular exercise, meditation, deep breathing exercises, or engaging in hobbies and activities that bring joy and relaxation.

6. **Regular Check-ups:** Schedule regular check-ups with healthcare professionals to monitor and manage your physical health. Routine screenings and assessments help identify potential health issues early on.

Remember, improving physical health is a continuous process that requires consistency and commitment. By incorporating these strategies into your daily life, you can enhance your physical well-being and enjoy the benefits of a healthy body.

Example: Understanding Macronutrients

Macronutrients, including carbohydrates, proteins, and fats, are essential for maintaining optimal physical health. Let's take a closer look at these macronutrients and their role in our body:

- **Carbohydrates:** Carbohydrates are the primary source of energy for our body. They are divided into two types: simple carbohydrates, found in foods like fruits and processed sugars, and complex carbohydrates, found in whole grains, legumes, and vegetables. Carbohydrates provide fuel for physical activity and aid in replenishing glycogen stores in muscles.

- **Proteins:** Proteins are important for muscle growth, repair, and maintenance. They are composed of amino acids, which are the building blocks of our body. High-quality protein sources include lean meats, fish, eggs, dairy products, and plant-based sources like beans, lentils, and tofu.

- **Fats:** Fats are a concentrated source of energy and provide essential fatty acids that our body needs. They play a crucial role in absorbing fat-soluble vitamins and insulating and protecting organs. Healthy fat sources include avocados, nuts and seeds, olive oil, fatty fish, and plant-based oils.

It is important to strike a balance and choose high-quality sources of these macronutrients to support physical health. Incorporating a variety of foods from different macronutrient categories ensures a well-rounded and nutritious diet.

Key Takeaways

Physical health is a vital aspect of overall well-being. It encompasses various components such as cardiorespiratory endurance, muscular strength and endurance, flexibility, body composition, and balance and coordination. Prioritizing physical health through regular exercise, a balanced diet, sufficient rest, stress management, and regular check-ups helps prevent chronic diseases, boosts energy levels, enhances mental health, and promotes longevity. By understanding the importance of physical health and adopting healthy habits, we can lead fulfilling lives with optimal physical well-being.

Mental Health

Mental health is an essential component of overall well-being, encompassing a person's emotional, psychological, and social well-being. It affects how individuals think, feel, and behave, and influences how they handle stress, make decisions, and relate to others. In this section, we will explore the importance of mental health and discuss various aspects that contribute to maintaining and improving mental well-being.

Understanding Mental Health

Mental health is a multifaceted concept that involves various factors, including biological, psychological, and social elements. It is influenced by genetic predispositions, life experiences, and environmental factors. Mental health disorders can range from common conditions like anxiety and depression to more severe conditions like bipolar disorder and schizophrenia.

To maintain good mental health, it is important to address both internal and external factors. Factors like self-esteem, resilience, coping skills, and the ability to form positive relationships contribute to mental well-being. Additionally, environmental factors such as social support, access to healthcare, and safe living conditions play a role in protecting mental health.

The Importance of Mental Health

Promoting mental health is crucial not only for individuals but also for society as a whole. Mental health impacts every aspect of a person's life, including their ability to perform daily activities, maintain relationships, and contribute to their community. Here are some key reasons why mental health should be prioritized:

1. **Enhanced well-being:** Good mental health leads to greater life satisfaction, improved overall well-being, and a sense of purpose and fulfillment in life.

2. **Optimal cognitive function:** Mental health influences cognitive processes such as concentration, memory, and problem-solving abilities. By maintaining good mental health, individuals can optimize their cognitive function.

3. **Healthy relationships:** Mental health affects our ability to form and maintain healthy relationships. Good mental health allows individuals to communicate effectively, empathize with others, and build meaningful connections.

4. **Productivity and success:** When mental health is prioritized, individuals can thrive in their personal and professional lives. Good mental health promotes productivity, creativity, and success in various domains.

5. **Reduced healthcare costs:** By investing in mental health promotion and prevention, the burden on healthcare systems can be reduced. Effective mental health interventions can mitigate the risk of developing severe mental health disorders and the associated healthcare costs.

Factors Influencing Mental Health

Several factors contribute to an individual's mental health. Understanding these factors can help individuals make informed decisions and take appropriate actions to protect and improve their mental well-being. Let's explore some of the key factors influencing mental health:

1. **Biological factors:** Genetic predispositions and imbalances in brain chemicals (neurotransmitters) can influence an individual's susceptibility to mental health disorders.

2. **Psychological factors:** Individual traits such as self-esteem, coping skills, and resilience can significantly impact mental health. The ability to manage stress, adapt to change, and maintain a positive outlook plays a crucial role.

3. **Social factors:** Our connections with family, friends, and the broader community influence our mental health. Social support, acceptance, and a sense of belonging contribute to positive mental well-being.

4. **Environmental factors:** The physical and social environment in which individuals live can affect their mental health. Factors such as exposure to violence, poverty, discrimination, or a lack of access to healthcare can increase the risk of mental health problems.

5. **Lifestyle factors:** Engaging in healthy lifestyle practices, such as regular exercise, a balanced diet, adequate sleep, and stress management techniques, can protect and promote mental health.

Common Mental Health Disorders

Mental health disorders are prevalent worldwide, affecting individuals of all ages and backgrounds. Let's explore some of the common mental health disorders:

1. **Anxiety disorders:** Anxiety disorders are characterized by excessive worry, fear, and various physical symptoms. Generalized anxiety disorder, panic disorder, and social anxiety disorder are examples of common anxiety disorders.

2. **Depressive disorders:** Depressive disorders involve persistent feelings of sadness, loss of interest, and a variety of physical and cognitive symptoms. Major depressive disorder and persistent depressive disorder are examples of depressive disorders.

3. **Bipolar disorder:** Bipolar disorder involves alternating periods of extreme mood swings, including manic episodes (elevated mood, heightened energy) and depressive episodes.

4. **Schizophrenia:** Schizophrenia is a severe mental disorder characterized by hallucinations, delusions, disorganized thinking, and other cognitive impairments.

5. **Eating disorders:** Eating disorders, such as anorexia nervosa and bulimia nervosa, involve distorted body image and unhealthy eating behaviors.

6. **Substance use disorders:** Substance use disorders involve the excessive use of drugs or alcohol, resulting in significant distress and impairment in daily life.

Promoting Mental Health

Promoting mental health is a collective responsibility that requires efforts from individuals, communities, healthcare systems, and policymakers. Here are some strategies to promote and maintain good mental health:

1. **Self-care practices:** Engaging in activities that promote well-being, such as exercise, relaxation techniques, hobbies, and healthy lifestyle choices, can contribute to good mental health.

2. **Social support:** Building and maintaining positive relationships with family, friends, and support networks contribute to mental well-being. Seeking support during challenging times is essential.

3. **Stress management:** Developing effective coping mechanisms and stress reduction techniques, such as mindfulness, meditation, and problem-solving skills, can help manage stress and protect mental health.

4. **Education and awareness:** Educating individuals about mental health, reducing stigma, and promoting awareness can encourage early intervention and improve access to mental health services.

5. **Access to mental health services:** Ensuring access to affordable and quality mental health services, including therapy, counseling, and medications when necessary, is crucial for those who need support.

Case Study: Workplace Mental Health

Mental health in the workplace is a significant concern, as it affects employee well-being, job satisfaction, and productivity. Let's consider a case study to illustrate the importance of addressing mental health in the workplace:

Case Study: Sarah's Story

Sarah works in a high-stress corporate environment known for its long working hours and competitive culture. Over time, Sarah starts experiencing symptoms of chronic stress, including insomnia, irritability, and difficulty focusing. Her job performance declines, and she starts withdrawing from social activities.

In this case, Sarah's mental health is negatively impacted by workplace stress. To support Sarah and promote a mentally healthy workplace, the following strategies could be implemented:

1. **Stress management programs:** Introducing programs that teach stress reduction techniques and provide resources for employees to manage work-related stress effectively.

2. **Flexible work arrangements:** Offering flexible work schedules or remote work options to enhance work-life balance and reduce stress.

3. **Mental health resources:** Providing access to mental health support services, such as counseling or employee assistance programs, to ensure employees have the necessary resources to address their mental health needs.

4. **Promoting open communication:** Fostering a culture of open communication, where employees feel comfortable discussing mental health concerns without fear of judgment or negative repercussions.

5. **Training and education:** Providing training sessions and workshops on mental health awareness and stress management for both employees and managers.

By implementing these strategies, organizations can create a supportive and mentally healthy work environment, ultimately benefiting the well-being and productivity of their employees.

Conclusion

Prioritizing mental health is fundamental to leading a fulfilling and balanced life. Understanding the factors that influence mental health, recognizing common mental health disorders, and promoting strategies for maintaining good mental well-being are crucial for individuals, communities, and society as a whole.

By embracing a holistic approach that addresses biological, psychological, social, and environmental aspects, we can create a culture that fosters mental well-being, reduces stigma, and provides support to those in need. Let us strive to promote mental health, challenge prejudice and bias, and foster a culture of inclusivity and empathy for the betterment of all.

Emotional Health

Emotional health is a crucial aspect of overall well-being. It refers to the ability to understand, manage, and express our emotions in a healthy and balanced way. It involves being aware of our feelings, having the capacity to cope with stress and adversity, and maintaining positive relationships with others. Emotional health encompasses various dimensions, including emotional awareness, emotional regulation, resilience, and empathy.

Understanding Emotions

Emotions are complex psychological and physiological experiences that arise in response to stimuli, events, or thoughts. They play a fundamental role in our lives and have a significant impact on our mental and physical well-being. Common emotions include happiness, sadness, anger, fear, and love. Understanding our emotions and recognizing their triggers is essential for maintaining emotional health.

Emotional Regulation

Emotional regulation refers to the ability to effectively manage and control our emotions. It involves recognizing and understanding our emotional responses and finding healthy ways to express and cope with them. People with good emotional regulation skills are better equipped to handle stress, conflicts, and challenges. They can respond to situations in a calm and rational manner, reducing the risk of impulsive or harmful behaviors.

Resilience

Resilience is the capacity to bounce back from adversity, trauma, or significant life changes. It is the ability to adapt and recover from stress, setbacks, or disappointments. Resilient individuals can maintain their emotional well-being even in the face of challenges, remaining optimistic and confident. Building resilience involves developing strong coping mechanisms, fostering a positive mindset, and seeking support when needed.

Empathy

Empathy is the ability to understand and share the feelings of others. It involves putting ourselves in someone else's shoes and experiencing their emotions. Cultivating empathy is essential for healthy relationships, effective communication, and social connection. It allows us to form meaningful connections with others, show compassion, and provide support during difficult times.

The Role of Emotional Health in Overall Well-being

Emotional health is interconnected with other aspects of well-being, such as physical, mental, and social health. When we prioritize emotional well-being, we increase our resilience, enhance our relationships, and improve our overall quality of life. Conversely, neglecting our emotional health can lead to a range of negative outcomes, including increased stress, mental health issues, and reduced life satisfaction.

Strategies to Promote Emotional Health

There are several strategies that can help promote emotional health:

- **Self-reflection and self-awareness:** Take time to understand your emotions, triggers, and patterns of behavior. Reflect on your feelings and thoughts to gain insight into yourself.

- **Emotion regulation techniques:** Practice techniques such as deep breathing, mindfulness meditation, and journaling to manage and regulate your emotions effectively.

- **Social support:** Foster strong relationships with family, friends, and supportive communities. Seek support and guidance from trusted individuals during challenging times.

- **Physical activity:** Engage in regular physical activity as it can help reduce stress, improve mood, and increase overall well-being.

- **Healthy coping mechanisms:** Develop healthy coping mechanisms to deal with stress, such as engaging in hobbies, practicing relaxation techniques, or seeking professional help if needed.

- **Positive mindset:** Cultivate a positive outlook on life, practice gratitude, and focus on the present moment. Engage in activities that bring you joy and fulfillment.

- **Limits on social media usage:** Be mindful of the impact of social media on emotional well-being. Limit the time spent on social media platforms that may contribute to comparison, self-doubt, or negative emotions.

It is important to note that emotional health is a lifelong journey, and everyone's experience is unique. It's okay to seek professional help from therapists or counselors if you are facing challenges that impact your emotional well-being. Remember to be kind to yourself, practice self-compassion, and prioritize your emotional well-being as an integral part of your overall health.

Spiritual Health

Spiritual health is an integral aspect of overall well-being that encompasses a person's connection to their inner self, others, and the universe. It goes beyond religious beliefs and practices and focuses on finding meaning, purpose, and a sense of transcendence in life. In this section, we will explore the importance of spiritual health and its impact on physical, mental, and emotional well-being.

Understanding the Essence of Spiritual Health

Spiritual health is a deeply personal experience that is unique to each individual. It involves nurturing and developing a connection with one's inner self, higher power, nature, or the universe. It provides a framework for understanding the meaning of life, coping with challenges, and experiencing a sense of purpose and fulfillment.

While spirituality is often associated with religious practices, it is important to note that it transcends traditional religious boundaries. It can be expressed through religious beliefs, meditation, mindfulness, yoga, contemplative practices, nature appreciation, and other avenues that help individuals explore their inner selves and connect with something greater.

The Holistic Connection

Spiritual health is an essential component of the holistic approach to well-being, which recognizes the interconnectedness of the body, mind, and spirit. Neglecting spiritual health can lead to an imbalance in the holistic system and impact overall health.

When individuals cultivate their spiritual health, it can positively impact their physical health. Research has shown that spiritual practices such as meditation and prayer can reduce stress, lower blood pressure, and boost the immune system. Engaging in activities that promote spiritual well-being, such as spending time in nature or practicing mindfulness, can also improve mental and emotional health by reducing anxiety, depression, and negative emotions.

Finding Meaning and Purpose

Spiritual health provides individuals with a sense of meaning and purpose in their lives. It helps them make sense of their experiences and find significance in the face of challenges and adversity. Having a strong sense of purpose is linked to a lower risk of mental health disorders and improved overall well-being.

Exploring spirituality can involve reflecting on existential questions, discovering personal values, and seeking answers to life's mysteries. It can involve engaging in activities that bring joy, creativity, and fulfillment, such as art, music, or volunteering. By aligning their actions with their spiritual beliefs and values, individuals can experience a greater sense of purpose and fulfillment.

Connecting with Others and the Universe

Spiritual health also involves building connections with others and cultivating a sense of unity with the universe. By recognizing our interconnectedness, individuals can develop a deep sense of empathy, compassion, and love for others.

Engaging in practices that promote connection, such as participating in community activities, volunteering, or engaging in acts of kindness, can enhance spiritual well-being. It fosters a sense of belonging and nurtures social health by strengthening relationships and promoting a sense of support and care in the community.

Furthermore, connecting with the universe, whether through nature appreciation, stargazing, or contemplative practices, can create a profound sense of awe, wonder, and transcendence. It allows individuals to experience something greater than themselves and tap into a source of inspiration and wisdom.

Promoting Spiritual Health

To promote spiritual health, individuals can incorporate various practices into their daily lives. Some suggestions include:

1. Meditation and Mindfulness: Engaging in meditation or mindfulness practices can help individuals quiet the mind, cultivate self-awareness, and enhance their connection with their inner selves.

2. Exploring Nature: Spending time in nature can be a powerful way to connect with the natural world and experience a sense of awe and wonder. Taking hikes, gardening, or simply observing the beauty of the environment can promote a deeper sense of spirituality.

3. Reflective Writing: Journaling or reflective writing allows individuals to explore their thoughts, feelings, and beliefs. It can be a tool for self-exploration, self-reflection, and deeper understanding of one's spiritual journey.

4. Engaging in Rituals or Ceremonies: Participating in rituals or ceremonies that are meaningful to you can provide a sense of connection, meaning, and celebration. This might include attending religious services, lighting candles, or creating personal rituals that align with your spiritual beliefs.

5. Connecting with Others: Engaging in meaningful relationships and nurturing connections with loved ones, friends, and the broader community can enhance spiritual well-being. Acts of kindness, compassion, and empathy promote a sense of unity and connection with others.

Remember, spirituality is a personal journey, and what works for one person may not resonate with another. It is important to explore different practices and find what aligns with your beliefs, values, and individual needs.

Conclusion

Spiritual health plays a crucial role in our overall well-being, providing meaning, purpose, and connection in our lives. By exploring and deepening our spiritual beliefs and practices, we can enhance our physical, mental, and emotional health. Remember to approach spirituality with an open mind and embrace different perspectives, as spirituality is a deeply personal and individual experience.

Social Health

Social health refers to one's ability to interact and form meaningful connections with others. It encompasses the quality of relationships, social support networks, and the level of satisfaction derived from social interactions. Social health is an essential component of overall well-being, as it has been linked to improved physical and mental health outcomes.

Importance of Social Health

Humans are social beings, and our need for social connection and belonging is ingrained in our biology. Numerous studies have shown that individuals with strong social ties tend to have better overall health and longevity compared to those who are socially isolated.

Strong social connections contribute to social support, which serves as a buffer against stress and adversity. In times of difficulty, having a supportive network of friends, family, and community members can provide emotional support, practical assistance, and a sense of belonging. Social support has been shown to reduce the risk of developing mental health disorders, such as depression and anxiety.

Furthermore, social interactions and relationships can positively impact our emotional well-being. Sharing experiences, receiving validation, and having a sense of belonging can increase feelings of happiness and life satisfaction. Engaging in social activities also provides opportunities for personal growth, learning, and self-discovery.

Social Determinants of Health

Social health is influenced by various social determinants that can either promote or hinder the development of healthy relationships. These determinants include:

1. **Family dynamics:** The quality of family relationships, communication patterns, and support systems greatly influence an individual's social health. Positive family relationships foster a sense of security and provide a foundation for healthy social development.

2. **Peer relationships:** Interactions with friends and peers play a crucial role in social health, particularly during adolescence and young adulthood. Positive peer relationships can boost self-esteem, enhance social skills, and provide emotional support.

3. **Community engagement:** The social environment in which individuals live can impact their social health. Access to community resources, such as recreation centers, community organizations, and social events, can facilitate social connections and foster a sense of belonging.

4. **Socioeconomic status:** Economic limitations can create barriers to social participation and access to resources. Socioeconomic disparities can lead to social exclusion and can negatively impact social health.

5. **Cultural and societal norms:** Cultural values, beliefs, and societal expectations shape our social interactions and influence our social health. Understanding and respecting cultural diversity contribute to positive social relationships and inclusivity.

Promoting Social Health

Promoting social health involves creating an environment that nurtures positive social interactions and fosters a sense of community. Here are some strategies to enhance social health:

1. **Building and maintaining relationships:** Invest time and effort in cultivating meaningful connections with family, friends, and colleagues. Engage in activities that promote socializing, such as joining groups or clubs with shared interests.

2. **Effective communication:** Develop effective communication skills, including active listening, assertiveness, and empathy. Clear and respectful communication lays the foundation for positive relationships and prevents misunderstandings.

3. **Creating a supportive environment:** Foster a supportive environment by offering help and support to others. Acts of kindness and empathy strengthen social connections and contribute to a sense of community.

4. **Participating in community activities:** Engage in community events, volunteer work, or local organizations to foster a sense of belonging and contribute to the well-being of the community.

5. **Addressing social isolation:** Recognize the signs of social isolation in oneself or others and take steps to address it. Encouraging social participation, connecting with support groups or community services can help combat loneliness and improve social health.

6. **Developing social skills:** Enhance social skills through activities such as group discussions, role-playing, or social skills training. Building confidence in social interactions can improve relationships and overall social health.

Example: Social Health and College Life

Let's consider the example of college life and its impact on social health. Starting college can be a significant transition, often involving moving away from home, making new friends, and adapting to a new environment. Here are some factors that can influence social health in the college setting:

- **Residence halls and communal living:** Living in on-campus residence halls or shared apartments can provide opportunities for building friendships and social connections. It can create a sense of belonging and facilitate social interactions.

- **Extracurricular activities and clubs:** Engaging in extracurricular activities or joining clubs allows students to meet individuals with shared interests and values. Participating in group activities fosters social connections and provides a platform for personal growth and development.

- **Supportive social networks:** College campuses often provide support services, such as counseling centers or peer support groups, which can help students navigate the challenges of college life and foster social connections.

- **Sense of community:** Building a sense of community within the college environment can contribute to social health. Creating inclusive and supportive spaces, organizing events, and encouraging collaboration and teamwork can foster positive social interactions among students.

- **Communication and conflict resolution skills:** College provides an opportunity for students to develop and refine their communication and conflict resolution skills. Learning effective communication techniques and strategies for resolving conflicts can enhance social health and facilitate positive relationships.

- **Social media and online interactions:** Virtual platforms, such as social media, play an increasingly significant role in college students' social lives. While online interactions provide opportunities for connection, it is important to strike a balance between online and face-to-face interactions to maintain social health.

In conclusion, social health is a crucial component of overall well-being and is influenced by various factors such as family dynamics, peer relationships, community engagement, and cultural norms. Promoting social health involves building and maintaining relationships, effective communication, creating a supportive environment, participating in community activities, addressing social isolation, and developing social skills. In the context of college life, fostering a sense of community, engaging in extracurricular activities, and developing effective communication skills are vital for enhancing social health.

Role of Diet in Overall Health

Macronutrients

In order to understand the role of diet in overall health, it is important to explore the concept of macronutrients. Macronutrients are the nutrients that our bodies require in large quantities to function properly and provide energy. These macronutrients include carbohydrates, proteins, and fats. Each macronutrient plays a unique and essential role in our bodies, and a balanced intake of these nutrients is crucial for maintaining optimal health.

Carbohydrates

Carbohydrates are the main source of energy for our bodies. They are broken down into glucose, which provides fuel for our cells. Carbohydrates can be found in various foods such as grains, fruits, vegetables, and dairy products. There are two types of carbohydrates: simple carbohydrates and complex carbohydrates.

Simple carbohydrates, also known as sugars, are found in foods like table sugar, honey, and fruit. They provide quick energy but can cause rapid fluctuations in blood sugar levels. On the other hand, complex carbohydrates are found in foods like whole grains, legumes, and vegetables. They contain fiber, which helps regulate blood sugar levels and promote a feeling of fullness.

It is important to choose complex carbohydrates over simple carbohydrates as they provide sustained energy and are more nutrient-dense. Incorporating whole grains, vegetables, and legumes into your diet can help you maintain a balanced intake of carbohydrates.

Proteins

Proteins are essential for growth, repair, and maintenance of body tissues. They are made up of amino acids, which are the building blocks of protein. Proteins can be found in both animal and plant sources, such as meat, poultry, fish, dairy products, beans, nuts, and seeds.

Proteins play a vital role in various functions of the body, including the formation of enzymes, hormones, and antibodies. They also contribute to the structure of muscles, bones, and skin. Additionally, proteins provide a source of energy when carbohydrates and fats are not available in sufficient amounts.

It is important to consume a variety of protein sources to ensure an adequate intake of essential amino acids. Aim for a balanced mix of animal and plant-based proteins to meet your body's protein needs.

Fats

Contrary to popular belief, not all fats are bad for you. In fact, fats are an essential component of a healthy diet. Fats provide energy, help absorb fat-soluble vitamins, and support proper brain function. However, it is important to choose healthy fats and limit the intake of unhealthy fats.

Healthy fats, such as monounsaturated fats and polyunsaturated fats, can be found in foods like avocados, nuts, seeds, and fatty fish. These fats have been associated with a reduced risk of heart disease and inflammation.

On the other hand, unhealthy fats, such as saturated fats and trans fats, can increase the risk of heart disease and other health problems. Saturated fats are found in foods like red meat, butter, and full-fat dairy products, while trans fats are found in processed foods and baked goods.

It is important to prioritize healthy fats in your diet and limit the intake of unhealthy fats. Incorporating foods rich in healthy fats can help support overall health and well-being.

Energy Balance

Maintaining a healthy balance of macronutrients is essential for overall health, but it is also important to consider energy balance. Energy balance refers to the relationship between the energy we consume through food and the energy we expend through physical activity and bodily functions.

Consuming more energy than we expend can lead to weight gain, while consuming less energy than we expend can lead to weight loss. It is important to find an appropriate balance between calorie intake and energy expenditure to maintain a healthy weight.

To achieve and maintain energy balance, it is important to be mindful of portion sizes, choose nutrient-dense foods, and engage in regular physical activity. Consulting a healthcare professional or registered dietitian can provide personalized guidance on achieving and maintaining energy balance.

Conclusion

In this section, we explored the concept of macronutrients and their role in overall health. Carbohydrates, proteins, and fats are essential for providing energy and supporting various bodily functions. A balanced intake of these macronutrients is crucial for maintaining optimal health.

It is important to choose complex carbohydrates over simple carbohydrates, consume a variety of protein sources, and prioritize healthy fats in our diets. Understanding the concept of energy balance is also crucial for maintaining a healthy weight.

By incorporating a balanced mix of macronutrients and maintaining energy balance, we can support our overall health and well-being. It is important to adopt a holistic approach to nutrition and make informed choices to promote a healthy lifestyle.

Micronutrients

Micronutrients are essential nutrients required by the body in small quantities to ensure optimal health and functioning. Unlike macronutrients (such as proteins, carbohydrates, and fats), micronutrients are not a source of energy but instead play critical roles in various physiological processes. In this section, we will explore the importance of micronutrients, their types, and their role in maintaining overall health.

Types of Micronutrients

There are several types of micronutrients that the body needs for proper functioning. These include vitamins and minerals. Let's dive deeper into each of these categories:

Vitamins: Vitamins are organic compounds that are necessary for the body to perform various metabolic processes. They are classified into two categories: water-soluble vitamins and fat-soluble vitamins.

Water-soluble vitamins include vitamin C and the eight B vitamins (thiamin, riboflavin, niacin, pantothenic acid, pyridoxine, biotin, folic acid, and cobalamin). These vitamins are not stored in the body and must be consumed regularly through a balanced diet. They play vital roles in energy production, immune function, DNA synthesis, and nervous system health.

Fat-soluble vitamins include vitamins A, D, E, and K. These vitamins are stored in the body's fat tissues and liver, allowing the body to tap into them when needed. They are involved in processes such as vision, bone health, blood clotting, and antioxidant protection. It's important to note that fat-soluble vitamins require the presence of dietary fat for absorption.

Minerals: Minerals are inorganic substances that the body needs to carry out various physiological functions. They can be divided into two categories: macrominerals and trace minerals.

Macrominerals are needed in larger amounts and include calcium, phosphorus, magnesium, sodium, potassium, and chloride. These minerals are involved in processes such as bone health, muscle contraction, fluid balance, nerve function, and maintaining a stable pH level in the body.

Trace minerals are required in much smaller quantities but are equally essential. Some examples of trace minerals include iron, zinc, copper, manganese, iodine, selenium, and molybdenum. These minerals play crucial roles in enzyme function, immune system support, hormone synthesis, and antioxidant defense.

Functions of Micronutrients

Micronutrients are involved in a wide range of physiological functions, working together to support overall health. Here are some key functions of micronutrients:

Energy Production: Many micronutrients, such as B vitamins, play a crucial role in converting macronutrients (carbohydrates, proteins, and fats) into energy. They act as coenzymes, facilitating various metabolic reactions involved in the production of ATP (adenosine triphosphate), the body's primary energy source.

Cellular Health: Micronutrients serve as cofactors for enzymes involved in cellular processes. For instance, minerals like zinc and copper are essential for DNA synthesis, cell growth, and repair. Antioxidant vitamins, such as vitamin C and vitamin E, help protect cells from oxidative stress and maintain their integrity.

Immune Function: Several micronutrients, including vitamins A, C, D, E, and minerals like zinc and selenium, support the immune system. They help in the production and functioning of immune cells and play a vital role in fighting off pathogens and infections.

Bone Health: Minerals like calcium, phosphorus, and magnesium are crucial for maintaining healthy bones and teeth. They provide structural support and contribute to bone mineral density, reducing the risk of conditions like osteoporosis.

Brain Function: Micronutrients, particularly B vitamins and omega-3 fatty acids, are important for brain health and cognitive function. They support the production and functioning of neurotransmitters, which are essential for communication between brain cells. Adequate intake of these micronutrients is associated with improved memory, concentration, and overall mental well-being.

Mood Regulation: Certain micronutrients, such as vitamin D and omega-3 fatty acids, have been linked to mood regulation and the prevention of mental health conditions like depression and anxiety. These micronutrients support the synthesis and activity of neurotransmitters involved in mood regulation.

Ensuring Adequate Micronutrient Intake

To ensure optimal micronutrient intake, it is crucial to consume a varied and balanced diet that incorporates a wide range of nutrient-dense foods. Here are some tips to consider:

Eat a Rainbow of Fruits and Vegetables: Different fruits and vegetables contain various micronutrients. By consuming a colorful array of produce, you can increase the diversity of micronutrients in your diet. Aim for at least five servings of fruits and vegetables per day.

Choose Whole Grain Foods: Whole grains, such as quinoa, brown rice, and whole wheat bread, are rich in B vitamins and minerals like magnesium and selenium. Opt for whole grain versions of bread, cereals, pasta, and rice to maximize your micronutrient intake.

Include Lean Protein Sources: Protein-rich foods like lean meats, fish, legumes, and tofu can provide essential micronutrients such as iron, zinc, and B vitamins. Incorporate a variety of protein sources into your meals to diversify your micronutrient intake.

Don't Fear Healthy Fats: Some micronutrients, like vitamins A, D, E, and K, require the presence of dietary fat for absorption. Including sources of healthy fats, such as avocados, nuts, seeds, and olive oil, can enhance the bioavailability of fat-soluble vitamins.

Consider Supplementation if Necessary: While a well-balanced diet is the ideal way to obtain micronutrients, certain populations (such as pregnant women, strict vegetarians/vegans, and individuals with malabsorption issues) may benefit from specific micronutrient supplements. Consult with a healthcare professional to determine your individual needs.

Be Mindful of Cooking Methods: The way you prepare and cook your food can affect the micronutrient content. Overcooking or prolonged heat exposure can lead to nutrient loss. Opt for gentle cooking methods like steaming or stir-frying to preserve micronutrients.

Conclusion

Micronutrients are essential components of a healthy diet, playing crucial roles in various bodily functions. Vitamins and minerals, in particular, are necessary for energy production, cellular health, immune function, bone health, brain function, and mood regulation. By adopting a balanced and varied diet that includes a wide range of nutrient-dense foods, you can ensure adequate intake of micronutrients to support overall health and well-being. Remember, nutrition is not just about macronutrients; the power of micronutrients should not be underestimated.

Dietary Guidelines

When it comes to maintaining a healthy diet, following dietary guidelines is crucial. These guidelines provide evidence-based recommendations on the types and amounts of food to consume in order to promote good health and prevent chronic diseases. In this section, we will explore the importance of dietary guidelines and discuss some key principles that can help individuals make informed choices about their diet.

What are Dietary Guidelines?

Dietary guidelines are a set of recommendations developed by nutritionists and health experts to guide individuals in making healthy food choices. They are based on scientific research and take into account the nutritional needs of different age groups, genders, and activity levels.

The primary goal of dietary guidelines is to promote nutritionally balanced and adequate diets that contribute to overall health and well-being. They provide information on the recommended daily intake of essential nutrients, such as

ROLE OF DIET IN OVERALL HEALTH

vitamins, minerals, proteins, carbohydrates, and fats, as well as guidance on maintaining a healthy body weight.

Key Principles of Dietary Guidelines

1. Balance and Variety: Dietary guidelines emphasize the importance of consuming a variety of foods from different food groups. This ensures that individuals get a wide range of nutrients necessary for optimal health. A balanced diet includes fruits, vegetables, whole grains, lean proteins, and healthy fats in appropriate portions.

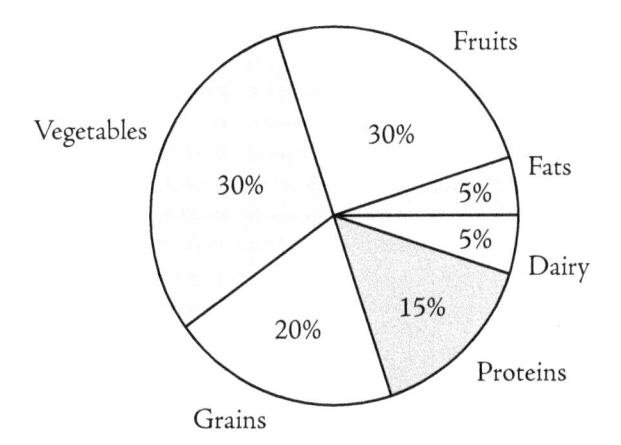

Figure 0.1: Suggested portion distribution of different food groups in a balanced diet.

2. Moderation: Dietary guidelines emphasize moderation in the consumption of certain foods and beverages that are high in added sugars, saturated fats, and sodium. While these foods can be enjoyed occasionally, excessive intake can lead to adverse health effects, such as obesity, heart disease, and high blood pressure. Being mindful of portion sizes and limiting the frequency of indulgence in these foods is important.

3. Adequacy: Dietary guidelines promote the consumption of nutrient-dense foods that provide essential nutrients without excessive calories. Nutrient-dense foods include fruits, vegetables, whole grains, lean proteins, and low-fat dairy products. These foods are rich in vitamins, minerals, and antioxidants that support overall health and well-being.

4. Energy Balance: Dietary guidelines emphasize the importance of maintaining a balance between energy intake and energy expenditure. Consuming more calories than the body needs can lead to weight gain, while consuming fewer calories than

the body requires can lead to weight loss. Adjusting portion sizes and incorporating physical activity can help achieve and maintain a healthy weight.

5. Hydration: Adequate hydration is essential for health. Dietary guidelines recommend consuming an adequate amount of water and fluids throughout the day to stay properly hydrated. Water is the best choice for hydration, but other beverages like herbal teas and low-sugar drinks can also contribute to hydration.

Putting Dietary Guidelines into Practice

Following dietary guidelines can sometimes seem challenging, especially with the abundance of unhealthy food options available. However, there are several strategies individuals can use to incorporate these guidelines into their daily lives:

- Meal Planning: Planning meals in advance can help ensure a balanced and nutritious diet. It allows individuals to include a variety of foods from different food groups and make conscious choices about portion sizes and nutrient intake.

- Reading Food Labels: Understanding food labels can empower individuals to make informed choices. It allows them to identify nutrient-dense foods and avoid those that are high in added sugars, unhealthy fats, and sodium.

- Cooking at Home: Cooking meals at home gives individuals control over the ingredients used and the cooking methods. It enables them to choose healthier options and reduce the consumption of processed and fast foods that are often high in unhealthy fats, sodium, and added sugars.

- Seeking Professional Advice: Consulting with a registered dietitian or nutritionist can provide personalized guidance and support. These professionals can help individuals create a tailored meal plan that meets their specific nutritional needs and goals.

It is important to note that dietary guidelines are intended to be flexible and can accommodate various cultural preferences and dietary restrictions. They provide a framework for individuals to make healthier choices while still enjoying a diverse range of foods.

Summary

Dietary guidelines play a critical role in promoting good health and preventing chronic diseases. They provide evidence-based recommendations on the types and amounts of food to consume in order to achieve a balanced and nutrient-dense diet. By following dietary guidelines, individuals can make informed choices about their diet and prioritize their overall well-being.

In the next section, we will explore the different perspectives on health benefits, including Western medicine, traditional medicine, holistic approaches, integrative medicine, and cultural influences. Understanding these perspectives can provide valuable insights into the diverse ways in which individuals approach health and wellness.

Impact of Diet on Chronic Diseases

Diet plays a crucial role in maintaining overall health and preventing chronic diseases. In this section, we will explore the significant impact of diet on chronic diseases and how making informed dietary choices can lead to a healthier life.

Chronic diseases, such as heart disease, diabetes, obesity, and certain types of cancer, are prevalent in our society today. These conditions often develop over time and are influenced by a variety of factors, including genetic predisposition, lifestyle choices, and environmental factors. While genetics may play a role in the development of chronic diseases, research has shown that diet is a modifiable risk factor that can significantly influence their occurrence.

Dietary Factors and Chronic Diseases

1. **Obesity and Weight Management:** Obesity is a major risk factor for various chronic diseases, including cardiovascular disease, type 2 diabetes, and certain types of cancer. Poor dietary choices, such as consuming high-calorie foods that are rich in saturated fats, added sugars, and refined carbohydrates, contribute to weight gain and obesity. On the other hand, a balanced diet that includes a variety of nutrient-dense foods can help maintain a healthy weight and reduce the risk of chronic diseases.

2. **Cardiovascular Health:** The consumption of unhealthy fats, high sodium intake, and inadequate intake of fruits and vegetables are associated with an increased risk of cardiovascular diseases, including heart disease and stroke. A diet rich in antioxidants, omega-3 fatty acids, and fiber, found in fruits, vegetables, whole grains, fish, and nuts, can help reduce the risk of cardiovascular diseases and promote heart health.

3. **Blood Pressure Management:** Excessive intake of sodium (salt) is a significant risk factor for high blood pressure, a major risk factor for heart disease and stroke. A diet low in sodium and high in potassium, which can be achieved by

consuming fruits, vegetables, and low-fat dairy products while limiting processed foods, can help maintain healthy blood pressure levels.

4. **Diabetes Prevention and Management:** A poor diet that is high in refined carbohydrates, sugary beverages, and unhealthy fats can increase the risk of developing type 2 diabetes. In contrast, a diet rich in whole grains, lean proteins, healthy fats, and low in added sugars can help prevent and manage diabetes.

5. **Cancer Prevention:** Several dietary factors have been associated with an increased risk of certain types of cancer. For instance, high consumption of processed and red meats is linked to colorectal cancer, while diets high in fruits, vegetables, whole grains, and low-fat dairy products have been found to reduce the risk of various cancers. Antioxidants, found in abundance in fruits and vegetables, can help protect against cellular damage that can lead to cancer.

Strategies to Improve Diet Quality

Improving diet quality involves adopting healthy eating patterns that focus on nutrient-dense foods while limiting the intake of processed, high-calorie foods. Here are some strategies to consider:

1. **Balanced Macronutrient Intake:** A balanced diet includes a proper distribution of macronutrients, such as carbohydrates, proteins, and fats. It is important to consume a variety of whole grains, lean sources of protein (e.g., poultry, fish, legumes), and healthy fats (e.g., avocados, nuts, olive oil) to meet the body's nutritional needs.

2. **Portion Control:** Controlling portion sizes can help prevent overeating and promote weight management. It is essential to be mindful of portion sizes and listen to your body's hunger and satiety cues.

3. **Emphasis on Plant-based Foods:** Including a wide range of fruits, vegetables, whole grains, legumes, and nuts in your diet provides essential nutrients, fiber, and antioxidants. These plant-based foods have been associated with a lower risk of chronic diseases.

4. **Reducing Added Sugars and Sodium:** Limiting the consumption of foods and beverages high in added sugars and sodium can help prevent obesity, high blood pressure, and other chronic diseases. Reading food labels and being aware of hidden sources of sugar and sodium is crucial in making healthier choices.

5. **Moderation in Alcohol Consumption:** Excessive alcohol consumption has been linked to an increased risk of chronic diseases such as liver disease, cardiovascular disease, and certain types of cancer. Moderation is key, and it is recommended to limit alcohol intake to moderate levels (up to one drink per day for women and up to two drinks per day for men).

6. **Educating Yourself:** Staying informed about nutrition and maintaining a critical mindset towards food marketing claims can help you make better dietary choices. Learning how to identify reliable sources of nutrition information and distinguishing between fact and fiction is essential in improving your diet quality.

Real-world Example: The Mediterranean Diet

The Mediterranean diet serves as an excellent example of a dietary pattern associated with lower rates of chronic diseases. This eating pattern emphasizes the consumption of plant-based foods, such as fruits, vegetables, whole grains, legumes, and nuts, along with moderate amounts of fish, poultry, and dairy products. It incorporates healthy fats, such as olive oil, and limits the intake of red and processed meats, sweets, and sugary beverages. Research has shown that adherence to the Mediterranean diet is associated with a reduced risk of cardiovascular diseases, cancer, and overall mortality.

By adopting a Mediterranean-inspired eating pattern, individuals can significantly improve their overall health and reduce the risk of chronic diseases.

Resources and Further Reading

1. World Health Organization (WHO) - *Noncommunicable diseases and their risk factors* - Available at: https://www.who.int/news-room/fact-sheets/detail/noncommunicable-diseases

2. American Heart Association (AHA) - *Diet and Lifestyle Recommendations* - Available at: https://www.heart.org/en/healthy-living/healthy-eating/eat-smart/nutrition-basics/dietary-recommendations-for-healthy-children

3. Mayo Clinic - *The Mediterranean Diet: What is it and how can it help?* - Available at: https://www.mayoclinic.org/healthy-lifestyle/nutrition-and-healthy-eating/in-depth/mediterranean-diet/art-20047801

Remember, making informed dietary choices is essential in promoting health and preventing chronic diseases. By adopting a balanced and nutrient-rich diet, you can take control of your well-being and enjoy a healthier life.

Strategies to Improve Diet Quality

Maintaining a healthy and balanced diet is essential for overall well-being. A diet that is rich in essential nutrients can help prevent chronic diseases, promote good physical and mental health, and enhance the body's immune system. In this section, we will explore various strategies to improve diet quality and ensure optimal nutrition.

Understanding Macronutrients

Macronutrients are the key nutrients that our bodies need in large quantities to function properly. They include carbohydrates, proteins, and fats. Understanding the role and importance of each macronutrient can help individuals make informed decisions about their diet.

Carbohydrates Carbohydrates are a vital source of energy for the body. However, not all carbohydrates are created equal. In order to improve diet quality, it is essential to choose complex carbohydrates, such as whole grains, legumes, and vegetables, over simple carbohydrates like sugary snacks and refined grains. Complex carbohydrates provide sustained energy, fiber, and essential nutrients.

Proteins Proteins are necessary for growth, repair, and maintenance of body tissues. Including high-quality protein sources in your diet is crucial. Opt for lean meats, poultry, fish, eggs, dairy products, and plant-based protein sources like beans, lentils, and tofu. These protein sources provide essential amino acids and are low in saturated fats, making them ideal for improving diet quality.

Fats Fats play a vital role in our body by providing energy, aiding in the absorption of fat-soluble vitamins, and supporting brain function. However, not all fats are beneficial for our health. To improve diet quality, it is important to choose healthy fats such as those found in avocado, nuts, seeds, and fatty fish. Limiting the intake of saturated and trans fats, commonly found in processed foods and fried snacks, is also crucial.

Incorporating Micronutrients

Micronutrients are essential vitamins and minerals that our bodies require in smaller quantities but are still important for proper functioning. Including a variety of micronutrient-rich foods in our diets is key to improving diet quality.

Fruits and Vegetables Fruits and vegetables are packed with vitamins, minerals, and dietary fiber. Aim to include a rainbow of colors in your diet to ensure a variety of nutrients. Incorporating leafy greens, berries, citrus fruits, and cruciferous vegetables like broccoli and cauliflower can provide a wide range of micronutrients.

Whole Grains   Whole grains are an excellent source of fiber, vitamins, minerals, and antioxidants. Choose whole grain options like brown rice, quinoa, whole wheat bread, and oatmeal over refined grains to improve diet quality.

Dairy and Alternatives   Dairy products, such as milk, cheese, and yogurt, provide calcium, vitamin D, and other essential nutrients. If you are lactose intolerant or prefer plant-based options, choose fortified alternatives like soy milk or almond milk to ensure adequate intake of these micronutrients.

Nuts and Seeds   Nuts and seeds are rich in healthy fats, protein, fiber, vitamins, and minerals. Incorporating a variety of nuts and seeds like almonds, walnuts, chia seeds, and flaxseeds can be a great way to improve diet quality.

Balancing Macronutrients

While macronutrients are essential, balancing their proportions is equally important. Here are some strategies to achieve a well-balanced diet:

Portion Control   Maintaining appropriate portion sizes is crucial to avoid overeating and ensure a balanced intake of macronutrients. Use measuring cups or a kitchen scale to portion out your meals and snacks.

Meal Planning   Plan your meals in advance to ensure a well-balanced diet throughout the week. Include a combination of all macronutrients and incorporate a variety of fruits, vegetables, whole grains, and lean proteins.

Food Pairing   Pairing different food groups can optimize nutrient absorption and provide a balanced intake of macronutrients. For example, combining whole grains with legumes creates a complete protein source.

Exploring Different Cultural Diets

Cultural diets offer a wealth of knowledge about balanced nutrition, as they have evolved over generations to meet specific dietary needs. Exploring different cultural diets can provide inspiration for improving diet quality. Some examples of healthy cultural diets include the Mediterranean diet, Japanese diet, and Indian diet.

Mediterranean Diet The Mediterranean diet is rich in fruits, vegetables, legumes, whole grains, fish, and olive oil. This diet is known for its health benefits, including a reduced risk of heart disease and improved overall well-being.

Japanese Diet The Japanese diet is based on fish, seafood, tofu, vegetables, fermented foods, and rice. It is low in saturated fats and high in essential nutrients. This diet has been associated with longevity and a lower risk of chronic diseases.

Indian Diet The Indian diet is diverse and includes a variety of spices, whole grains, lentils, vegetables, and dairy products. It is rich in antioxidants and beneficial compounds. Including traditional Indian dishes can improve diet quality and provide a wide range of nutrients.

Sustainability and Ethical Considerations

Improving diet quality also involves considering the sustainability and ethical implications of our food choices. Here are some strategies to align our diets with environmental and ethical concerns:

Choose Organic and Locally Sourced Foods Opt for organic and locally sourced foods whenever possible. Organic foods are grown without the use of synthetic pesticides and fertilizers, while supporting local farmers minimizes the carbon footprint associated with transportation.

Reduce Food Waste Reducing food waste not only helps the environment but also improves diet quality by ensuring that the food we consume is fresh and nutritious. Plan meals based on what is available in your pantry and make use of leftovers creatively.

Plant-based Alternatives Incorporating more plant-based meals in your diet can significantly reduce the environmental impact of food production. Consider substituting animal-based proteins with plant-based alternatives like tofu, tempeh, and legumes.

Teaching Critical Thinking Skills

In today's world, where food myths and fads abound, it is crucial to develop critical thinking skills to navigate through the noise and make informed decisions about our diets. Here are some strategies to improve critical thinking skills related to nutrition:

Questioning Information Sources When encountering new information or nutrition advice, it is important to critically evaluate the credibility and reliability of the sources. Rely on evidence-based research published in reputable scientific journals rather than relying solely on anecdotes or popular opinions.

Understanding Research Studies Learn how to interpret research studies and understand the limitations of different study designs. This will enable you to distinguish between significant findings and preliminary, inconclusive data.

Considering Individual Differences Recognize that individual nutritional needs may vary based on factors such as age, sex, activity level, and overall health. Avoid one-size-fits-all approaches and tailor your diet to meet your specific requirements.

Promoting Balanced Meal Planning

Planning meals in advance can significantly improve diet quality. Here are some tips for promoting balanced meal planning:

Include All Food Groups Ensure that each meal includes a combination of macronutrients and incorporates a variety of fruits, vegetables, whole grains, and proteins.

Practice Mindful Eating Eat mindfully, savoring the flavors and textures of your food. This can help you maintain a healthy relationship with food and prevent overeating.

Experiment with New Recipes To avoid monotony and increase adherence to a well-balanced diet, try new recipes that incorporate a variety of ingredients and flavors. This can make healthy eating more enjoyable.

Meal Prep Consider meal prepping for the week to save time and ensure that nutritious meals are readily available. This involves preparing larger batches of meals and portioning them into individual servings.

Conclusion

Improving diet quality is a lifelong journey that requires careful consideration of macronutrients, micronutrients, cultural influences, and individual differences. By following these strategies, individuals can make more informed choices about their diet, leading to better health outcomes and overall well-being. Remember to balance diverse food choices, practice critical thinking skills, and prioritize sustainable and ethical considerations in your dietary decisions. Embrace the power of nutrition and embark on a path to a healthier, happier life.

Different Perspectives on Health Benefits

Western Medicine

In the field of healthcare, Western medicine is often referred to as allopathic medicine or conventional medicine. It is a system of medical practice that is based on the principles of scientific evidence, empirical observation, and the diagnosis and treatment of diseases primarily using pharmaceutical drugs and surgery.

Principles of Western Medicine

Western medicine is based on several core principles:

- **Evidence-based practice:** Western medicine emphasizes the use of scientific evidence to guide medical decision-making. Clinical trials, epidemiological studies, and other research methods are used to evaluate the safety and efficacy of medical interventions.

- **Reductionism:** Western medicine often takes a reductionist approach, where complex physiological processes are broken down into smaller, more manageable components. This reductionist mindset allows for a better understanding of the underlying mechanisms of disease and the development of targeted treatments.

- **Holism:** While reductionism is a core principle, Western medicine also acknowledges the importance of considering the whole person. This includes understanding the interplay between physical, psychological, and social factors in determining health outcomes.

- **Standardization:** Western medicine aims to establish standardized guidelines and protocols for the diagnosis and treatment of various diseases. This helps to ensure consistency of care and improve patient outcomes.

Diagnostic Approaches

In Western medicine, the diagnostic process often involves the following steps:

1. **Medical history:** Gathering information about the patient's symptoms, medical conditions, and family history to identify potential risk factors and provide contextual information for further evaluation.

2. **Physical examination:** Physicians use various techniques, such as inspection, palpation, percussion, and auscultation, to assess the patient's overall health and identify any abnormal findings.

3. **Laboratory tests:** Blood tests, urine tests, imaging studies (such as X-rays and CT scans), and other diagnostic tests can help to confirm or rule out certain conditions.

4. **Specialized procedures:** In some cases, specialized procedures such as biopsies, endoscopies, or genetic testing may be necessary to obtain further diagnostic information.

Treatment Approaches

The treatment approaches employed in Western medicine primarily include:

- **Pharmacotherapy:** Prescription medications are frequently used to treat various health conditions. These medications are designed to target specific molecular pathways and physiological processes associated with the disease.

- **Surgery:** In cases where medication alone may not be sufficient, surgical interventions may be employed. Surgery can range from simple outpatient procedures to complex interventions aimed at correcting anatomical abnormalities or removing diseased tissues.

- **Physical interventions:** Physical therapies, such as physiotherapy, occupational therapy, and rehabilitation, are commonly used to help patients regain or improve their physical function and quality of life.

- **Psychological interventions:** Western medicine recognizes the importance of mental health and incorporates psychological interventions, such as cognitive-behavioral therapy, to address conditions such as anxiety and depression.

- **Preventive measures:** Western medicine places a strong emphasis on preventive healthcare, aiming to reduce the risk of developing diseases through interventions like vaccinations, counseling on healthy lifestyle behaviors, and routine screenings.

Challenges and Criticisms

While Western medicine has made significant contributions to healthcare, it is not without its challenges and criticisms. Some of these include:

- **Overreliance on pharmaceutical drugs:** Western medicine is often criticized for its heavy reliance on pharmaceutical drugs, with concerns about potential side effects and the rising cost of medication.

- **Focus on treating symptoms rather than addressing root causes:** Western medicine's reductionist approach can sometimes result in treating symptoms without fully addressing the underlying causes of diseases.

- **Limited integration of traditional medicine:** Western medicine historically has had minimal integration with traditional medicine practices, which may limit a more holistic understanding and treatment of certain conditions.

- **Healthcare disparities:** In many Western countries, there are significant disparities in access to healthcare, resulting in unequal health outcomes for different populations.

- **Medicalization of normal conditions:** Western medicine has been criticized for medicalizing normal conditions, such as certain aspects of aging or natural variations in human physiology, which may lead to overtreatment or unnecessary medical interventions.

In conclusion, Western medicine is a system of medical practice that is based on scientific evidence, empirical observation, and the use of pharmaceutical drugs and surgery to diagnose and treat diseases. It emphasizes evidence-based practices, reductionism, and standardized protocols. While Western medicine has its strengths, it also faces challenges and criticisms, including overreliance on pharmaceutical drugs and a sometimes narrow focus on treating symptoms rather than addressing root causes.

Traditional Medicine

Traditional medicine is a system of healthcare that has been practiced for centuries in various cultures around the world. It encompasses a wide range of healing practices, beliefs, and therapies that are often passed down through generations. Traditional medicine is deeply rooted in the cultural, social, and spiritual values of a community and takes a holistic approach to health and well-being.

Principles of Traditional Medicine

Traditional medicine is based on several key principles that guide its practices and beliefs:

1. **Holistic approach**: Traditional medicine views the human body as a complex ecosystem where physical, mental, emotional, and spiritual aspects are interconnected. It focuses on restoring balance and harmony within the individual to promote health and prevent or treat diseases.

2. **Individualized treatment**: Traditional medicine recognizes that each person is unique and requires personalized care. Treatment plans are tailored to an individual's specific needs, taking into account their constitution, lifestyle, and environment.

3. **Natural remedies**: Traditional medicine utilizes natural substances derived from plants, animals, and minerals for healing purposes. These remedies are believed to contain inherent healing properties and are often used in their whole or minimally processed forms.

4. **Prevention-oriented**: Traditional medicine places a strong emphasis on preventive measures to maintain health and well-being. It advocates for a balanced lifestyle, proper nutrition, exercise, and the avoidance of harmful behaviors or substances.

Traditional Medical Systems

Traditional medicine encompasses various medical systems, each with its own unique principles and approaches. Some commonly practiced traditional medical systems include:

1. **Traditional Chinese Medicine (TCM)**: Originating in ancient China, TCM is based on the concepts of Yin and Yang, the Five Elements, and Qi (vital

energy). It comprises practices such as acupuncture, herbal medicine, cupping therapy, and tai chi. TCM aims to restore balance and harmony in the body to promote health.

2. **Ayurveda:** Originating in ancient India, Ayurveda is a holistic system that focuses on aligning an individual's body, mind, and spirit. It involves techniques such as herbal medicine, dietary changes, yoga, and meditation to maintain health and prevent diseases.

3. **Traditional African Medicine:** Practiced across many African countries, traditional African medicine is deeply rooted in cultural beliefs and practices. It often combines herbal remedies, spiritual rituals, divination, and counseling to address physical, mental, and spiritual ailments.

4. **Native American Medicine:** Native American medicine encompasses various indigenous healing traditions that have been passed down through generations. It involves the use of medicinal plants, ceremonies, and rituals to promote well-being and restore harmony within the community.

5. **Traditional Medicine in Indigenous Cultures:** Indigenous cultures around the world have their own unique traditional medical systems that are based on their deep connection with nature and spirituality. These systems often incorporate herbal remedies, rituals, and traditional healing practices to maintain health and treat diseases.

Treatment Modalities

Traditional medicine employs a variety of treatment modalities to promote healing and restore balance. Some common modalities include:

1. **Herbal Medicine:** Plant-based remedies are commonly used in traditional medicine to treat a wide range of ailments. These remedies may be taken orally, applied topically, or inhaled. Herbal medicine relies on the medicinal properties of plants to restore health and treat diseases.

2. **Acupuncture:** This practice involves the insertion of thin needles into specific points on the body to manipulate the flow of energy or Qi. Acupuncture is believed to restore balance and relieve various physical and mental health conditions.

3. **Massage and Bodywork:** Therapeutic massage and bodywork techniques are used in traditional medicine to promote relaxation, reduce muscular tension, improve circulation, and enhance overall well-being.

4. **Meditation and Mindfulness:** These practices are often employed to calm the mind, reduce stress, and enhance mental clarity. They are an integral part of many traditional medical systems, promoting overall health and well-being.

5. **Dietary Changes:** Traditional medicine recognizes the importance of nutrition in maintaining health. Dietary changes and recommendations are often prescribed to address specific health conditions and promote overall well-being.

6. **Exercise and Movement:** Physical activity, such as yoga, tai chi, or specific exercises, is commonly recommended in traditional medicine to improve energy flow, build strength, and promote overall vitality.

Integration with Modern Medicine

In recent years, there has been a growing recognition of the potential benefits of integrating traditional medicine with modern healthcare approaches. This integration, known as integrative medicine, aims to combine the strengths of both systems to provide comprehensive and holistic care for individuals.

Integrative medicine acknowledges the evidence-based practices of modern medicine while incorporating traditional medical systems and therapies. It recognizes the importance of individualized care and promotes a patient-centered approach that considers a person's physical, mental, and emotional well-being.

By integrating traditional medicine into modern healthcare, individuals can potentially benefit from a wider range of treatment options, improved symptom management, and a more personalized approach to their health. Moreover, integrative medicine encourages collaboration and communication between healthcare providers from different disciplines, fostering a multidimensional approach to patient care.

Cultural Considerations

Traditional medicine is deeply influenced by cultural beliefs, practices, and values. It considers the social and spiritual aspects of health, emphasizing the interconnectedness of individuals within their communities and natural environments.

When working with individuals from diverse cultural backgrounds, it is important for healthcare providers to understand and respect these cultural contexts. This includes recognizing the traditional medical beliefs and practices that may be integral to an individual's worldview and incorporating them into their healthcare plan, where appropriate.

Engaging in culturally sensitive care ensures that individuals receive treatment that aligns with their cultural beliefs, promotes trust and rapport, and supports their overall well-being. It is crucial to approach traditional medicine with an open mind, respect for cultural diversity, and a willingness to learn from different healing traditions.

Conclusion

Traditional medicine is a valuable and rich healthcare system that offers unique insights into holistic health and well-being. Its principles, modalities, and cultural contexts provide a diverse and comprehensive approach to healthcare. Integrating traditional medicine into modern healthcare practices can enhance patient care and promote a more holistic understanding of health.

As we explore the health benefits of soy consumption and debunk the myths surrounding soy boys and snowflakes, it is important to consider the perspectives and contributions of traditional medicine. By embracing diverse approaches to health and wellness, we can foster a culture of inclusivity, acceptance, and personal growth.

Holistic Approaches

In the realm of healthcare, holistic approaches aim to address the person as a whole, taking into consideration various aspects of their being, including physical, mental, emotional, and spiritual health. These approaches emphasize the interconnectedness of these dimensions and their impact on overall well-being. Holistic medicine seeks to promote balance, harmony, and integration within the individual.

Principles of Holistic Approaches

Holistic medicine is built upon several key principles that guide its practice:

1. **Individuality**: Each person is unique and requires personalized care. Holistic approaches recognize the importance of tailoring treatments to

meet the specific needs of an individual rather than adopting a one-size-fits-all approach.

2. **Whole-person care:** Holistic medicine views the individual as a complex system of interconnected parts. Instead of focusing solely on symptoms or specific ailments, holistic approaches consider the entire person and aim to identify and address the root causes of health issues.

3. **Integration of mind, body, and spirit:** Holistic approaches recognize the intricate interplay between the physical, mental, and spiritual aspects of an individual. They aim to restore balance and harmony within these dimensions, as imbalances can lead to illness or disease.

4. **Prevention and wellness:** Holistic medicine places great emphasis on prevention as the best form of healthcare. By promoting healthy lifestyle choices, proper nutrition, stress management techniques, and regular exercise, holistic approaches aim to prevent the onset of diseases and maintain overall wellness.

5. **Collaboration and partnership:** Holistic healthcare providers work in partnership with individuals, encouraging active participation in their own healing process. This collaborative approach ensures that individuals are empowered to make informed decisions about their health and well-being.

Modalities in Holistic Approaches

Holistic approaches encompass a wide range of modalities that address multiple dimensions of health. Here are some common modalities used in holistic medicine:

- **Acupuncture:** This ancient Chinese practice involves the insertion of thin needles at specific points on the body to promote healing, balance energy flow, and alleviate pain and discomfort.

- **Ayurveda:** Originating in India, Ayurveda is a holistic healing system that focuses on harmonizing the body, mind, and spirit through diet, herbal remedies, yoga, meditation, and lifestyle modifications.

- **Homeopathy:** Homeopathy is based on the principle of "like cures like" and uses highly diluted substances to stimulate the body's self-healing abilities.

- **Massage therapy:** Massage techniques are used to manipulate soft tissues, muscles, and joints, promoting relaxation, stress reduction, pain relief, and overall well-being.

- **Meditation and mindfulness:** These practices aim to quiet the mind, reduce stress, and increase self-awareness. They involve focusing one's attention and achieving a state of mental clarity and relaxation.

- **Naturopathy:** Naturopathic medicine combines traditional healing practices with modern medical knowledge. It emphasizes the body's innate ability to heal itself and focuses on natural therapies, such as herbal medicine, nutrition, physical manipulation, and lifestyle counseling.

- **Yoga:** Yoga is a holistic practice that combines physical postures, breathing exercises, meditation, and ethical principles. It promotes flexibility, strength, stress reduction, and overall mind-body balance.

The Role of Holistic Approaches in Health

Holistic approaches can play a significant role in promoting and maintaining health. By addressing the physical, mental, emotional, and spiritual aspects of an individual, these approaches provide a comprehensive framework for disease prevention and wellness.

Physical health: Holistic modalities, such as acupuncture, massage therapy, and yoga, can help improve physical well-being by reducing pain, increasing flexibility, enhancing overall fitness, and supporting the body's ability to heal itself.

Mental health: Holistic approaches emphasize the connection between the mind and body. Practices like meditation, mindfulness, and yoga can help reduce stress, improve focus, enhance cognitive function, and promote a positive outlook on life.

Emotional health: Holistic approaches recognize the impact of emotions on overall health. By integrating techniques like counseling, art therapy, and journaling, these approaches aim to improve emotional well-being, promote self-expression, and facilitate healing from past traumas.

Spiritual health: Holistic medicine acknowledges the importance of addressing the spiritual dimension of a person. Practices like meditation, yoga, and connecting with nature can nurture a sense of purpose, inner peace, and interconnectedness, enhancing spiritual well-being.

Holistic Approaches in Practice

To illustrate the application of holistic approaches, let's consider the example of a person experiencing chronic back pain. In addition to physical therapies and medications, a holistic approach would explore the underlying causes of the pain, considering factors such as stress, emotions, lifestyle choices, and posture. The treatment plan might include acupuncture sessions, yoga exercises to improve posture and flexibility, counseling to address emotional stressors, and mindfulness techniques to reduce anxiety. By addressing all dimensions of health, a holistic approach can provide a more comprehensive and effective solution.

Considering the Whole Picture

While holistic approaches have numerous benefits, it is important to acknowledge that they are not a substitute for conventional medical care. Instead, holistic approaches can complement traditional treatments by addressing the individual as a whole. By integrating various modalities, individuals can achieve a balanced approach to health that encompasses physical, mental, emotional, and spiritual well-being. It is crucial for healthcare providers and individuals to work together and consider the whole picture when designing treatment plans and promoting wellness.

Further Exploration

To delve deeper into the world of holistic approaches, consider reading the following resources:

- Chopra, D., & Simon, D. (2004). *The Chopra Center Herbal Handbook: Forty Natural Prescriptions for Perfect Health*. Harmony Publishing.

- Dossey, L. (1999). *Reinventing Medicine: Beyond Mind-Body to a New Era of Healing*. HarperOne.

- Jonas, W. B., & Levin, J. S. (Eds.). (2015). *Essentials of Complementary and Alternative Medicine*. Wolters Kluwer Health.

- Weil, A. (1993). *Spontaneous Healing: How to Discover and Enhance Your Body's Natural Ability to Maintain and Heal Itself*. Knopf.

- Wren-Lewis, J. (2000). *The Art of Jin Shin: Physio-Philosophy*. Jin Shin Institute.

By exploring these resources, you will gain a deeper understanding of holistic approaches and their potential benefits for overall wellness. Remember, the integration of various modalities and a personalized approach are key to holistic healthcare.

Integrative Medicine

Integrative medicine is a holistic approach to healthcare that combines conventional medical practices with complementary and alternative therapies. It focuses on treating the whole person - body, mind, and spirit - and recognizes the importance of addressing the root causes of illness rather than just treating symptoms.

Principles of Integrative Medicine

Integrative medicine is guided by several key principles that distinguish it from traditional medicine:

- **Patient-centered care:** Integrative medicine emphasizes the importance of building a strong doctor-patient relationship and involves the active participation of the patient in their own healing process. The patient's individual needs, preferences, and values are taken into account when developing a treatment plan.

- **Personalized medicine:** Each individual is unique, and integrative medicine recognizes that there is no one-size-fits-all approach to healthcare. It takes into consideration the patient's unique genetic makeup, lifestyle, and environmental factors in order to tailor treatment plans to meet their specific needs.

- **Evidence-based practice:** While integrative medicine incorporates complementary and alternative therapies, it does not abandon the principles of science and evidence-based medicine. All interventions and treatments are rigorously evaluated to ensure their safety and effectiveness.

- **Collaborative approach:** Integrative medicine encourages collaboration among healthcare providers from different disciplines. This interdisciplinary approach allows for a comprehensive evaluation of the patient's condition and the development of a well-rounded treatment plan.

DIFFERENT PERSPECTIVES ON HEALTH BENEFITS

- **Focus on prevention:** In integrative medicine, prevention is seen as the best way to maintain optimal health. It emphasizes the importance of healthy lifestyle choices, such as nutrition, exercise, stress management, and adequate sleep, in preventing chronic diseases.

Integrative Approaches to Health

Integrative medicine incorporates a wide range of therapies and practices to promote health and well-being. Some common modalities include:

1. **Nutritional therapy:** Nutrition plays a vital role in overall health, and integrative medicine emphasizes the importance of a balanced diet rich in whole foods, fruits, vegetables, and lean proteins. Nutritional therapy may also include the use of herbs, supplements, and therapeutic diets to address specific health concerns.

2. **Mind-body medicine:** The mind and body are interconnected, and integrative medicine recognizes the profound impact of thoughts, emotions, and beliefs on physical health. Mind-body practices like meditation, yoga, tai chi, and relaxation techniques are used to promote stress reduction, resilience, and emotional well-being.

3. **Complementary therapies:** Integrative medicine incorporates a range of complementary therapies, such as acupuncture, chiropractic care, massage therapy, and naturopathy. These therapies aim to restore balance and enhance the body's natural healing processes.

4. **Energy medicine:** Energy-based therapies, such as Reiki and therapeutic touch, are used in integrative medicine to manipulate the body's energy fields to promote healing and restore balance.

5. **Herbal medicine:** Herbal remedies have been used for centuries to treat various health conditions. Integrative medicine incorporates evidence-based herbal medicine to support overall health and address specific ailments.

Integrative Medicine in Practice

Integrative medicine can be applied in various clinical settings, from primary care to specialized clinics. Here are a few examples of how integrative medicine is used in practice:

- **Geriatric care:** Integrative medicine approaches are particularly beneficial for elderly patients who may have complex health needs. Integrative interventions, such as acupuncture for pain management, nutritional therapy for age-related conditions, and mind-body practices for stress reduction, can improve their quality of life.

- **Cancer care:** Integrative medicine is often used alongside conventional cancer treatments to support patients through their cancer journey. Complementary therapies, such as acupuncture and massage, can help manage treatment side effects, while nutrition and mind-body practices can improve overall well-being and enhance treatment outcomes.

- **Chronic disease management:** Integrative medicine can be effective in managing chronic conditions like diabetes, heart disease, and autoimmune disorders. By combining conventional medical treatments with lifestyle modifications, nutritional therapy, and mind-body practices, patients can experience greater symptom relief and improved quality of life.

- **Pain management:** Chronic pain is a complex condition that often requires a multidisciplinary approach. Integrative medicine offers a range of options, including acupuncture, physical therapy, massage, and mindfulness techniques, to help patients find relief from pain while minimizing the use of opioid medications.

Challenges and Critics of Integrative Medicine

While integrative medicine has gained popularity in recent years, it still faces some challenges and critics. Here are a few common concerns:

- **Lack of regulation:** The field of integrative medicine encompasses a wide range of therapies, some of which may lack standardized training or regulation. This can make it difficult for healthcare providers and patients to navigate the options and ensure safety and efficacy.

- **Limited insurance coverage:** Integrative medicine therapies are not always covered by insurance, making them inaccessible to many individuals. Lack of reimbursement can limit patients' ability to pursue integrative approaches that may benefit their health.

- **Contradictory evidence:** Some critics argue that the evidence base for certain integrative therapies is limited or contradictory. While some therapies may have substantial research support, others may still require further investigation to establish their effectiveness.

- **Integration with conventional medicine:** Integrating complementary therapies with conventional medical treatments can be challenging. Communication and collaboration between healthcare providers from different disciplines are essential to ensure a cohesive treatment plan that addresses the patient's needs and preferences.

Despite these challenges, integrative medicine holds great promise in improving patient outcomes and promoting holistic well-being. By embracing a patient-centered, evidence-based, collaborative, and preventive approach, integrative medicine has the potential to transform the healthcare landscape and enhance the quality of care provided to individuals. It encourages open-mindedness, critical thinking, and a willingness to explore innovative approaches to healing, ultimately empowering individuals to take an active role in their own health and well-being.

Conclusion

In this section, we explored the concept of integrative medicine, which combines conventional medical practices with complementary and alternative therapies to promote holistic health and well-being. We discussed the principles of integrative medicine, the various approaches it employs, and its application in clinical settings.

Integrative medicine recognizes the importance of personalized, patient-centered care, evidence-based practice, collaboration among healthcare providers, and a focus on prevention. It incorporates therapies such as nutritional therapy, mind-body medicine, complementary therapies, energy medicine, and herbal medicine.

While integrative medicine has gained popularity, it also faces challenges such as the lack of regulation, limited insurance coverage, contradictory evidence, and integration with conventional medicine. However, by addressing these challenges and promoting open-mindedness, critical thinking, and collaboration, integrative medicine has the potential to greatly enhance patient outcomes and improve the overall healthcare landscape.

Embracing diversity and wellness is crucial in nurturing a healthy lifestyle. By encouraging acceptance, empathy, and educated discussions, we can challenge prejudice and bias and foster a culture of inclusivity. Striving for personal and societal growth, we can create a healthcare system that values the whole person -

body, mind, and spirit - and empowers individuals to take control of their own health journey.

As we move forward, let us remember the importance of balanced perspectives and the power of integrative medicine in promoting health, healing, and well-being. By embracing the principles of integrative medicine and nurturing a culture of inclusivity, we can work towards a future where everyone has access to comprehensive, compassionate, and personalized healthcare.

Cultural Influences on Health Beliefs

Culture plays a significant role in shaping individuals' beliefs, values, and behaviors, including their perspectives on health and wellness. Cultural influences can impact various aspects of health, including dietary choices, health-seeking behaviors, and beliefs about the causes and treatments of illness. In this section, we will explore the cultural influences on health beliefs and their implications for overall well-being.

Cultural Diversity and Health Beliefs

Cultural diversity refers to the presence of multiple cultures within a society, each with its own unique values, traditions, and customs. These cultural differences can profoundly influence individuals' health beliefs and practices. For example, in some cultures, the consumption of certain foods is considered essential for good health, while in others, specific dietary restrictions may be observed for religious or cultural reasons.

In the context of health beliefs, cultural diversity highlights the need for healthcare professionals to be culturally sensitive and aware. Understanding and respecting individuals' cultural beliefs and practices can improve the effectiveness of healthcare interventions and promote better health outcomes. It is important to acknowledge and value cultural diversity, as it enriches the overall healthcare experience and contributes to the development of more inclusive and equitable healthcare systems.

Cultural Beliefs about Illness and Disease

Cultural beliefs about illness and disease vary across different cultures and can significantly influence individuals' health-seeking behaviors and treatment preferences. For example, in some cultures, illness may be viewed as a result of spiritual imbalance or disharmony, while in others, it may be attributed to external factors such as exposure to specific environmental conditions.

Understanding cultural beliefs about illness is crucial for healthcare professionals in effectively communicating with and providing care to individuals from diverse cultural backgrounds. This knowledge helps foster trust and enhance patient-provider relationships, leading to improved health outcomes. It also allows healthcare providers to tailor treatment plans that align with patients' cultural beliefs and preferences, increasing treatment adherence and overall satisfaction.

Cultural Practices and Health Behaviors

Cultural practices have a significant impact on health behaviors and lifestyle choices. For example, in some cultures, physical activity may be woven into everyday life through traditional dance or agricultural practices, promoting overall wellness. In contrast, sedentary lifestyles may be more prevalent in cultures where technological advancements have reduced the need for physical labor.

Dietary habits also vary across cultures, influenced by factors such as geography, climate, availability of resources, and cultural traditions. For instance, some cultures emphasize the consumption of specific foods or food groups believed to have medicinal properties, while others follow dietary restrictions based on religious or cultural beliefs.

Understanding these cultural practices and their influence on health behaviors is essential for promoting healthy lifestyles and preventing disease. By recognizing the importance of cultural beliefs and practices, healthcare professionals can work collaboratively with individuals and communities to develop culturally appropriate strategies for health promotion and disease prevention.

Cultural Perspectives on Treatment and Healing

Cultural perspectives on treatment and healing encompass a wide range of practices, including traditional medicine, herbal remedies, spiritual rituals, and Western medicine. The choice of treatment and healing practices varies according to cultural beliefs, available resources, and accessibility to healthcare services.

It is crucial to respect and acknowledge cultural perspectives on treatment and healing while providing healthcare services. Integrating traditional and culturally sensitive approaches with evidence-based Western medicine can lead to more comprehensive and holistic healthcare. This approach not only acknowledges the value of cultural practices but also promotes better patient satisfaction, treatment adherence, and health outcomes.

Challenges and Recommendations

While cultural influences on health beliefs are important, certain challenges may arise in addressing cultural diversity in healthcare. These challenges include language barriers, limited cultural competence among healthcare providers, and the potential clash between cultural beliefs and evidence-based medicine. To overcome these challenges and provide culturally sensitive care, various strategies can be implemented:

1. Cultural competence training: Healthcare professionals should receive training on cultural competence to enhance their understanding of diverse cultural beliefs and practices. This training should focus on developing skills to communicate effectively and provide culturally appropriate care.

2. Interpreting services: To overcome language barriers and ensure effective communication, healthcare facilities should provide interpreting services or employ multilingual staff.

3. Collaborative approach: Healthcare providers need to adopt a collaborative approach with patients and their families, respecting their cultural beliefs and preferences. This approach involves active listening, mutual respect, and shared decision-making.

4. Incorporating cultural beliefs into care plans: Healthcare providers should consider cultural beliefs and practices when developing care plans, incorporating patient preferences and cultural norms.

5. Community engagement: Healthcare organizations can engage with communities to understand their cultural beliefs, promote health education programs, and collaborate on developing culturally relevant interventions.

By recognizing and addressing cultural influences on health beliefs, we can create a healthcare system that is more inclusive, equitable, and effective in meeting the diverse needs of individuals and communities.

Conclusion

Cultural influences shape individuals' health beliefs, values, and behaviors and have a significant impact on overall well-being. Understanding and respecting cultural diversity, beliefs about illness, cultural practices, and perspectives on treatment and healing are crucial for healthcare professionals in providing effective, patient-centered care. By incorporating cultural sensitivity into healthcare practices, we can foster better communication, improve health outcomes, and promote a more inclusive and equitable healthcare system.

Debunking Soy Boy Myths

Dispelling Misconceptions about Soy

Soy and Estrogen Levels

Estrogen is a hormone that plays a crucial role in the development and regulation of the female reproductive system. It is also present in males, although in significantly lower levels. There has been a longstanding concern that the consumption of soy products, which contain natural compounds called phytoestrogens, may lead to increased estrogen levels in both men and women. However, extensive research has debunked this myth and shown that the relationship between soy and estrogen levels is more complex than initially believed.

Phytoestrogens are plant compounds that structurally resemble human estrogen but have a weaker activity. They can bind to estrogen receptors in the body and exert both estrogenic and anti-estrogenic effects. Soybeans and soy products, such as tofu and soy milk, are rich sources of phytoestrogens, particularly a type called isoflavones.

Contrary to popular belief, the consumption of soy does not lead to a significant increase in estrogen levels. In fact, several studies have shown that soy intake has no discernible effect on the levels of circulating estrogen in both men and women. One study published in the Journal of Nutrition found that there was no difference in estrogen levels between postmenopausal women who consumed soy protein isolate and those who consumed a milk protein isolate.

The reason for this lack of effect on estrogen levels is thought to be due to the presence of specific enzymes in the body that can metabolize and eliminate phytoestrogens. These enzymes help prevent any significant buildup of phytoestrogens in the bloodstream, thereby minimizing their hormonal effects.

Moreover, soy consumption has been found to have several beneficial effects on female reproductive health. For premenopausal women, soy isoflavones have been shown to alleviate symptoms of menopause, such as hot flashes and night sweats. They can also help promote bone health and reduce the risk of osteoporosis, a condition commonly associated with declining estrogen levels.

In men, the fear of soy consumption leading to feminizing effects is unfounded. A study published in the Journal of the American College of Nutrition found that high soy consumption had no adverse effects on testosterone levels or sperm quality in healthy males. Another meta-analysis of 15 studies concluded that soy protein intake did not have a significant effect on testosterone levels in both men and women.

It is important to note that the majority of research indicates that soy consumption is safe and does not lead to hormonal imbalances. However, as with any dietary component, moderation is key. Consuming a varied diet that includes a balance of different plant-based proteins, such as beans, legumes, and grains, can provide a range of nutritional benefits.

In summary, the idea that soy consumption significantly affects estrogen levels is a myth. The phytoestrogens found in soy products do not have a noticeable impact on circulating estrogen levels in men or women. Soy consumption can be part of a healthy diet and may provide various health benefits, particularly for female reproductive health. It is essential to approach nutrition with a balanced perspective and include a variety of plant-based protein sources in our diets for optimal health and well-being.

Soy and Testosterone

Testosterone is a hormone that plays a crucial role in the development and maintenance of male sexual characteristics. It is responsible for regulating various bodily functions, including muscle growth, bone density, and sex drive. There have been claims suggesting that soy consumption could lower testosterone levels, leading to concerns about its potential effects on male health.

Understanding Testosterone

Before delving into the relationship between soy and testosterone, it is essential to have a basic understanding of testosterone and its functions. Testosterone is primarily produced in the testes in men and in smaller amounts in the ovaries and adrenal glands in women. It is a steroid hormone belonging to the androgen group, which also includes dihydrotestosterone (DHT) and androstenedione.

Testosterone is responsible for the development of male reproductive tissues, including the testes and prostate. It stimulates the growth of muscle and bone mass and helps regulate the production of red blood cells. In addition, testosterone influences libido and plays a role in mood regulation.

Soy and Isoflavones

Soy is a legume native to East Asia and is widely consumed in various forms, including whole soybeans, soy milk, tofu, and tempeh. It is a rich source of protein and contains all essential amino acids. Soy also contains various bioactive compounds, including isoflavones.

Isoflavones are naturally occurring phytoestrogens found in soy. Phytoestrogens are compounds that have a similar structure to estrogen, a hormone primarily associated with female reproductive health. Isoflavones can bind to estrogen receptors in the body, but their effects are much weaker compared to natural estrogen.

The two main isoflavones in soy are genistein and daidzein. These isoflavones have been extensively studied for their potential health benefits, including their role in preventing chronic diseases such as cardiovascular disease, osteoporosis, and certain types of cancer.

Debunking Soy and Testosterone Relationship

There is a popular belief that soy consumption can lead to a decrease in testosterone levels in men. This misconception stems from the fact that isoflavones in soy can mimic estrogenic effects in the body. However, research has consistently shown that the impact of soy on testosterone levels is negligible and unlikely to have any significant physiological effects.

Numerous studies have investigated the relationship between soy consumption and testosterone levels in men. A comprehensive review published in the Journal of Clinical Endocrinology and Metabolism analyzed 15 randomized control trials and concluded that neither soy foods nor isoflavone supplements had any effect on testosterone levels.

Moreover, a study published in the Journal of the American College of Nutrition found that increased soy consumption did not lead to changes in testosterone concentrations in healthy adult men. The study involved a six-week intervention, during which the participants consumed soy protein shakes daily.

Hormonal Balance and Phytoestrogens

It is important to note that hormonal balance is a complex interplay between various hormones and their receptors in the body. In the case of soy consumption, the presence of phytoestrogens may have a regulatory effect on estrogen receptors, influencing the hormonal balance. However, this modulation does not necessarily lead to a decrease in testosterone levels.

For instance, phytoestrogens can competitively inhibit the aromatase enzyme, which converts testosterone to estrogen. By inhibiting this enzyme, phytoestrogens may indirectly help maintain testosterone levels by preventing excess conversion to estrogen. This mechanism of action suggests that soy consumption can actually be beneficial for testosterone balance rather than detrimental.

Real-World Examples and Considerations

To further illustrate the negligible impact of soy on testosterone levels, it is worth examining populations with high soy consumption. In various Asian countries where soy is a dietary staple, such as Japan and China, there is no evidence of widespread hormonal imbalances or feminization of men attributed to soy consumption.

Moreover, Olympic athlete Carl Lewis, known for his remarkable athletic achievements, followed a vegan diet that included soy products. His exemplary performance demonstrates that soy consumption did not hinder his testosterone levels or athletic abilities.

It is essential to approach the topic of soy and testosterone with a balanced perspective. Incorporating moderate amounts of soy products into a well-rounded diet is unlikely to have any adverse effects on testosterone levels in men. An overall healthy lifestyle, regular exercise, and a diverse diet are more crucial factors in maintaining hormonal balance and overall well-being.

Summary

In summary, the claim that soy consumption negatively impacts testosterone levels in men lacks scientific evidence. Soy isoflavones, including genistein and daidzein, can bind to estrogen receptors but have weak estrogenic effects. Their influence on testosterone levels in men is negligible and unlikely to have any physiological impact.

Maintaining hormonal balance involves a complex interplay between various hormones and receptors in the body. Phytoestrogens present in soy may help regulate estrogen receptors, indirectly assisting in maintaining testosterone levels by inhibiting excess conversion to estrogen.

Real-world examples and scientific studies have consistently shown that soy consumption, even in higher amounts, does not lead to feminization or hormonal imbalances in men. A balanced perspective on soy and testosterone is necessary, emphasizing the importance of overall healthy lifestyle choices and a diverse diet in maintaining optimal hormonal health.

Impact of Soy on Muscle Mass

In the pursuit of physical health and fitness, muscle mass plays a crucial role. Many individuals who engage in strength training or sports activities aim to increase their muscle mass to enhance their performance and achieve their desired physique. In recent years, there have been discussions about the impact of soy consumption on muscle mass. In this section, we will explore the relationship between soy and muscle mass, debunking myths and shedding light on scientific evidence.

Understanding Muscle Growth

Before delving into the specific effects of soy on muscle mass, let's first understand the process of muscle growth. Muscle growth, also known as muscle hypertrophy, occurs when muscle fibers increase in size. This process is driven by a combination of factors, including resistance exercise, adequate protein intake, and hormonal regulation.

During resistance exercise, such as weightlifting, the muscle fibers experience small tears, triggering a process known as muscle protein synthesis (MPS). MPS is the mechanism by which the body repairs and rebuilds these damaged muscle fibers, leading to muscle growth.

Protein, as one of the essential macronutrients, plays a fundamental role in muscle growth. When we consume dietary protein, it gets broken down into amino acids, which are the building blocks of muscle tissue. These amino acids are then used by the body to repair and build new muscle fibers, promoting muscle growth.

Hormones, particularly testosterone and growth hormone, also contribute to muscle growth. These hormones stimulate protein synthesis and play a role in muscle repair and recovery.

Examining Soy Protein and Muscle Mass

Soy protein, derived from soybeans, has gained attention in recent years due to its potential benefits for overall health and well-being. However, there have been concerns and misconceptions regarding the impact of soy protein on muscle mass. Let's explore the scientific evidence and debunk some of these myths.

Myth 1: Soy protein lacks essential amino acids necessary for muscle growth.

Soy protein is known as a complete protein as it contains all the essential amino acids required by the body. Essential amino acids cannot be produced by the body and must be obtained through dietary sources. Soy protein, therefore, provides a good source of amino acids necessary for muscle protein synthesis and overall muscle growth.

Myth 2: Soy protein is inferior to animal-based proteins for muscle growth.

Some individuals believe that animal-based proteins, such as whey protein, are superior to soy protein for muscle growth. However, research studies have shown that soy protein is equally effective in promoting muscle protein synthesis and muscle growth when compared to animal-based proteins. The timing and distribution of protein intake throughout the day, rather than the specific source of protein, seem to be more critical for muscle growth.

Myth 3: Soy protein negatively affects testosterone levels.

There is a common misconception that soy protein consumption can lower testosterone levels, which could potentially hinder muscle growth. However, numerous studies have shown that soy protein does not have a significant impact on testosterone levels in men. In fact, a review of the scientific literature suggests that there is no clinically relevant effect of soy protein on testosterone levels in both men and women.

Optimizing Muscle Growth with Soy

Now that we have debunked some of the myths surrounding soy protein and muscle mass, we can explore how soy can be optimized for muscle growth.

Balance protein intake throughout the day: To support muscle growth, it is important to distribute protein intake evenly throughout the day, rather than consuming a large amount in a single meal. Including soy protein in meals and snacks can help meet daily protein requirements and support muscle protein synthesis.

Combine soy protein with resistance exercise: Resistance exercise plays a significant role in muscle growth. To maximize the benefits of soy protein, it is recommended to combine its consumption with regular resistance training workouts. This combination enhances muscle protein synthesis and allows for optimal muscle growth.

Consider soy-based protein supplements: For individuals who struggle to meet their protein needs through whole food sources alone, soy-based protein supplements can be a convenient option. These supplements provide a concentrated source of protein and can be used as part of a well-balanced diet to support muscle growth.

Real-world Example

Let's consider the case of Alex, a young adult who is interested in building muscle mass. Alex's diet includes a variety of plant-based foods, and they have recently incorporated soy protein into their meals and snacks. Alex follows a consistent resistance training program to stimulate muscle growth.

By combining resistance training with regular soy consumption, Alex ensures an adequate intake of protein and essential amino acids necessary for muscle growth. In addition, Alex incorporates other plant-based protein sources, such as legumes, nuts, and seeds, to further diversify their protein intake and provide a wide range of nutrients.

Over time, with consistent effort and adherence to a well-balanced diet, including soy protein, Alex experiences improvements in muscle mass, strength, and overall physical performance.

Conclusion

Contrary to misconceptions, soy protein can be a valuable component of a diet aimed at optimizing muscle growth. Soy protein provides all the essential amino acids necessary for muscle protein synthesis and demonstrates comparable effectiveness to animal-based proteins. By combining soy protein consumption with resistance exercise and balancing protein intake throughout the day, individuals can achieve their muscle mass goals. It is important to remember that a well-rounded and diverse diet is key to overall health and fitness.

Soy and Femininity

In this section, we will explore the relationship between soy consumption and femininity. There are certain misconceptions and stereotypes surrounding soy and its effects on femininity, which we will debunk using scientific evidence. We will also discuss the potential benefits of soy for women's health and address any concerns that may arise.

Dispelling Misconceptions

One common misconception is that consuming soy products can make women more feminine or increase estrogen levels excessively. However, this is not supported by scientific research. Soy contains phytoestrogens, which are plant compounds that have similar structures to estrogen. These phytoestrogens have weaker estrogenic effects compared to the estrogen produced by the human body.

Research has shown that soy consumption does not significantly increase estrogen levels in women. In fact, a systematic review and meta-analysis conducted in 2019 found that soy consumption had no effect on estrogen levels in both premenopausal and postmenopausal women.

Another misconception is that soy can feminize men or lower their testosterone levels. However, evidence suggests that soy does not have a feminizing effect on men. A study published in the Journal of Clinical Endocrinology and Metabolism in 2010 found that soy protein consumption had no significant effect on testosterone levels in men.

Benefits of Soy Protein

While soy does not have a direct impact on femininity, it offers several health benefits for women. Soy protein is a high-quality plant-based protein that can be an excellent alternative to animal-based proteins. It contains all the essential amino acids needed for optimal health.

Including soy protein in the diet can help women maintain muscle mass and support overall physical fitness. Regular physical activity, along with a balanced diet that includes soy protein, can contribute to a healthy body composition and overall well-being.

Soy protein may also have benefits for women's bone health. Soy isoflavones, a type of phytoestrogen found in soy, have been shown to have a positive effect on bone mineral density. A study published in the American Journal of Clinical Nutrition in 2017 found that soy isoflavones significantly improved bone mineral density in postmenopausal women.

In addition, soy consumption has been associated with a reduced risk of certain types of cancer, including breast and ovarian cancer. The isoflavones in soy have been found to possess anti-cancer properties, potentially inhibiting the growth of cancer cells.

Exploring Femininity and Masculinity

It is important to note that femininity and masculinity are complex concepts that cannot be solely determined by dietary choices. Gender identity and expression are personal and subjective, influenced by a wide range of factors beyond diet.

Individuals define their own femininity and masculinity based on their values, beliefs, and identity. These definitions can vary across cultures and societies, reflecting the diverse perspectives of gender.

It is essential to create a supportive and inclusive environment where individuals can embrace their own unique expressions of femininity and masculinity without judgment. Emphasizing the importance of healthy dietary choices, including the inclusion of soy protein, can be part of promoting overall well-being for both women and men.

Empowering Individuals

Rather than perpetuating stereotypes or promoting rigid gender norms, it is crucial to empower individuals to make informed choices about their nutrition and overall health. Educating individuals about the benefits of soy protein, backed by scientific evidence, can help dispel any misconceptions and foster a positive relationship with food.

Promoting a balanced approach to nutrition that includes a variety of plant-based proteins, in addition to soy, can ensure that individuals receive the full spectrum of nutrients needed for optimal health. Encouraging open and respectful discussions on the topic of gender expression and identity can also contribute to a more inclusive and supportive society.

By challenging assumptions and addressing concerns related to soy consumption and femininity, we can promote a more nuanced understanding of how dietary choices can impact women's health while respecting individual autonomy and diversity of expression.

Benefits of Soy Protein

Soy protein is derived from soybeans and is a complete protein source, containing all the essential amino acids needed for optimal health. Incorporating soy protein into your diet can have numerous health benefits. In this section, we will explore the specific advantages of consuming soy protein.

Cardiovascular Health

One of the key benefits of soy protein is its positive impact on cardiovascular health. Numerous studies have shown that regular consumption of soy protein can reduce the risk of heart disease.

Impact of Soy on Cholesterol Levels Soy protein has been found to lower low-density lipoprotein (LDL) cholesterol levels, which is commonly referred to as "bad" cholesterol. Elevated LDL cholesterol levels are a major risk factor for heart disease. Soy protein contains components called isoflavones, which have been shown to lower LDL cholesterol levels by inhibiting cholesterol absorption and promoting its excretion.

Soy and Heart Disease Prevention In addition to reducing LDL cholesterol, consuming soy protein can also reduce the risk of heart disease by improving other risk factors. Studies have demonstrated that soy protein can lower triglyceride levels, decrease blood pressure, and improve blood vessel function. These effects contribute to lower overall cardiovascular risk and improve heart health.

Bone Health

Soy protein has also been associated with positive effects on bone health.

Soy and Calcium Absorption Soy protein consumption has been shown to enhance calcium absorption in the body. Calcium is essential for maintaining strong bones and teeth. By promoting calcium absorption, soy protein can help prevent conditions such as osteoporosis, which is characterized by low bone density and increased risk of fractures.

Soy and Bone Density In addition to aiding calcium absorption, soy protein may also directly influence bone density. Several studies have shown that regular soy consumption can increase bone mineral density, especially in postmenopausal women. This is particularly significant because postmenopausal women are at a higher risk of developing osteoporosis due to hormonal changes.

Cancer Prevention

Another important benefit of soy protein is its potential to reduce the risk of certain types of cancer.

Soy and Breast Cancer Soy protein contains phytoestrogens, plant compounds that have a similar structure to estrogen. These phytoestrogens can bind to estrogen receptors in the body and may exert anti-cancer effects. Studies suggest that consuming soy protein during adolescence and adulthood may reduce the risk of breast cancer later in life.

Soy and Prostate Cancer   Evidence also suggests that soy protein consumption may be protective against prostate cancer. Epidemiological studies have found an inverse relationship between soy intake and prostate cancer risk, particularly among Asian populations where soy consumption is traditionally higher.

Hormonal Balance

Contrary to popular belief, soy protein does not negatively impact hormone levels in men or women. Instead, it can help maintain hormonal balance.

Impact of Soy on Estrogen Levels   Soy contains phytoestrogens, which can weakly mimic the effects of estrogen in the body. Concerns have been raised regarding the potential adverse effects of soy on hormone levels, particularly in women. However, comprehensive reviews of the scientific literature have consistently demonstrated that soy protein consumption does not significantly affect estrogen levels in either men or women.

Soy and Menopause Symptoms   Soy protein's phytoestrogens may offer relief from some menopausal symptoms, such as hot flashes and night sweats. Phytoestrogens can act as weak estrogen agonists in the body, potentially reducing the severity and frequency of these symptoms. However, individual responses may vary, and further research is needed to fully understand the mechanisms behind soy's effects on menopause.

In conclusion, soy protein offers a range of health benefits, including improvements in cardiovascular health, bone health, cancer prevention, and hormonal balance. Incorporating soy protein into your diet can be a nutritious and valuable addition, contributing to an overall healthy lifestyle. It is important to note that while soy protein provides numerous advantages, a balanced approach to nutrition is essential. Variety in diet and incorporating other plant-based proteins is important to ensure optimal nutrient intake.

Unraveling Soy Boy Stereotypes

Soy Boys and Emotional Intelligence

In this section, we will explore the connection between soy boys and emotional intelligence. Emotional intelligence refers to the ability to understand, manage, and express emotions effectively.   It encompasses skills such as self-awareness, self-regulation, empathy, and social skills. The term "soy boy" is often used as a derogatory label to mock men who are perceived as weak or overly emotional. However, it is essential to understand that emotional intelligence is not limited to any particular gender or dietary choice.

Emotional intelligence plays a crucial role in promoting mental well-being and healthy social relationships. It involves the ability to perceive, understand, and manage one's emotions and the emotions of others. People with high emotional intelligence are more likely to have better mental health outcomes, increased relationship satisfaction, and effective stress management skills.

Now, let's delve deeper into the relationship between soy boys and emotional intelligence:

Stereotypes and Misconceptions

The labeling of soy boys is often based on stereotypes and misconceptions surrounding masculinity and emotional expression. Society has long perpetuated the notion that men should suppress their emotions and appear strong and stoic. This societal expectation can create a barrier for men in developing emotional intelligence and expressing their feelings effectively. However, it is important to recognize that emotional intelligence is not a sign of weakness but rather an asset that promotes psychological well-being.

Breaking Down Emotional Intelligence

To better understand the concept of emotional intelligence, let's explore its key components:

1. **Self-awareness:** This component involves recognizing and understanding one's emotions. It includes being aware of what triggers certain emotions and how they affect thoughts and behaviors. Developing self-awareness allows individuals to better regulate their emotional response and make informed decisions.

2. **Self-regulation:** Self-regulation refers to the ability to manage and control one's emotions effectively. It involves being able to respond to challenging situations without becoming overwhelmed by emotions such as anger, frustration, or sadness. Self-regulation also includes the ability to redirect negative emotions into more positive and constructive actions.

3. **Empathy:** Empathy is the ability to understand and share the feelings of others. It involves recognizing and appreciating different perspectives and

being able to communicate empathy and compassion to others. Empathy plays a crucial role in building healthy and meaningful relationships.

4. **Social skills:** Social skills encompass the ability to navigate social interactions successfully. This includes effective communication, active listening, conflict resolution, and cooperation. Having strong social skills allows individuals to build and maintain healthy relationships with others.

The Intersection of Soy Boys and Emotional Intelligence

Now, let's examine the intersection between soy boys and emotional intelligence. While the term "soy boy" often carries negative connotations, it is vital to note that there is no inherent relationship between soy consumption and emotional intelligence. Emotional intelligence is a personal attribute that can be developed and nurtured through various means, including self-reflection, education, and practice.

With regards to dietary choices, including soy in one's diet does not inherently impact emotional intelligence. Soy is a plant-based protein source that offers various nutritional benefits, but it does not directly influence emotional or psychological aspects of an individual's well-being.

It is essential to separate the stereotypes and misconceptions from the reality when discussing emotional intelligence and soy boys. Emotional intelligence is a valuable skill set that anyone, regardless of their dietary choices or gender, can cultivate. It is a vital aspect of personal growth and overall well-being.

Promoting Emotional Intelligence and Well-being

Promoting emotional intelligence requires creating an environment that supports open and honest communication, encourages self-reflection, and fosters empathy and understanding. Here are some strategies to promote emotional intelligence and well-being:

1. **Education and awareness:** Educate individuals about the importance of emotional intelligence and its positive impact on mental well-being. Raise awareness about stereotypes and misconceptions regarding emotional expression and masculinity.

2. **Emotional literacy:** Teach individuals how to identify and label their emotions accurately. Encourage emotional self-expression and provide resources for individuals to develop effective coping strategies.

3. **Empathy-building activities:** Provide opportunities for individuals to practice empathy and understand different perspectives. This can be done through group activities, discussions, and community engagement.

4. **Mental health support:** Offer resources and support for individuals struggling with emotional well-being. This can include access to mental health professionals, counseling services, and workshops on stress management and self-care.

By promoting emotional intelligence and providing support for well-being, we can create a society that values emotional expression, nurtures healthy relationships, and empowers individuals to live fulfilling lives.

In conclusion, emotional intelligence is not limited to any particular gender or dietary choice. The term "soy boy" should not be used to undermine or dismiss the importance of emotional intelligence. Instead, it is crucial to recognize the value of emotional intelligence and promote its development for the benefit of all individuals, regardless of their dietary preferences.

Soy Boys and Body Image

In this section, we will explore the relationship between soy boys and body image. The term "soy boy" has gained popularity in recent years, often used as a derogatory label for men who are perceived as weak, feminine, or lacking in masculinity. These stereotypes are often based on misconceptions and prejudice. In reality, body image is a complex issue that affects individuals from all walks of life, regardless of their dietary choices.

Body Image Concerns

Body image refers to the way individuals perceive and feel about their own bodies. It encompasses both physical appearance and body functionality. In today's society, there is immense pressure to conform to certain beauty standards, which can lead to body dissatisfaction and negative self-perception.

Men, like women, can experience body image concerns. Traditional masculine ideals often emphasize strong, muscular bodies, which can cause men to feel inadequate or self-conscious if they do not meet these standards. Such unrealistic expectations can lead to body dysmorphia, eating disorders, and other psychological issues.

Misconceptions about Soy and Body Image

One common misconception is that consuming soy products can feminize men and negatively impact their body image. This notion stems from the belief that soy contains high levels of estrogen, a hormone typically associated with femininity.

However, it is important to understand that the estrogen in soy is plant-based and structurally different from the estrogen found in human bodies. The human body metabolizes phytoestrogens, such as those found in soy, differently than endogenous estrogen. Numerous scientific studies have shown that moderate consumption of soy does not lead to feminization or any negative effects on male bodies.

Soy and Muscle Development

Another concern related to body image is the belief that soy consumption hinders muscle development. Some individuals argue that soy protein is inferior to animal-based protein sources, such as whey protein, in promoting muscle growth.

In reality, soy protein is a high-quality source of protein, containing all essential amino acids necessary for muscle synthesis. Research has shown that soy protein supplementation can lead to increases in muscle mass and strength, comparable to animal-based protein sources. Additionally, soy protein has the added benefits of being cholesterol-free and lower in saturated fats.

Diverse Body Image Representations

Promoting diverse body image representations is essential for cultivating a healthy and inclusive society. Embracing different body types, including those that deviate from traditional masculine ideals, can help counteract the harmful effects of body image dissatisfaction.

Encouraging acceptance and respect for all body types, regardless of dietary choices, can contribute to a more positive and inclusive culture. A holistic approach to body image should focus on overall well-being, self-care, and mental health, rather than solely on physical appearance.

Promoting Body Positivity

To foster a positive body image for all individuals, it is crucial to challenge stereotypes and promote body positivity. This can be achieved through education, awareness, and open conversations about the harmful impact of body shaming and unrealistic beauty standards.

Additionally, encouraging individuals to focus on self-acceptance, self-compassion, and self-care can help counteract negative body image issues. Holistic practices like mindfulness, gratitude, and engaging in physical activities that bring joy rather than solely concentrating on appearance can also contribute to a healthier body image.

Case Study: Xavier's Journey

To illustrate the impact of body image concerns and the role of soy consumption in promoting a positive body image, let's consider a case study of Xavier, a young man struggling with self-esteem and body image issues.

Xavier had always felt pressure to conform to societal expectations of masculinity, including having a muscular physique. However, he found it challenging to gain muscle despite his efforts in the gym. He started to doubt his own worth and masculinity, which negatively affected his mental health.

Upon researching the benefits of soy protein, he decided to incorporate soy-based protein shakes into his diet. He learned about the nutritional value of soy and how it could contribute to muscle growth and recovery. With time, Xavier noticed positive changes in his physique, which boosted his self-confidence.

Furthermore, Xavier began to challenge traditional standards of masculinity and body image. He realized that true strength lies in individuality and self-acceptance, rather than conforming to societal expectations. Xavier's journey highlights the importance of embracing diverse body image representations and debunking misconceptions about soy and masculinity.

In conclusion, body image concerns affect men and women alike, and stereotypes regarding soy boys and body image can be harmful and misleading. Consuming soy does not feminize men or hinder muscle development. By promoting diverse body images, challenging stereotypes, and fostering body positivity through education and self-acceptance, we can cultivate a healthier and more inclusive society.

Exploring Femininity and Masculinity

Society often associates certain characteristics and behaviors with femininity and masculinity. These societal expectations can influence individuals' perceptions of themselves and their choices, including their dietary preferences. In this section, we will delve into the concept of femininity and masculinity, exploring how they intersect with diet and health.

Defining Femininity and Masculinity

Femininity and masculinity are social constructs that define qualities and behaviors traditionally associated with women and men, respectively. These constructs vary across cultures, and there is no one-size-fits-all definition. However, there are some commonly recognized characteristics often attributed to femininity and masculinity.

Femininity may be associated with qualities such as nurturing, empathy, and emotional sensitivity. Traditionally, women have been expected to embody these characteristics and play roles associated with childbearing and caregiving. On the other hand, masculinity has often been linked to attributes like physical strength, assertiveness, and independence. Men have typically been expected to take on the roles of providers and protectors.

Gender Roles and Dietary Preferences

Societal expectations about femininity and masculinity have influenced not only how individuals perceive themselves but also their dietary preferences. For example, women have historically and culturally been associated with being more health-conscious and attentive to their diet. Consequently, they may be more likely to incorporate fruits, vegetables, and other nutrient-dense foods in their diet.

On the other hand, masculinity has been linked to meat consumption, particularly red meat, which is often associated with strength and vitality. Men may feel societal pressure to consume larger quantities of protein, including animal products, to meet expectations related to physical appearance and strength.

However, it is essential to recognize that these associations are not inherently tied to biological sex. The concept of femininity and masculinity is fluid and can be experienced by individuals of all gender identities.

Challenging Stereotypes and Expanding Definitions

As our society becomes more inclusive and diverse, it is crucial to challenge and expand our understanding of femininity and masculinity. By doing so, we can break free from rigid stereotypes that limit individuals' choices and perpetuate harmful gender norms.

When it comes to diet and health, promoting a more expansive definition of femininity and masculinity can help create a more inclusive and accepting environment. This means recognizing that individuals of all genders can make diverse choices based on personal preferences, cultural background, and health needs.

Embracing a Balanced Approach to Diet

Instead of adhering to rigid gender norms, it is essential to adopt a balanced approach to diet that focuses on individual needs and overall health. This means incorporating a variety of nutrient-rich foods, including fruits, vegetables, whole grains, legumes, and lean proteins, regardless of gender identity.

Focusing on macronutrient balance, such as the appropriate ratio of carbohydrates, proteins, and fats, can also contribute to overall well-being. Additionally, considering individual dietary restrictions and preferences can help create a sustainable and enjoyable eating pattern.

Promoting Healthy Body Image

Challenges related to body image are not exclusive to a particular gender. Both men and women can face societal pressure to conform to certain beauty standards. The concept of masculinity, specifically, can create expectations related to muscularity and physical appearance.

It is essential to promote body positivity and self-acceptance for individuals of all gender identities. Encouraging regular exercise, engaging in activities that promote mental and emotional well-being, and fostering positive relationships with food can contribute to a healthier body image.

Cultural and Individual Differences

Cultural and individual factors play a significant role in shaping dietary choices and preferences. Cultural norms and traditions can influence what foods and eating rituals are considered appropriate for individuals of different genders.

Respecting and embracing cultural diversity is crucial in promoting inclusivity and dismantling stereotypes. Recognizing that individuals may have unique dietary needs and preferences based on cultural heritage can help create a more inclusive and respectful environment.

Promoting Conversation and Understanding

Open and respectful communication is key in promoting understanding and acceptance of diverse dietary choices. Creating a safe space for individuals to discuss their experiences, concerns, and aspirations can foster empathy and combat stereotypes.

Promoting educational programs and initiatives that celebrate diversity and challenge gender norms is essential. These initiatives can help individuals develop critical thinking skills and cultivate respect for diverse dietary choices.

Encouraging Personal Growth

Ultimately, exploring femininity and masculinity in the context of diet and health is about encouraging personal growth and self-discovery. By challenging existing stereotypes, individuals can better understand and embrace their own unique preferences and needs.

Encouraging individuals to explore their relationship with food, their bodies, and their overall well-being can lead to personal empowerment and a healthier mindset. Providing resources, support, and guidance can help individuals navigate societal expectations and make choices that align with their genuine selves.

In conclusion, exploring femininity and masculinity in the context of diet and health involves challenging stereotypes, expanding definitions, and promoting inclusivity. By embracing a balanced approach to diet, promoting healthy body image, recognizing cultural and individual differences, and encouraging open conversations, we can create a more accepting and empowering environment for all individuals.

The Intersection of Gender and Diet

In today's society, gender roles and stereotypes heavily influence various aspects of our lives, including our dietary choices. The intersection of gender and diet explores how cultural norms and societal expectations shape the food preferences, eating habits, and nutritional needs of individuals based on their gender identity. Understanding this intersection is crucial for promoting gender equality, promoting healthy eating behaviors, and addressing specific health concerns.

Gender Identity and Food Preferences

Gender identity refers to an individual's deeply-held sense of being male, female, or another gender. It is important to note that gender identity is not determined by biological sex, and individuals may identify as transgender, non-binary, or genderqueer, among other identities. Gender identity can influence food preferences and dietary choices for several reasons.

1. Cultural and Social Factors: Cultural norms and social expectations often dictate specific roles and behaviors associated with each gender. These influences can extend to dietary choices, with certain foods and cuisines considered more masculine

or feminine. For example, salads and fruits may be associated with femininity, while grilled meats and protein-rich foods may be associated with masculinity.

2. Marketing and Advertising: Food advertising often reinforces gender stereotypes, targeting specific genders with different products. For example, advertisements for diet-related products are often aimed at women, while ads for high-protein foods or energy drinks may be geared towards men. These marketing strategies can influence individuals' perception of what is appropriate or desirable to consume based on their gender.

3. Peer Influence: Peer pressure and social norms can also play a significant role in shaping food preferences. Individuals may conform to the dietary patterns of their social groups or strive to fit in by adopting specific eating habits commonly associated with their gender.

4. Body Image Concerns: Gender norms and societal expectations regarding appearance and body image can influence dietary choices. For instance, societal pressure to conform to a thin ideal may lead some individuals to adopt restrictive eating behaviors, particularly among women.

Nutritional Considerations Based on Gender

While there are undeniable social and cultural influences on dietary choices, it is important to recognize that nutrient requirements and health concerns can vary between genders. These differences stem from physiological variations, such as hormonal fluctuations, reproductive functions, and body composition. Adapting dietary patterns to meet specific nutritional needs can help reduce the risk of gender-specific health issues.

1. Nutrient Requirements: - Men often have higher calorie needs due to a higher percentage of lean muscle mass and higher metabolic rates. Adequate protein intake is crucial for muscle repair and growth. - Women, particularly during pregnancy and lactation, have increased nutrient requirements to support fetal and infant development. Nutrients like folate, iron, and calcium are of particular importance. - Hormonal changes in women, such as menstruation and menopause, require careful attention to specific nutrients like iron and calcium.

2. Health Concerns: - Women have higher rates of osteoporosis, making adequate calcium and vitamin D intake crucial for bone health. - Men may have a higher risk of cardiovascular disease, necessitating a diet low in saturated and trans fats and rich in heart-healthy nutrients like omega-3 fatty acids. - Hormonal imbalances can affect both men and women, necessitating dietary interventions (e.g., managing symptoms of menopause and supporting prostate health).

Promoting Gender-Inclusive and Balanced Eating Habits

To promote a gender-inclusive and balanced approach to diet, it is essential to challenge gender stereotypes and encourage individuals to make food choices based on their own preferences, health needs, and values. Here are some approaches to fostering inclusivity and healthy eating habits:

1. Education and Awareness: - Promote nutrition education that emphasizes the importance of individual needs and preferences over gender-based stereotypes. - Raise awareness about the potential harmful effects of rigid gender norms on both physical and mental well-being. - Encourage critical thinking skills to analyze and question gender-biased marketing and advertising strategies.

2. Diverse Dietary Options: - Encourage a range of food choices that are culturally diverse and cater to different nutritional needs and preferences, rather than prescribing certain foods as masculine or feminine. - Promote the inclusion of plant-based proteins, whole grains, and diverse fruits and vegetables to ensure a balanced and nutrient-rich diet for all genders.

3. Mindful Eating: - Encourage individuals to develop a healthy relationship with food, focusing on mindful eating practices rather than restrictive or excessive eating behaviors influenced by societal expectations. - Highlight the benefits of intuitive eating, which emphasizes self-awareness, honoring hunger and fullness cues, and finding pleasure in eating without judgment.

4. Addressing Body Image Concerns: - Promote body positivity and self-acceptance, discouraging dieting practices aimed at conforming to unrealistic standards of beauty and attractiveness. - Encourage body diversity and challenge stereotypes associated with body shape, size, and appearance.

By recognizing the intersection of gender and diet, we can promote a more inclusive and supportive environment that empowers individuals to make informed and healthy food choices based on their unique needs, preferences, and overall well-being.

Remember, food is not gendered. Everyone, regardless of gender identity, deserves to have a positive relationship with food and access to proper nutrition. Let's break free from gender stereotypes and embrace a more inclusive approach to diet and health.

Key Takeaways:

- Gender identity can influence food preferences and dietary choices due to cultural, social, and marketing influences, as well as body image concerns. - Nutritional considerations differ between genders based on physiological variations and health concerns. - Promoting gender-inclusive and balanced eating habits involves education, diverse dietary options, mindful eating practices, and addressing body image concerns. - Encouraging individuals to make food choices based on their own needs and preferences fosters a healthier and more inclusive approach to diet.

Empowering Men to Make Nutritious Choices

In today's society, there is a growing awareness of the importance of nutrition and its impact on overall health and well-being. However, men often face unique challenges when it comes to making nutritious choices. Societal norms and stereotypes may discourage men from prioritizing their health, leading to unhealthy habits and dietary choices. In this section, we will explore strategies to empower men to make nutritious choices and improve their overall health.

Understanding the Barriers

Before we can empower men to make nutritious choices, it is crucial to understand the barriers they may face. Societal expectations often place an emphasis on masculinity associated with eating large portions of meat, fried foods, and high-calorie snacks. This can make it difficult for men to adopt healthier eating habits, as they may fear judgment or criticism.

Additionally, men are often targeted by marketing campaigns promoting unhealthy foods and beverages. Advertisements for sugary drinks, fast food, and processed snacks often perpetuate the idea that these choices are inherently masculine. Such advertisements can influence men's perceptions of what constitutes a "manly" diet, further reinforcing unhealthy behaviors.

Building Awareness

One essential strategy for empowering men to make nutritious choices is to build awareness of the benefits of a healthy diet. Emphasizing the positive impacts of proper nutrition on physical performance, mental clarity, and overall well-being can help men see the value in making healthier choices.

Educational campaigns targeted specifically at men can provide information on the nutritional needs of the male body and the long-term health benefits of a balanced diet. By highlighting the link between nutrition and performance in areas that men may prioritize, such as exercise, sports, and overall vitality, we can motivate men to take charge of their health through their food choices.

Changing Perceptions

To empower men to make nutritious choices, we must challenge and change the perception that healthy eating is incompatible with masculinity. This can be achieved by promoting positive role models who embody both strength and a healthy lifestyle.

Using social media platforms and other channels, we can showcase men who prioritize their health and nutrition, debunking the notion that healthy choices are feminine or weak. By highlighting athletes, fitness enthusiasts, and everyday men who embody a balanced and nutritious lifestyle, we can inspire men to shift their perception of what it means to be healthy.

Educating on Nutrient Diversity

One effective way to empower men to make nutritious choices is by educating them on the importance of nutrient diversity. Men often tend to focus on macronutrients, such as protein, and overlook the role of micronutrients in maintaining overall health.

By providing comprehensive information on various nutrients and their sources, we can encourage men to incorporate a wide range of foods into their diet. This can help them meet their nutrient requirements, enhance their energy levels, and support optimal physical and mental performance.

Promoting Practical Strategies

In order to make nutritious choices, men need practical strategies that fit into their busy lifestyles. Providing easy-to-follow guidelines and tips can help them navigate grocery shopping, meal planning, and cooking.

Additionally, encouraging men to develop basic culinary skills and explore new recipes can make healthy eating more enjoyable and accessible. By equipping men with the knowledge and skills to prepare nutritious meals, they are more likely to adopt long-lasting healthy habits.

Creating a Supportive Environment

Creating a supportive environment is crucial for empowering men to make nutritious choices. Men are more likely to embrace healthy behaviors when they receive support from their peers, family, and healthcare professionals.

By fostering open and non-judgmental conversations about nutrition, we can create spaces for men to share their challenges and successes. Peer support groups, cooking clubs, and online communities can provide a platform for men to connect, seek advice, and share their experiences in adopting a healthier lifestyle.

Summary

In conclusion, empowering men to make nutritious choices is essential for their overall health and well-being. By understanding the barriers they face, building awareness, changing perceptions, educating on nutrient diversity, promoting practical strategies, and creating a supportive environment, we can empower men to prioritize their health and make positive changes in their dietary choices. By challenging societal norms and stereotypes, we can redefine what it means to be a healthy man and encourage men to embrace a balanced and nutritious lifestyle.

Exploring the Snowflake Phenomenon

Understanding the Snowflake Generation

Definition of the Snowflake Generation

The term "Snowflake Generation" has gained popularity in recent years, often used to describe a specific group of young people who are perceived as being overly sensitive, easily offended, and lacking resilience. However, it is essential to approach this term with caution, as it is heavily loaded with stereotypes and often used in a derogatory manner.

Origins of the Term

The term "Snowflake Generation" originated from the phrase "every snowflake is unique." It was initially used to emphasize and celebrate the individuality and uniqueness of each person. Over time, however, the term has evolved and taken on a negative connotation.

In the context of the Snowflake Generation, the term is used to imply that young people are fragile, delicate, and unable to handle criticism or discomfort. It suggests that they need constant validation and safe spaces, leading to the perception that they are easily offended or triggered by opposing viewpoints.

Factors Influencing the Snowflake Phenomenon

Understanding the factors that contribute to the development of the Snowflake Generation is crucial. Several societal and cultural shifts have shaped the attitudes and behaviors associated with this phenomenon:

- **Parenting Styles:** The parenting styles prevalent in recent decades have placed a strong emphasis on shielding children from adversity and promoting self-esteem. While well-intentioned, overprotective parenting may have unintentionally hindered the development of resilience and coping mechanisms.

- **Education System:** Modern education systems have shifted towards prioritizing emotional well-being and creating safe spaces for students. While this is beneficial for mental health support, critics argue that it may contribute to a lack of exposure to diverse perspectives and challenges.

- **Technology and Social Media:** The rise of social media has increased the exposure to negativity, cyberbullying, and online criticism. Constant connectivity and online comparison can impact the mental well-being of individuals, leading to heightened emotional responses.

- **Generational Differences:** Each generation has unique experiences and perspectives shaped by historical events. The Snowflake Generation, typically characterized as Millennials and Gen Z, has grown up in a time of rapid technological advancements, economic uncertainty, and increased emphasis on inclusivity and social justice issues.

Generational Differences in Health Perspectives

Generational differences play a significant role in shaping health perspectives. The Snowflake Generation often showcases distinct attitudes towards health and well-being. These differences can be attributed to various factors, including exposure to new information, cultural shifts, and advancements in healthcare:

- **Mental Health Awareness:** The Snowflake Generation has been at the forefront of raising awareness about mental health. They emphasize the significance of emotional well-being, accessible mental health support, and reducing the stigma associated with seeking help.

- **Inclusivity and Diversity:** This generation prioritizes inclusivity and challenges existing norms and stereotypes. They advocate for diverse representation and equal access to healthcare for marginalized groups.

- **Preventive Health Practices:** With increased access to information, the Snowflake Generation is more inclined to engage in preventive health practices, such as regular exercise, healthy eating, and proactive healthcare.

- **Holistic Approaches:** There is a growing interest in holistic health approaches that encompass physical, mental, emotional, and spiritual well-being. This generation recognizes the interconnectedness of these aspects and seeks a balanced approach to health.

- **Environmental Consciousness:** The Snowflake Generation is more environmentally conscious and recognizes the importance of sustainable practices for personal and planetary health.

It is essential to approach generational differences with understanding and respect, recognizing that each generation brings unique perspectives and experiences to the table. Emphasizing dialogue and collaboration can bridge the gaps and foster mutual learning and growth.

Navigating Mental Health Concerns

Navigating mental health concerns is a critical aspect of addressing the Snowflake Generation phenomenon. It is crucial to provide support and resources to promote mental well-being while also encouraging the development of resilience and coping skills.

- **Access to Mental Health Services:** Collaborative efforts are required to improve accessibility and affordability of mental health services. This includes destigmatizing mental health concerns and providing adequate resources within educational institutions, workplaces, and communities.

- **Youth Empowerment:** Encouraging young people to voice their concerns, actively participate in decision-making processes, and engage in advocacy efforts can empower them and contribute to their mental well-being.

- **Resilience-building Programs:** Developing programs that focus on building resilience can help individuals navigate challenges effectively. These programs can include techniques such as mindfulness, stress management, and goal-setting.

- **Promoting Open Conversations:** Educating individuals about mental health, facilitating open conversations, and promoting empathy and understanding can help combat the stigma and stereotypes associated with the Snowflake Generation.

Conclusion

Understanding the complexities surrounding the Snowflake Generation requires moving beyond stereotypes and embracing a holistic approach. Recognizing generational differences, fostering dialogue, providing mental health support, and promoting resilience are essential steps towards creating a society that values the well-being of all individuals.

By debunking misconceptions and focusing on their unique contributions and perspectives, we can pave the way for a more inclusive and empathetic future. Let us move forward by embracing diversity, nurturing a healthy lifestyle, and encouraging acceptance and empathy.

Factors Influencing the Snowflake Phenomenon

The emergence of the "snowflake generation" phenomenon can be attributed to several key factors. In this section, we will explore and discuss these factors, shedding light on the societal changes and influences that have contributed to the development of this phenomenon.

Challenging Economic Landscape

One of the significant factors shaping the snowflake phenomenon is the challenging economic landscape that the younger generation has faced. The global financial crisis and subsequent economic downturns have resulted in limited job opportunities, job insecurity, and increased competition in the job market. These circumstances have created a sense of uncertainty and anxiety among young people, impacting their outlook on life and their propensity to take risks.

The pressure to succeed in a competitive job market has fostered a sense of fragility among young individuals, as they fear failure and struggle to live up to societal expectations. Moreover, the burden of mounting student loans and escalating living costs adds to the economic challenges faced by the snowflake generation.

Helicopter Parenting and Overprotection

Another factor contributing to the snowflake phenomenon is the prevalence of helicopter parenting and overprotection. Over the years, there has been a shift in parenting styles, with many parents becoming overly involved in their children's lives. This overinvolvement often includes shielding them from any form of discomfort, failure, or disappointment. As a result, young individuals may lack the necessary resilience and coping mechanisms to navigate challenges independently.

Being constantly shielded from difficult situations can hinder their development of problem-solving skills, self-reliance, and emotional regulation. This overprotective approach may inadvertently contribute to an increased vulnerability and perceived fragility among young individuals, thus fueling the snowflake phenomenon.

Internet and Social Media Influence

The widespread use of the internet and social media has had a profound impact on the snowflake phenomenon. Social media platforms offer a constant stream of curated content that reinforces specific ideals, norms, and expectations. On social media, individuals are more likely to present a filtered version of their lives, highlighting only the positive aspects.

This constant exposure to idealized, unrealistic representations of life can lead to feelings of inadequacy, comparison, and a fear of missing out. Additionally, online platforms provide avenues for online harassment, cyberbullying, and the spread of offensive or triggering content. The constant connectivity and exposure to such negative experiences can contribute to heightened sensitivity and emotional vulnerability among the younger generation.

Emphasis on Mental Health and Well-being

In recent years, there has been a significant shift in societal attitudes towards mental health and well-being. While this shift is generally positive, it has also resulted in a heightened awareness and focus on mental health issues. While it is crucial to acknowledge and address mental health concerns, the emphasis on vulnerability and emotional well-being has also perpetuated the snowflake phenomenon.

The focus on emotional well-being, combined with the increased availability of mental health support and services, has led to a greater recognition and openness about mental health struggles. This has created a generation that is more comfortable in expressing their emotions and seeking help when needed. However, it has also contributed to the perception of increased fragility and sensitivity among young individuals.

Educational and Workplace Changes

Changes in the educational and workplace environments have also played a role in shaping the snowflake phenomenon. In the educational system, there has been a shift towards a greater emphasis on inclusivity, emotional support, and creating safe spaces for students. While these changes are positive in many ways, they have also contributed to the perception of increased fragility and sensitivity among the snowflake generation.

In the workplace, there has been an increased focus on employee well-being, mental health support, and workplace diversity. This shift towards a more inclusive and supportive work environment is beneficial, but it has also contributed to the perception that younger individuals require more emotional support and accommodation.

Conclusion

The snowflake generation phenomenon is a complex and multifaceted issue influenced by various societal factors. The challenging economic landscape, parenting styles, internet and social media influence, emphasis on mental health and well-being, and changes in educational and workplace environments have all contributed to the development of the snowflake phenomenon.

It is important to approach the snowflake phenomenon with empathy and understanding, recognizing the unique challenges faced by young individuals in contemporary society. By acknowledging and addressing these factors, we can promote a more inclusive and supportive environment that nurtures resilience and personal growth among the younger generation.

Generational Differences in Health Perspectives

Generational differences play a significant role in shaping people's perspectives on health and wellness. Various factors such as cultural norms, technological advancements, and societal changes contribute to the differences in health beliefs and practices between generations. Understanding these generational differences is essential for promoting effective communication, bridging gaps in knowledge, and providing appropriate healthcare interventions.

Definition of Generational Cohorts

Before delving into the specific differences, it is important to define the generational cohorts being discussed. The key generational cohorts often referenced in discussions about health perspectives are:

- Baby Boomers (born 1946-1964): This generation experienced significant societal changes, including the Vietnam War, the civil rights movement, and the advent of television. They generally have a more traditional approach to health and tend to prioritize physical fitness and preventive healthcare.

- Generation X (born 1965-1980): Growing up during the rapid rise of technology, Generation X is considered the "middle child" between Baby Boomers and Millennials. They adopt a more individualistic approach to health and place importance on work-life balance, mental health, and self-care practices.

- Millennials (born 1981-1996): This generation witnessed the digital revolution and came of age during the turn of the millennium. They prioritize holistic health approaches, are more open-minded to alternative therapies, and value convenience and accessibility in healthcare.

- Generation Z (born 1997 and onwards): Often referred to as the "digital natives," Generation Z has grown up fully immersed in the digital world. They are more aware of social and environmental issues, tend to seek immediate gratification and personalized healthcare, and are receptive to technology-enabled healthcare solutions.

It is important to note that individuals within each generational cohort can still have diverse perspectives and beliefs. These generalizations serve as a starting point to understand the broader health perspectives within each generation.

Influence of Cultural Norms and Socioeconomic Factors

Cultural norms and socioeconomic factors have a significant impact on health perspectives across generations. Older generations, such as Baby Boomers, often hold onto traditional beliefs and practices influenced by their cultural background. For example, certain immigrant communities may rely heavily on traditional medicine or home remedies for treating ailments.

In contrast, younger generations, like Millennials and Generation Z, are more likely to embrace cultural diversity and explore various health practices from different cultures. They are open to integrating alternative therapies like acupuncture or Ayurveda into their health routines.

Socioeconomic factors also play a role in shaping health perspectives. For instance, Baby Boomers, who grew up during a period of economic prosperity, may have more access to healthcare resources and be more proactive about preventive screenings. On the other hand, younger generations, especially those facing economic challenges, may prioritize affordability and seek cost-effective healthcare options.

Technological Advances and Health Information Seeking

Technological advancements have revolutionized the way health information is accessed and shared. Each generation's exposure to technology influences their approach to health and wellness.

Baby Boomers, who witnessed the rise of television and print media, tend to rely on traditional sources of information such as books, newspapers, and television programs. They may be more skeptical of online health information and value face-to-face interactions with healthcare providers.

Generation X was the first generation to grow up with personal computers and the internet. They are comfortable navigating online resources, but they also value expert opinions and seek a balanced view between traditional and digital sources of health information.

Millennials and Generation Z, being digital natives, heavily rely on technology for health-related information. They are more likely to turn to online platforms, social media influencers, and health apps for advice and guidance. However, there is a need to educate younger generations about the importance of reliable sources and critical evaluation of health information.

Shift towards Preventive and Holistic Approaches

There has been a noticeable shift in recent generations towards a preventive and holistic approach to health and wellness. Baby Boomers, influenced by a post-World War II focus on prosperity and disease prevention, tend to prioritize physical fitness, regular check-ups, and a balanced diet.

Generation X, deeply impacted by the high-stress work culture of the 80s and 90s, gravitates towards practices that promote work-life balance, stress reduction, and mental health. They are more open to seeking therapy or practicing mindfulness techniques.

Millennials and Generation Z, surrounded by a culture of convenience and multi-tasking, often look for quick, accessible, and individualized healthcare solutions. They prioritize well-being in all aspects of life, including physical, mental, emotional, and social dimensions. They are more open to trying alternative therapies such as yoga, meditation, and natural remedies.

Challenges and Opportunities

Understanding and bridging the generational differences in health perspectives present both challenges and opportunities for healthcare providers, policymakers, and educators. Some key considerations include:

- Tailoring healthcare strategies: Healthcare providers need to adopt patient-centered approaches that align with each generation's unique needs and preferences. This includes developing personalized care plans and utilizing digital health tools to enhance accessibility and engagement.

- Effective health communication: Clear and concise health communication is essential to break through generational barriers. Providers should use appropriate language, leverage various communication channels, and engage in shared decision-making to promote understanding and collaboration.

- Promoting intergenerational learning: Encouraging intergenerational learning and dialogue can foster mutual understanding and bridge gaps in health perspectives. Platforms for knowledge exchange, such as community health programs or mentorship initiatives, can create opportunities for different generations to learn from one another.

- Addressing healthcare disparities: Generational differences can contribute to disparities in healthcare access and utilization. Policymakers should address these disparities by implementing policies that consider key generational factors, such as improving access to healthcare for underserved communities or incentivizing preventive care across all generations.

In conclusion, generational differences in health perspectives are shaped by a range of factors, including cultural norms, socioeconomic status, and technological advancements. Understanding these differences is crucial for promoting effective healthcare communication, developing tailored interventions, and fostering a more inclusive and holistic approach to health and wellness across generations. By recognizing and respecting these generational differences, we can work towards a future where healthcare is accessible, comprehensive, and meaningful for people of all ages.

Impact of Social Media on the Snowflake Generation

Social media has become an integral part of our lives, shaping the way we communicate, gather information, and form opinions. For the Snowflake Generation, those born in the 1990s and early 2000s, social media platforms have had a profound impact on their experiences and perspectives. This section explores how social media has affected the Snowflake Generation and its influence on their mental health, self-perception, and societal expectations.

The Influence of Social Media

Social media platforms such as Facebook, Instagram, Twitter, and Snapchat provide a constant stream of information and a platform for self-expression. The Snowflake Generation has grown up with these platforms, which has influenced their behaviors and attitudes in unique ways.

One significant impact of social media is the perpetuation of unrealistic standards of beauty and success. The curated images and posts that flood these platforms often present an idealized version of life, leading young people to compare themselves and feel inadequate. They are bombarded with images showcasing perfectly sculpted bodies, luxurious lifestyles, and seemingly effortless achievements. This constant exposure to highly curated content can create feelings of self-doubt, anxiety, and low self-esteem.

The Role of Validation and Likes

The like button, a prominent feature on most social media platforms, has had a profound effect on the Snowflake Generation. The number of likes and positive feedback received on a post or photo is often seen as an indicator of popularity and self-worth. This quest for validation can become a driving force behind the need to create and share content that is likely to receive positive feedback. As a result, young people may feel pressured to mold themselves into an image that will gain approval from their peers, rather than embracing their true selves.

The reliance on likes and validation also fuels a fear of judgment and a desire for perfection. This fear of being criticized or ridiculed can lead to self-censorship and a reluctance to express opinions or ideas that might be considered controversial or unpopular. Social media becomes a place where conformity thrives, limiting the diversity of thought and stifling individuality.

Escaping the Fear of Missing Out (FOMO)

One of the negative consequences of social media is the fear of missing out (FOMO). This phenomenon occurs when individuals see their peers engaging in exciting activities or social events online, leading them to feel excluded and left behind. The constant updates on others' lives can create a sense of anxiety and pressure to participate in every social gathering or experience in order to feel validated.

FOMO can also lead to excessive use of social media, as individuals try to stay connected and up-to-date with the latest trends and happenings. This constant need to stay plugged in can be exhausting and detrimental to mental health, as it is difficult to disconnect and find genuine moments of rest and relaxation.

The Echo Chamber Effect

The nature of social media algorithms often filters content based on an individual's preferences and interests. While this curates personalized newsfeeds, it can also create a bubble where opposing viewpoints are seldom encountered. This echo chamber effect can lead to confirmation bias, where individuals only see information that aligns with their existing beliefs and values.

Being constantly exposed to a limited range of perspectives can hinder critical thinking skills and the ability to consider alternative viewpoints. It fosters an environment where differing opinions are dismissed, and the echo chamber reinforces preexisting biases. This lack of exposure to diverse ideas can restrict personal growth and hinder the development of empathy and compassion.

Mitigating the Negative Effects

While the impact of social media on the Snowflake Generation can be significant, it is important to recognize that social media is a tool that can be harnessed for good. It provides a platform for connection and sharing valuable information. Therefore, it is essential to promote healthy and responsible social media usage.

Education and awareness are key in helping young people navigate the world of social media. Teaching critical thinking skills, media literacy, and encouraging individuals to question the content they consume can empower them to make conscious choices. Highlighting the carefully curated nature of social media posts can help break the illusion of perfection and foster a more realistic understanding of the diversity of experiences.

Encouraging users to diversify their social media feeds by following accounts from different backgrounds, cultures, and perspectives can help create a more open-minded and inclusive online environment. Additionally, promoting self-care practices, such as digital detoxes and setting boundaries with social media usage, can enable individuals to find a healthier balance between online and offline experiences.

Building Resilience and Self-Empowerment

To counteract the negative impact of social media, it is crucial to foster resilience and self-empowerment in the Snowflake Generation. By emphasizing the importance of self-acceptance, self-worth, and authenticity, young people can develop a stronger sense of identity and resist the pressures to conform.

Promoting face-to-face interactions and offline activities can help reduce reliance on social media for validation and connection. Encouraging hobbies, physical exercise, and creative pursuits can offer opportunities for personal growth and well-being outside the digital realm.

Furthermore, providing spaces for open dialogue and promoting empathy and understanding can combat the echo chamber effect. Creating safe environments where individuals can express their opinions without fear of judgment encourages the development of critical thinking, empathy, and active listening skills.

Managing Mental Health on Social Media

Mental health concerns among young people have risen alongside the increased use of social media. The constant exposure to curated content and the pressure to present a picture-perfect life can exacerbate feelings of anxiety, depression, and loneliness.

To address these concerns, it is vital to promote mental health support and educate young people about self-care practices. Teaching strategies for managing stress, recognizing warning signs of mental health issues, and providing access to resources can empower individuals to seek help when needed.

Encouraging digital empathy and fostering supportive online communities can also contribute to a healthier social media environment. Emphasizing the importance of kindness and respect in online interactions can counteract the negative impacts of cyberbullying and harassment.

Conclusion

Social media has become an influential force in the lives of the Snowflake Generation, shaping their self-perception, societal expectations, and mental well-being. While social media can have negative consequences, it also offers opportunities for connection, expression, and activism.

By promoting healthy usage, critical thinking, and self-empowerment, we can mitigate the negative effects of social media and create a more inclusive and supportive online environment. By fostering resilience, empathy, and personal growth, we empower young people to navigate social media responsibly and to embrace their individuality without succumbing to the pressures of conformity.

Navigating Mental Health Concerns

Mental health is a crucial aspect of overall well-being, and it is important to address the unique challenges faced by individuals, including those within the snowflake generation. This section aims to explore different strategies for navigating mental health concerns and promoting positive mental well-being.

Understanding Mental Health

Before delving into the challenges and strategies, it is important to have a clear understanding of mental health. Mental health refers to a person's emotional, psychological, and social well-being. It affects how individuals think, feel, and act, and also influences how they handle stress, make choices, and interact with others.

Mental health concerns can range from common issues such as stress, anxiety, and depression to more severe disorders like bipolar disorder and schizophrenia. It is important to recognize that mental health is a spectrum, and each individual's experiences and challenges may be different.

Stigmatization and Stereotypes

One of the significant barriers to addressing mental health concerns is the stigma and stereotypes surrounding these issues. The snowflake generation, in particular, faces criticism for being overly sensitive or easily triggered, which can trivialize their experiences and discourage seeking help.

To overcome this stigma, it is essential to promote open and inclusive conversations about mental health. Education and awareness campaigns can help challenge misconceptions and stereotypes, emphasizing that mental health concerns are real and valid. Sharing personal stories of individuals who have successfully managed their mental health can also help reduce stigmatization.

Promoting Mental Well-being

Navigating mental health concerns requires a comprehensive approach that addresses various aspects of well-being. Here are some strategies to promote positive mental well-being:

1. Seeking professional help: Encouraging individuals to seek professional help from mental health practitioners, such as psychologists or therapists, can provide them with the support and guidance they need. These professionals can offer evidence-based treatments, therapy, and coping strategies tailored to their specific concerns.

2. Building a support network: Encouraging individuals to build a strong support network comprising friends, family, and trusted individuals can provide a sense of belonging and emotional support. This includes promoting healthy communication and interpersonal relationships.

3. Practicing self-care: Emphasizing the importance of self-care activities, such as exercise, relaxation techniques, hobbies, and adequate sleep, can help individuals manage stress and maintain emotional well-being. Self-care looks different for everyone, so it is important to encourage individuals to explore activities that bring them joy and relaxation.

4. Promoting healthy lifestyle choices: Highlighting the role of physical health in mental well-being is essential. Regular exercise, a balanced diet, and adequate rest play a significant role in maintaining positive mental health. Educating individuals on the connections between physical and mental health can empower them to make healthy lifestyle choices.

5. Developing coping mechanisms: Teaching individuals effective coping mechanisms can help them navigate challenging situations. This includes strategies such as deep breathing exercises, mindfulness practices, journaling, and seeking social support.

6. Encouraging help-seeking behavior: Creating a safe and non-judgmental environment that promotes help-seeking behavior is vital. Individuals should feel comfortable reaching out to friends, family, or mental health professionals when they are struggling. Providing resources and information about available support services can empower individuals to seek help when needed.

The Role of Technology

In the digital age, technology plays a significant role in mental health concerns. While social media platforms can offer connection and support, they can also contribute to feelings of isolation, comparison, and excessive screen time, leading to negative mental health outcomes.

To navigate these challenges, it is crucial to educate individuals about healthy technology use. This includes setting boundaries with technology, taking breaks from social media, and engaging in activities that promote face-to-face interactions and real-life connections. Encouraging the use of mental health apps and online support communities can also be beneficial, but it is essential to emphasize the importance of balancing virtual connections with real-life interactions.

Addressing Systemic Issues

While individual strategies are important for navigating mental health concerns, it is equally important to address systemic issues that contribute to mental health challenges. This includes advocating for mental health resources in schools, workplaces, and communities, as well as challenging societal norms and beliefs that perpetuate stigma and discrimination.

Promoting mental health education and awareness programs in educational institutions and workplaces can help foster a culture of understanding and support. Encouraging policy changes that prioritize mental health, such as increased funding for mental health services and insurance coverage, is also crucial.

Example: Promoting Mental Well-being in College Settings

In college settings, where mental health concerns are prevalent, it is essential to implement comprehensive strategies to support students' well-being. This can include:

1. Offering accessible and affordable mental health services on campus, including counseling and therapy sessions.

2. Providing mental health workshops and training for students, faculty, and staff to increase awareness and reduce stigma.

3. Creating student-led mental health support groups and clubs to foster a sense of community and peer support.

4. Incorporating mental health awareness into the curriculum, ensuring students have a comprehensive understanding of mental health and well-being.

5. Promoting a healthy work-life balance by offering support services related to time management, stress reduction, and effective study habits.

By implementing these strategies, colleges can create an environment that supports students' mental well-being, promoting their overall academic success and personal growth.

Conclusion

Navigating mental health concerns requires a multi-faceted approach that addresses individual needs, societal challenges, and systemic issues. By promoting education, awareness, destigmatization, and accessible resources, we can create a culture that prioritizes mental well-being and supports individuals in the snowflake generation and beyond. Through these efforts, we can foster a healthy and inclusive society where everyone feels understood, accepted, and supported.

Debunking Snowflake Myths

Stereotypes and Misconceptions about Snowflakes

In recent years, the term "snowflake" has gained popularity as a derogatory label used to describe individuals who are deemed overly sensitive, easily offended, and lacking resilience. This section aims to explore the stereotypes and misconceptions associated with the snowflake generation, shedding light on the nuances often overlooked in these generalizations.

Defining the Snowflake Generation

To better understand the stereotypes surrounding snowflakes, it is important to define the generation to which they belong. The snowflake generation typically refers to individuals who were born in the 1990s and 2000s, who are often portrayed as being overly sensitive, entitled, and lacking in resilience. However, it is crucial to acknowledge that this generalization overlooks the diverse experiences and perspectives within this generation.

Misconception 1: Exaggerated Sensitivity

One of the most common stereotypes about snowflakes is that they are excessively sensitive, particularly when it comes to issues of race, gender, and social justice. While it is true that the snowflake generation tends to have a heightened awareness of social issues, it is unfair to dismiss their concerns as mere hypersensitivity. In fact, it is important to recognize the importance of empathizing with others and creating a more inclusive and equitable society. The ability to empathize and understand different perspectives should be celebrated rather than criticized.

Misconception 2: Lack of Resilience

Another misconception about snowflakes is that they lack resilience and are unable to cope with the challenges of the real world. However, it is essential to understand that resilience takes different forms and may not always conform to traditional expectations. Snowflakes often exhibit resilience through their ability to adapt to changing circumstances, their emphasis on self-care and mental well-being, and their commitment to advocating for positive change. Resilience can be seen in their ability to stand up against injustice and to create inclusive spaces for marginalized communities.

Misconception 3: Entitlement

Snowflakes are often characterized as entitled individuals who have unrealistically high expectations and a sense of special treatment. This stereotype arises from the perception that they demand trigger warnings, safe spaces, and accommodations in educational institutions and workplaces. However, it is crucial to recognize that these requests are often driven by a genuine desire for inclusivity and the acknowledgment of mental health concerns. By challenging the status quo, snowflakes seek to create environments that are more equitable, compassionate, and supportive for all.

Misconception 4: Avoidance of Discomfort

Another stereotype associated with snowflakes is their supposed avoidance of discomfort, particularly in relation to challenging conversations and differing opinions. While it is true that snowflakes place importance on creating safe spaces, it does not imply an avoidance of dialogue or conflict. Instead, it signals a need for open and respectful discussions, where everyone feels heard and valued. This emphasis on constructive dialogue lays the foundation for growth, understanding, and societal progress.

Misconception 5: Lack of Responsibility

Snowflakes are occasionally accused of shirking responsibility and relying on others to solve their problems. However, this oversimplification fails to recognize the commitment snowflakes have towards effecting positive change. Many individuals within this generation actively engage in volunteer work, activism, and social entrepreneurship, demonstrating a deep sense of responsibility towards creating a better world.

Addressing the Stereotypes

To counter these stereotypes, it is important to challenge our preconceived notions and examine the complexities within the snowflake generation. By engaging in open and respectful dialogue, we can foster understanding, empathy, and collaboration. Educating others about the diverse experiences and perspectives of this generation can help dispel misconceptions and promote inclusivity.

Promoting Understanding and Empathy

To foster a greater understanding of the snowflake generation, it is essential to foster empathy and compassion. Encouraging dialogue between different generations can bridge the gap in understanding and dispel stereotypes. By actively listening to one another and acknowledging the validity of different perspectives, we can create a more inclusive and supportive society.

Encouraging Personal Growth

Rather than dismissing the concerns and experiences of the snowflake generation, it is important to recognize the potential for personal growth and societal progress. By embracing the call for inclusivity and empathy, individuals can challenge their own biases and assumptions, leading to personal development and a more harmonious coexistence in society.

In conclusion, the stereotypes and misconceptions associated with the snowflake generation often fail to capture the complexities and diversity within this group. By challenging the prevailing narratives and engaging in meaningful conversations, we can promote understanding, empathy, and personal growth. It is crucial to move beyond stereotypes and embrace the opportunity for greater inclusivity and a more compassionate society.

Resilience and Emotional Well-being

Resilience is defined as the ability to bounce back from adversity, to recover quickly from setbacks, and to adapt to change. It is a crucial aspect of emotional well-being and plays a significant role in maintaining mental health. In our modern society, where stress, uncertainty, and challenges are prevalent, developing resilience is essential for individuals of all ages.

Understanding Resilience

Resilience is not a fixed trait that some people possess inherently while others do not. It is a skill that can be developed and strengthened over time. Resilience involves various psychological factors and coping mechanisms that contribute to our ability to navigate difficult situations successfully.

One component of resilience is self-awareness. Being aware of our emotions, thoughts, and reactions allows us to identify and address any negative patterns that may hinder our capacity to handle adversity. Moreover, having a strong support system, including family, friends, and professionals, is another vital factor in building resilience. These relationships provide emotional support, guidance, and a sense of belonging, all of which contribute to overall well-being.

Factors Influencing Resilience

Several factors influence an individual's resilience. These include genetics, early life experiences, personality traits, and external support systems. Additionally, the way we interpret and perceive adverse events also affects our ability to bounce back.

A growing body of research suggests that individuals who have experienced some level of adversity in their lives may develop higher levels of resilience. Adversity can foster important skills, such as problem-solving, emotional regulation, and coping mechanisms, which can enhance resilience.

Personality traits, such as optimism and flexibility, also play a significant role in developing resilience. Optimistic individuals tend to view setbacks as temporary and specific to a situation rather than a reflection of their own abilities, leading to more adaptive responses. Similarly, individuals who embrace change and are flexible in their thinking are better equipped to navigate challenges.

Building Resilience

Building resilience requires intentional effort and practice. Here are some strategies that can help individuals develop and enhance their resilience:

Developing a Growth Mindset A growth mindset entails believing that our abilities and intelligence can be developed through dedication and hard work. This mindset promotes resilience by fostering a belief in our capacity to learn, adapt, and overcome challenges.

Cultivating Emotional Intelligence Emotional intelligence involves recognizing and managing our emotions, as well as understanding and empathizing with others' emotions. Developing emotional intelligence can enhance resilience by improving our ability to regulate negative emotions, maintain positive relationships, and effectively communicate our needs.

Building Social Connections Maintaining healthy and supportive relationships is crucial for building resilience. Having people we trust and can rely on provides emotional support, encouragement, and different perspectives. Actively nurturing these relationships can help us navigate adversity more effectively.

Practicing Self-Care Engaging in activities that promote self-care, such as exercise, mindfulness, adequate sleep, and hobbies, helps reduce stress and promotes emotional well-being. Taking care of our physical and mental health enhances our ability to cope with challenges and increases resilience.

Resilience and Mental Health

Resilience is closely tied to mental health. Individuals with higher levels of resilience are better equipped to manage stress, anxiety, and depression. Building resilience can help prevent the onset of mental health conditions and reduce the severity of symptoms in individuals who are experiencing such challenges.

Resilience allows individuals to develop effective coping mechanisms, problem-solving skills, and healthy strategies for managing stress. It provides a protective factor against the negative impact of adversity, trauma, and difficult life events.

Promoting Resilience in Educational Settings

Educational institutions play a crucial role in fostering resilience among students. By creating a supportive and inclusive learning environment, educators can help students develop the necessary skills to navigate challenges and setbacks. Here are some strategies for promoting resilience in educational settings:

Teaching Coping Skills Incorporating social-emotional learning programs that teach coping skills, stress management techniques, and conflict resolution can empower students to build resilience.

Encouraging Growth Mindset Educators can promote a growth mindset by praising effort, persistence, and resilience instead of solely focusing on achievements. This encourages students to view challenges as opportunities for growth and development.

Providing Emotional Support Offering a safe space for students to express their emotions, talk about their challenges, and seek guidance is vital in promoting resilience. School counselors and mental health professionals can play a significant role in providing this support.

Fostering Connection and Belonging Creating opportunities for students to build positive relationships, promote inclusivity, and develop a sense of belonging within the school community can enhance their resilience.

Promoting Self-Care Practices Incorporating mindfulness exercises, physical activities, and self-care practices into the school routine can help students develop healthy habits that contribute to their overall well-being and resilience.

Real-World Example: Resilience in the Face of a Pandemic

The global COVID-19 pandemic has tested individuals' resilience worldwide. Many people have had to adapt to drastic changes, face uncertainty, and cope with increased stress levels. However, stories of resilience have emerged, showcasing individuals and communities who have effectively navigated through challenging times.

For example, healthcare workers have shown immense resilience by working tirelessly on the front lines, putting themselves at risk to care for others. They have demonstrated strength, adaptability, and a commitment to their profession despite the unprecedented circumstances.

Similarly, individuals who have lost their jobs due to the economic impact of the pandemic have displayed resilience by finding alternative sources of income, developing new skill sets, and exploring entrepreneurial opportunities. Their ability to bounce back and adapt to new realities demonstrates the power of resilience in the face of adversity.

Conclusion

Resilience is a valuable skill that contributes significantly to our emotional well-being. It is a skill that can be cultivated and strengthened through various strategies, including developing a growth mindset, nurturing social connections, practicing self-care, and seeking support when needed.

In educational settings, promoting resilience among students is essential for their overall development and success. By creating supportive environments, teaching coping skills, and fostering a growth mindset, educators can empower students to navigate challenges and setbacks effectively.

Ultimately, resilience allows individuals to thrive in the face of adversity, maintain mental health, and lead fulfilling lives. By embracing resilience and supporting its development in ourselves and others, we can create a more resilient and compassionate society.

Addressing the Snowflake Generation's Concerns

The Snowflake Generation is often criticized for their perceived sensitivity and desire for safe spaces. However, it is important to understand the underlying concerns and challenges they face in order to address them effectively. In this section, we will explore some of these concerns and provide strategies for addressing them.

Creating a Supportive Environment

One of the key concerns of the Snowflake Generation is the need for a supportive environment that recognizes and validates their experiences. This is especially important when it comes to mental health issues, as this generation faces unique challenges in terms of increased stress, anxiety, and depression.

To address these concerns, it is crucial to create safe spaces where individuals can openly discuss their mental health issues without fear of judgment or ridicule. This can be done through the establishment of support groups, counseling services, and mental health awareness campaigns. Providing resources and information about available support systems can help individuals navigate their mental health concerns and seek appropriate help when needed.

Promoting Emotional Intelligence

Emotional intelligence is another concern often associated with the Snowflake Generation. This refers to the ability to identify, understand, and manage one's own emotions, as well as recognize and empathize with the emotions of others. Developing emotional intelligence is important for building healthy relationships and effectively managing conflicts.

To address this concern, educational institutions can incorporate emotional intelligence training into their curriculum. This can include activities such as role-playing exercises, group discussions, and reflective writing assignments. Additionally, promoting open and inclusive communication can help individuals develop their emotional intelligence by encouraging them to express their thoughts and feelings in a constructive manner.

Encouraging Resilience and Self-Growth

A common stereotype associated with the Snowflake Generation is their perceived lack of resilience. However, it is important to recognize that resilience is a skill that can be developed and strengthened over time. By encouraging individuals to embrace challenges and learn from setbacks, we can empower them to become more resilient and overcome obstacles.

One way to promote resilience is by providing opportunities for personal growth and self-reflection. This can be done through workshops, seminars, and mentoring programs that focus on building self-confidence, problem-solving skills, and goal-setting. It is also important to emphasize the importance of learning from failures and providing support and encouragement to individuals as they navigate their personal and professional journeys.

Fostering Inclusivity and Acceptance

Another concern of the Snowflake Generation is the desire for a society that is inclusive and accepting of diverse identities and perspectives. This includes advocating for gender equality, LGBTQ+ rights, racial justice, and social equality.

To address these concerns, it is important to foster an inclusive environment that celebrates diversity and promotes acceptance. This can be done through educational initiatives that promote cross-cultural understanding, anti-discrimination policies, and inclusivity training. Additionally, providing platforms for open dialogue and collaboration can help individuals understand and appreciate different perspectives, fostering a culture of acceptance and empathy.

Developing Coping Mechanisms

Learning effective coping mechanisms is essential for managing stress, anxiety, and other mental health issues. This is particularly important for the Snowflake Generation, who often face high expectations and pressure from various sources.

To address this concern, it is important to educate individuals about different coping strategies and provide resources that promote mental well-being. This can include techniques such as mindfulness meditation, stress management exercises, and self-care practices. Additionally, encouraging healthy lifestyle habits, such as regular exercise and proper sleep, can play a significant role in managing stress and promoting overall well-being.

In conclusion, addressing the concerns of the Snowflake Generation requires a comprehensive approach that acknowledges their unique experiences and challenges. By creating a supportive environment, promoting emotional intelligence, fostering resilience, fostering inclusivity and acceptance, and developing coping mechanisms, we can empower individuals to navigate their personal and professional lives with confidence and well-being.

Promoting Conversation and Understanding

In today's polarized society, it is crucial to foster open and respectful dialogue in order to promote understanding and bridge divides. This is particularly important when it comes to addressing the concerns and perspectives of the Snowflake Generation. This section explores strategies for promoting productive conversations and creating an environment of empathy and comprehension.

Active Listening and Empathy

One of the keys to promoting conversation and understanding is the practice of active listening. Active listening involves fully focusing on and comprehending what the other person is saying, rather than simply waiting for your turn to speak. It requires setting aside preconceived notions and assumptions, and genuinely seeking to understand the other person's experiences and perspectives.

Empathy plays a vital role in active listening. By putting yourself in the shoes of another person, you can better understand their feelings and emotions. Empathy allows for a deeper connection and fosters a sense of shared understanding. Demonstrating empathy can be as simple as acknowledging and validating someone's emotions or experiences.

Creating Safe Spaces for Dialogue

Creating a safe and inclusive space for open dialogue is crucial for promoting conversation and understanding. It is necessary to establish ground rules that ensure respectful communication and the active participation of all individuals.

Some important ground rules may include:

- Respect each other's opinions and perspectives.
- Avoid personal attacks or derogatory language.
- Listen actively and avoid interrupting.
- Be open to learning and challenging your own beliefs.
- Be mindful of your nonverbal communication, such as body language and tone of voice.
- Encourage curiosity and ask questions to deepen understanding.

By setting these ground rules, participants can feel more comfortable expressing their viewpoints and engaging in meaningful discussions.

Promoting Critical Thinking

Critical thinking skills are essential for fostering conversation and understanding. Encouraging individuals to think critically helps them analyze and evaluate different perspectives and arguments. It enables them to separate facts from beliefs or opinions, and to identify logical fallacies and biases.

A useful strategy for promoting critical thinking is the Socratic method. This technique involves asking open-ended questions to stimulate thoughtful discussions and challenge assumptions. By asking probing questions, individuals can explore the underlying reasoning behind their beliefs and engage in deeper conversations.

Encouraging Cultural Competence

In a diverse society, cultural competence plays a crucial role in promoting conversation and understanding. Cultural competence involves understanding, appreciating, and respecting the values, beliefs, and behaviors of individuals from different cultures.

To encourage cultural competence, it is important to provide opportunities for individuals to learn about different cultures and engage in cross-cultural interactions. This can include organizing cultural events, inviting guest speakers from diverse backgrounds, or facilitating group discussions on cultural topics. By fostering cultural competence, individuals can better appreciate and understand the perspectives and experiences of others.

Overcoming Confirmation Bias

Confirmation bias is the tendency to seek and interpret information in a way that confirms one's preexisting beliefs or opinions. Overcoming confirmation bias is vital for promoting conversation and understanding. By actively seeking out diverse perspectives and challenging one's own biases, individuals can broaden their understanding and engage in more constructive conversations.

One effective way to overcome confirmation bias is through exposure to diverse media sources. Encouraging individuals to read, listen to, or watch news from a variety of perspectives can help them develop a more well-rounded understanding of different issues. Additionally, engaging in respectful conversations with people who hold differing opinions can provide valuable opportunities for growth and self-reflection.

Practicing Reflective Listening

Reflective listening is a technique that involves paraphrasing and summarizing what the other person has said to ensure mutual understanding. It helps clarify any potential misunderstandings and demonstrates active engagement in the conversation.

When practicing reflective listening, it is important to:

- Paraphrase the speaker's main points in your own words.

- Ask for clarification if something is unclear.

- Summarize the speaker's ideas at key intervals to ensure accurate understanding.

- Use open-ended questions to encourage the speaker to elaborate on their thoughts.

By practicing reflective listening, individuals can facilitate a deeper level of understanding and connection.

Conclusion

Promoting conversation and understanding is essential in building a society that values diversity and inclusivity. By actively listening, creating safe spaces, promoting critical thinking, encouraging cultural competence, overcoming confirmation bias, and practicing reflective listening, we can foster an environment of empathy, respect, and shared understanding. Through open and constructive dialogue, we can break down barriers, challenge stereotypes, and embrace the diverse perspectives of the Snowflake Generation and beyond. Let us continue on the journey toward personal and societal growth, and create a future where conversation and understanding thrive.

Encouraging Self-discipline and Personal Growth

Encouraging self-discipline and personal growth is essential in promoting overall wellbeing and success. In this section, we will explore strategies and practices that can help individuals develop self-discipline, enhance their personal growth, and achieve their goals. By adopting a balanced and holistic approach, individuals can cultivate self-discipline, develop resilience, and foster personal growth in various aspects of their lives.

Understanding Self-discipline

Self-discipline refers to the ability to control one's actions, thoughts, and emotions in order to achieve desired outcomes. It is the foundation of personal growth and plays a crucial role in maintaining a healthy and balanced lifestyle. When individuals exhibit self-discipline, they are better able to make conscious choices that align with their long-term goals, resist short-term temptations, and develop healthy habits.

Developing Self-discipline

Developing self-discipline requires practice, commitment, and a growth mindset. Here are some effective strategies that can help individuals cultivate self-discipline:

1. **Set Clear Goals:** Start by setting clear and specific goals that are meaningful to you. Having a clear vision of what you want to achieve will give you motivation and direction.

2. **Create a Routine:** Establishing a structured routine can provide a framework for self-discipline. Develop daily habits and rituals that align with your goals and prioritize tasks that contribute to your personal growth.

3. **Practice Mindfulness:** Cultivating mindfulness can improve self-awareness and help individuals stay focused on their goals. Practice being present in the moment and observe your thoughts, emotions, and behaviors without judgment. This can help you identify any distractions or barriers to self-discipline.

4. **Break Tasks Down:** Large tasks can be overwhelming and may hinder self-discipline. Break down your goals into smaller, manageable tasks, and focus on completing them one at a time. Celebrate small victories along the way to maintain motivation and momentum.

5. **Find Accountability Partners:** Engage with like-minded individuals or seek support from friends and family who can help keep you accountable. Share your goals with them, and regularly check-in to discuss progress and challenges.

6. **Practice Delayed Gratification:** Develop the ability to delay immediate gratification for long-term rewards. Train yourself to resist unnecessary distractions and temptations in order to stay focused on your goals.

Promoting Personal Growth

Personal growth is a lifelong journey of self-improvement and self-discovery. Encouraging personal growth involves continuous learning, self-reflection, and embracing new experiences. Here are some strategies to promote personal growth:

1. **Embrace Lifelong Learning:** Cultivate a growth mindset by seeking opportunities for learning and self-improvement. Take up new hobbies, attend workshops and seminars, read books, and engage in online courses to expand your knowledge and skills.

2. **Set Challenging Goals:** Set ambitious yet achievable goals that push you outside of your comfort zone. Challenging goals can motivate personal growth and foster a sense of achievement.

3. **Seek Feedback:** Feedback from others can be invaluable in identifying areas for improvement and personal growth. Be open to constructive criticism and use it as an opportunity to grow and develop.

4. **Reflect and journal:** Regularly reflect on your experiences, emotions, and lessons learned. Keeping a journal can help you gain insight into your thoughts and feelings, track your progress, and identify patterns of behavior.

5. **Step out of your comfort zone:** Embrace new experiences and take calculated risks. Stepping out of your comfort zone can lead to personal growth and expanded perspectives.

6. **Practice Self-care:** Prioritize self-care activities that promote physical, mental, and emotional well-being. Engage in activities such as exercise, meditation, and relaxation techniques to reduce stress and foster personal growth.

Unconventional Approaches to Self-discipline and Personal Growth

In addition to the conventional strategies mentioned above, it can be beneficial to explore unconventional approaches to self-discipline and personal growth. Here are a few examples:

1. **Gamification:** Gamification involves applying game design elements and principles to non-game contexts. By turning tasks and goals into a game, individuals can tap into their intrinsic motivation, making the process of self-discipline and personal growth more enjoyable and engaging.

2. **Vision Boards**: Creating a vision board involves visualizing your goals and desires by assembling images, quotes, and affirmations on a board. This visual representation can serve as a powerful reminder of what you want to achieve, enhancing motivation and self-discipline.

3. **Mind Mapping**: Mind mapping is a technique that helps individuals organize their thoughts, ideas, and goals visually. By creating a mind map, individuals can explore connections between different aspects of their lives, facilitating self-reflection and personal growth.

4. **Creative Expression**: Engaging in creative activities, such as painting, writing, or playing a musical instrument, can foster personal growth and self-expression. These activities provide an outlet for emotions and can serve as a form of therapy and self-discovery.

5. **Nature Immersion**: Spending time in nature has been shown to have numerous mental and physical health benefits. Immersing oneself in nature can promote self-discipline by providing a peaceful and rejuvenating environment for self-reflection and personal growth.

Conclusion

Encouraging self-discipline and personal growth is important for individuals to reach their full potential and live a fulfilling life. By incorporating strategies such as setting clear goals, creating routines, practicing mindfulness, and embracing new experiences, individuals can develop self-discipline, cultivate personal growth, and enhance their overall well-being. Remember that personal growth is a continuous process, and embracing a growth mindset will enable you to adapt, learn, and evolve throughout your life journey.

Health Benefits of Soy Consumption

Nutritional Profile of Soy

Macronutrients in Soy

In order to understand the health benefits of soy consumption, it is important to examine the macronutrient content of soy. Macronutrients are the nutrients that our bodies require in large amounts for energy and proper functioning. They include carbohydrates, proteins, and fats. Let's explore the macronutrient profile of soy and learn about the role each macronutrient plays in our overall health.

Carbohydrates

Soybeans are a rich source of carbohydrates, which are our body's primary source of energy. Carbohydrates are classified into two types: simple carbohydrates and complex carbohydrates. Simple carbohydrates, also known as sugars, provide quick energy to the body. Complex carbohydrates, on the other hand, are broken down more slowly and provide sustained energy.

Soybeans predominantly contain complex carbohydrates, making them an excellent choice for sustained energy release. The complex carbohydrates in soy are digested slowly, leading to a gradual and steady release of glucose into the bloodstream. This can help lower the risk of blood sugar spikes and crashes, making soy a suitable option for individuals with diabetes or those looking to maintain stable energy levels throughout the day.

Proteins

One of the most notable nutritional attributes of soy is its high protein content. Proteins are essential for the growth, repair, and maintenance of body tissues. They also play a crucial role in the production of enzymes, hormones, and antibodies.

Soybeans are considered a complete protein source, meaning they provide all essential amino acids required by the body. This makes soy an excellent option for individuals following vegetarian or vegan diets, as it can serve as a substitute for animal-based protein sources. In fact, studies have shown that the protein quality of soy is comparable to that of animal protein.

The protein content in soy can benefit individuals looking to build and maintain muscle mass. It is particularly beneficial for athletes, bodybuilders, and individuals engaging in regular physical activity. Consuming soy protein can support muscle recovery, promote muscle growth, and improve overall athletic performance.

Fats

Contrary to popular belief, soybeans contain healthy fats that are vital for various body functions. Soybeans are a significant source of polyunsaturated fats, including omega-3 and omega-6 fatty acids. These fats are essential for heart health, brain function, and reducing inflammation in the body.

Omega-3 fatty acids, in particular, have been extensively studied for their cardiovascular benefits. They can help lower cholesterol levels, reduce the risk of heart disease, and improve overall cardiovascular health. Incorporating soy-based products, such as tofu or soy milk, into your diet can be a feasible way to increase your omega-3 fatty acid intake.

It's important to note that while soybeans contain fats, they are also low in saturated fats. Saturated fats, found in animal products and some plant-based oils, are associated with increased risk of heart disease. Therefore, replacing foods high in saturated fats with soy-based alternatives can contribute to a heart-healthy diet.

Summary

Soybeans offer a well-rounded macronutrient profile, containing a good balance of carbohydrates, proteins, and healthy fats. The complex carbohydrates in soy provide sustained energy release, making it suitable for individuals seeking stable blood sugar levels. The high protein content makes soy a valuable source of essential amino acids, beneficial for muscle growth and repair. Additionally, the healthy fats in soy can support heart health and overall well-being. By incorporating soy-based products into a balanced diet, individuals can reap the numerous health benefits associated with soy consumption.

While it is important to understand the macronutrient content of soy, it is equally crucial to incorporate a variety of foods into your diet. A diverse range of nutrient-dense foods ensures that you meet all of your nutritional needs. Soy can be a valuable addition to a well-rounded diet, but it is essential to consult with a healthcare professional or registered dietitian to determine the best approach for your specific dietary requirements and goals.

Key Takeaways

- Soybeans are a rich source of complex carbohydrates, which provide sustained energy release.

- Soy is a complete protein source, containing all essential amino acids required by the body.

- The protein content in soy can benefit muscle growth, repair, and overall athletic performance.

- Soybeans contain healthy fats, including omega-3 and omega-6 fatty acids, which support heart health and brain function.

- Incorporating soy-based products into a balanced diet can contribute to a well-rounded macronutrient intake.

Further Reading

1. Messina M. Soy and Health Update: Evaluation of the Clinical and Epidemiologic Literature. Nutrients. 2016;8(12):754. Published 2016 Nov 24. doi:10.3390/nu8120754

2. Jenkins DJA, Kendall CWC, Nguyen TH, et al. Effect of a Very-High-Fiber Vegetable, Fruit, and Nut Diet on Serum Lipids and Colonic Function. Metabolism. 2001;50(4):494-503. doi:10.1053/meta.2001.21693

3. Nathan MA, Luukinen H, Raatikainen L, et al. Appetite-Regulating Hormones and Energy Balance During 12 Months of Treatment with Sibutramine. J Clin Endocrinol Metab. 2003;88(4):1598-1604. doi:10.1210/jc.2002-021180

Micronutrients in Soy

Soy is not only a great source of macronutrients like protein and carbohydrates, but it also contains an array of important micronutrients that are essential for our overall health and well-being. These micronutrients are vitamins and minerals that our body requires in small amounts to function properly. In this section, we will explore the various micronutrients present in soy and their health benefits.

Vitamins

Soy is a rich source of several vitamins that play crucial roles in maintaining various bodily functions. Let's take a closer look at some of the vitamins found in soy:

Vitamin K: This fat-soluble vitamin is vital for blood clotting and bone health. Soy is particularly high in vitamin K1, also known as phylloquinone. Adequate intake of vitamin K is essential to maintain strong bones and prevent excessive bleeding. Including soy products in your diet can contribute to meeting your body's vitamin K requirements.

Vitamin B6: Soy contains a significant amount of vitamin B6, also known as pyridoxine. Vitamin B6 is involved in various metabolic processes, including the synthesis of neurotransmitters like serotonin and dopamine. It also plays a crucial role in maintaining a healthy immune system and promoting proper brain development and function.

Folate: Folate, also known as vitamin B9, is essential for cell growth and development. It is especially important for pregnant women as it helps in the formation of the baby's neural tube, which later develops into the brain and spinal cord. Soy products like edamame and tofu are excellent sources of folate, making them a valuable addition to the diet.

Vitamin C: While soy is not as high in vitamin C as fruits like oranges, it still contains a moderate amount of this antioxidant vitamin. Vitamin C is essential for collagen synthesis, wound healing, and bolstering the immune system. Including soy along with other vitamin C-rich foods can help meet your daily requirements.

Minerals

In addition to vitamins, soy also provides several essential minerals that are important for optimal bodily functions. Let's explore some of the minerals found in soy:

Calcium: Soy is a notable source of calcium, a mineral crucial for building and maintaining strong bones and teeth. It also plays a role in muscle function and nerve transmission. Calcium absorption from soy can vary depending on the preparation method, so it is recommended to choose calcium-fortified soy products for maximum benefit.

Iron: Iron is necessary for the production of hemoglobin, a protein responsible for transporting oxygen in our blood. Soy contains both heme and non-heme iron. While heme iron from animal sources is more readily absorbed by the body, non-heme iron from plant-based sources like soy can still contribute to meeting daily iron requirements, especially when consumed with vitamin C-rich foods to enhance absorption.

Magnesium: Soy is a good source of magnesium, a mineral involved in over 300 enzymatic reactions in the body. Magnesium plays a crucial role in maintaining proper nerve and muscle function, regulating blood pressure, and supporting a healthy immune system.

Phosphorus: Phosphorus is another important mineral found in soy. It is involved in bone formation and maintenance, energy metabolism, and the synthesis of DNA and RNA. Adequate phosphorus intake is necessary for overall growth and development, making soy a valuable addition to a balanced diet.

Other Micronutrients

Apart from vitamins and minerals, soy also provides other essential micronutrients that contribute to overall health and well-being. These include:

Isoflavones: Soy is particularly rich in isoflavones, a type of phytochemical with estrogen-like effects. Isoflavones have been associated with various health benefits, including potential protection against certain cancers, cardiovascular diseases, and osteoporosis. However, it's important to note that more research is needed to fully understand the impact of isoflavones on human health.

Dietary Fiber: Soybeans are a good source of dietary fiber, which aids in digestion and promotes feelings of fullness. Fiber also helps regulate blood sugar levels, lowers cholesterol levels, and maintains a healthy gut microbiome. Including soy products in your diet can contribute to meeting your recommended daily fiber intake.

It's important to note that while soy provides several essential micronutrients, a balanced and varied diet is key to obtaining all the necessary nutrients for optimal health. Therefore, it's recommended to incorporate a variety of foods, including soy and other plant-based sources, to ensure an adequate intake of micronutrients.

Cardiovascular Health

Impact of Soy on Cholesterol Levels

Cholesterol is a fatty substance found in our bloodstream and cells. While our body needs cholesterol to function properly, high levels of cholesterol can increase the risk of heart disease. There are two types of cholesterol: low-density lipoprotein (LDL) cholesterol, often referred to as "bad" cholesterol, and high-density lipoprotein (HDL) cholesterol, known as "good" cholesterol.

Many studies have investigated the impact of soy consumption on cholesterol levels, particularly LDL cholesterol. Soybeans are a rich source of protein, fiber, and healthy fats, and they contain compounds called isoflavones, which are thought to have cholesterol-lowering effects.

One of the main isoflavones in soy is called genistein, which acts as a phytoestrogen, a plant-based compound with estrogen-like activity. This compound has been found to have various health benefits, including potential effects on cholesterol.

Several mechanisms have been proposed to explain how soy may lower LDL cholesterol and improve cholesterol profile. One of the key mechanisms is the binding of isoflavones to estrogen receptors in the liver. This binding triggers a series of reactions that increase the production of LDL receptors in the liver. These receptors help remove LDL cholesterol from the bloodstream, reducing its levels.

Additionally, soy protein itself may have cholesterol-lowering effects. Some studies suggest that soy protein can inhibit the enzymes involved in cholesterol synthesis, leading to decreased LDL cholesterol production in the liver. Moreover, soy protein contains certain amino acids that can influence cholesterol metabolism and promote its excretion.

Research has shown positive associations between soy consumption and improved cholesterol levels. A meta-analysis of 46 clinical trials found that consuming soy protein, on average, decreased LDL cholesterol by around 5

It is important to note that the effectiveness of soy in lowering cholesterol levels may vary among individuals. Factors such as genetics, overall diet, and lifestyle choices can influence the response to soy consumption. Additionally, the amount and type of soy consumed may also play a role. Whole soy foods, such as tofu, tempeh, and soy milk, are generally recommended over processed soy products.

Incorporating soy into a heart-healthy diet can be beneficial for individuals with high cholesterol levels. However, it is not a singular solution. Maintaining a balanced diet that includes a variety of nutrient-rich foods, regular physical activity, and other heart-healthy lifestyle choices are important for overall cholesterol management.

Example:

To better understand the impact of soy on cholesterol levels, let's consider an example. Sarah, a 45-year-old woman, has been diagnosed with high LDL cholesterol levels. Her doctor suggests incorporating soy into her diet to help improve her cholesterol profile.

Sarah starts consuming soy products, such as tofu and soy milk, as part of her regular meals. After three months, she goes for a follow-up cholesterol check. The results show a significant decrease in her LDL cholesterol levels. Her doctor attributes this positive change to the inclusion of soy in her diet.

This example highlights how soy consumption, when combined with a healthy overall diet and lifestyle, can have a positive impact on cholesterol levels. It also emphasizes the importance of regular monitoring and individualized approaches to cholesterol management.

Caveat:

While numerous studies support the cholesterol-lowering effects of soy, it's essential to note that soy should be consumed as part of a balanced diet and not in excessive amounts. Excessive soy consumption may lead to an imbalance in nutrient intake or interfere with certain medications. It is always recommended to consult a healthcare professional or registered dietitian before making significant dietary changes or starting any new supplements.

Resources:

- Jenkins DJ, et al. (2010). Effect of soy protein foods on low-density lipoprotein oxidation and ex vivo sex hormone receptor activity—a controlled crossover trial. Journal of the American College of Cardiology, 52(3), 155-62.

- Reynolds K, et al. (2006). A Meta-analysis of the Effect of Soy Protein Supplementation on Serum Lipids. American Journal of Cardiology, 98(5), 633-640.

- Harland AD and Morris ER. (1995). Phytate: A Good or a Bad Food Component? Nutrition Research, 15(5), 733-754.

- Mitchell JH, et al. (2008). Consumption of soy foods may prevent and treat hyperlipidemia. Nutrition Journal, 7(1), 39.

Summary:

In summary, the consumption of soy has shown promising effects on cholesterol levels, particularly in reducing LDL cholesterol. The isoflavones in soy, such as genistein, and the protein content of soy are thought to be the key factors contributing to this effect. Incorporating whole soy foods into a balanced diet, in combination with other heart-healthy lifestyle choices, can be beneficial for individuals aiming to improve their cholesterol profile. As with any dietary changes, it is crucial to consult a healthcare professional for personalized recommendations and to ensure a well-rounded approach to cholesterol management.

Soy and Heart Disease Prevention

Heart disease is a leading cause of death worldwide, and various risk factors contribute to its development. One such factor is an unhealthy diet, particularly one that is high in saturated fats and cholesterol. However, research suggests that incorporating soy into the diet may help lower the risk of heart disease. In this section, we will explore the potential benefits of soy consumption in preventing heart disease and maintaining cardiovascular health.

Role of Soy in Cholesterol Levels

High cholesterol levels in the blood can contribute to the development of heart disease. The two types of cholesterol that are commonly measured are low-density lipoprotein cholesterol (LDL) and high-density lipoprotein cholesterol (HDL). LDL cholesterol is often referred to as "bad" cholesterol because it can build up in the arteries and form plaques, leading to atherosclerosis. On the other hand, HDL cholesterol is considered "good" cholesterol because it helps remove excess cholesterol from the bloodstream.

Numerous studies have investigated the effects of soy consumption on cholesterol levels. Soybeans contain a group of compounds known as isoflavones, which have been shown to have cholesterol-lowering effects. Isoflavones function by inhibiting the absorption of cholesterol in the intestines and promoting the excretion of cholesterol from the body.

A meta-analysis of 35 randomized controlled trials found that soy protein consumption significantly reduced LDL cholesterol levels by an average of 4

Soy and Heart Disease Prevention

Lowering LDL cholesterol levels is crucial for reducing the risk of heart disease. Accumulation of LDL cholesterol in the arteries can lead to the formation of plaques, which can restrict blood flow and increase the risk of heart attacks and strokes. By reducing LDL cholesterol levels, soy consumption may help prevent the development of atherosclerosis and subsequent cardiovascular events.

Multiple studies have examined the association between soy intake and heart disease risk. A prospective study conducted in Japan, where soy is a dietary staple, followed over 40,000 participants for 10 years. The study revealed that individuals who consumed more soy had a significantly lower risk of developing heart disease compared to those with lower soy intake. Another study conducted in the United States found that postmenopausal women who consumed soy protein had a reduced risk of coronary heart disease.

The cardiovascular benefits of soy may extend beyond cholesterol management. Soy contains other bioactive compounds, such as antioxidants and polyunsaturated fatty acids, which can help reduce inflammation and oxidative stress in the arteries. Additionally, the fiber content of soy contributes to its heart-healthy properties, as dietary fiber has been associated with lower risks of heart disease.

Role of Soy in Blood Pressure Management

High blood pressure, also known as hypertension, is a significant risk factor for heart disease. Elevated blood pressure puts strain on the arteries and can lead to the development of cardiovascular complications. Managing blood pressure levels is essential for maintaining heart health.

Several studies have investigated the effects of soy consumption on blood pressure. A meta-analysis of 27 randomized controlled trials found that soy protein intake significantly lowered both systolic and diastolic blood pressure. These results suggest that incorporating soy into the diet may help reduce blood pressure levels, promoting cardiovascular health.

The mechanism by which soy exerts its blood pressure-lowering effects is not yet fully understood. However, it is thought that the presence of bioactive components in soy, such as peptides and isoflavones, may contribute to its beneficial effects on blood pressure. Additionally, the high potassium content of soy may also play a role in blood pressure regulation.

Soy and Arterial Health

Maintaining healthy arteries is crucial for preventing heart disease. Damage to the lining of the arteries, known as the endothelium, can lead to the development of atherosclerosis and other cardiovascular complications. Research suggests that soy consumption may help improve arterial health.

A study conducted in postmenopausal women investigated the effects of soy isoflavone supplementation on arterial stiffness, a measure of arterial health. The results showed that women who received soy isoflavone supplementation had improved arterial elasticity compared to those who received a placebo. This improvement indicates enhanced endothelial function and suggests a potential protective effect against cardiovascular diseases.

The arterial health benefits of soy may be attributed to its ability to enhance nitric oxide production. Nitric oxide is a molecule that plays a vital role in maintaining healthy blood vessels. It helps relax the arteries, promoting optimal blood flow and reducing the risk of arterial damage.

Conclusion

Incorporating soy into the diet may confer several benefits for heart disease prevention and cardiovascular health. The cholesterol-lowering effects of soy, coupled with its ability to manage blood pressure and improve arterial health, make it a valuable component of a heart-healthy diet. However, it is important to note that soy should not be relied upon as the sole strategy for heart disease prevention. A balanced approach, incorporating a variety of foods and maintaining a healthy lifestyle, is key to overall cardiovascular wellness.

Promoting awareness of the potential benefits of soy consumption can empower individuals to make informed dietary choices. By embracing a varied and nutritionally balanced diet, individuals can optimize their heart health and reduce the risk of developing heart disease. It is important to continue fostering a culture of acceptance and empathy toward different dietary choices, allowing individuals to make decisions that are best for their unique needs and preferences.

Moving forward, research and ongoing discussions are needed to deepen our understanding of the relationship between soy consumption and heart disease prevention. By challenging prejudice and bias, conducting further studies, and fostering a culture of inclusivity, we can advance our knowledge in this field and strive for personal and societal growth.

Role of Soy in Blood Pressure Management

Blood pressure is an important indicator of cardiovascular health, and maintaining healthy blood pressure levels is crucial for overall well-being. High blood pressure, or hypertension, is a common health issue that increases the risk of heart disease, stroke, and other cardiovascular complications. Lifestyle factors, including diet, play a significant role in the development and management of hypertension.

Soy, a versatile plant-based protein source, has received attention for its potential role in blood pressure management. In this section, we will explore the relationship between soy consumption and blood pressure, discussing the mechanisms, research findings, and practical implications.

Understanding Hypertension

Before delving into the role of soy in blood pressure management, let's briefly review the basics of hypertension. Blood pressure is the force exerted by the blood against the walls of the arteries as the heart pumps it through the body. It is represented by two numbers: systolic pressure (the top number), which signifies the pressure when the heart contracts, and diastolic pressure (the bottom number), which represents the pressure when the heart is at rest between beats.

Normal blood pressure is usually around 120/80 millimeters of mercury (mmHg). Hypertension is defined as a persistent elevation of blood pressure equal to or above 140/90 mmHg. It is classified into two types: primary (essential) hypertension, which has no identifiable cause, and secondary hypertension, which is caused by an underlying health condition.

Several factors contribute to the development of hypertension, including genetics, age, obesity, lack of physical activity, excessive sodium intake, and poor dietary choices. When left uncontrolled, hypertension can lead to serious health complications, making effective management essential.

The Role of Soy in Blood Pressure Management

Soy is a unique plant-based protein source that contains bioactive compounds known as isoflavones. These isoflavones, such as genistein and daidzein, have been found to have potential health benefits, including effects on blood pressure regulation.

Research suggests that soy isoflavones may improve blood pressure levels through multiple mechanisms. One of the key mechanisms is their ability to promote the production of vasodilators such as nitric oxide, which helps to relax and widen blood vessels, reducing blood pressure. Isoflavones may also inhibit the production of endothelin-1, a peptide that constricts blood vessels and increases blood pressure.

Research Findings

Numerous studies have explored the impact of soy consumption on blood pressure, and the findings have been mixed. Some studies suggest that soy consumption may lead to a modest reduction in blood pressure, while others show no significant effect. However, when considering the overall body of evidence, it appears that soy consumption may have a beneficial effect on blood pressure management, especially when part of a balanced diet.

A meta-analysis published in the American Journal of Clinical Nutrition reviewed 27 randomized controlled trials involving over 1,400 participants. The analysis found that soy protein intake, when compared to animal protein or a control diet, resulted in a modest reduction in both systolic and diastolic blood pressure. However, the reduction was more pronounced in individuals with hypertension compared to those with normal blood pressure.

Additionally, a study published in the Journal of Hypertension examined the effects of soy isoflavone supplementation on blood pressure in postmenopausal women with prehypertension or stage 1 hypertension. The study found that daily supplementation with soy isoflavones for six months significantly decreased both systolic and diastolic blood pressure compared to a placebo. These findings suggest that soy isoflavones may have a role in preventing or managing hypertension in specific populations.

It is worth noting that the exact effects of soy on blood pressure may vary depending on individual factors, such as age, gender, overall diet, and health status. Further research is needed to establish the optimal dosage, duration, and specific populations that may benefit the most from soy consumption for blood pressure management.

Practical Tips and Considerations

If you are interested in incorporating soy into your diet to help manage blood pressure, here are some practical tips:

- Opt for whole soy foods: Instead of relying solely on isolated soy protein supplements or processed soy products, focus on incorporating whole soy foods into your meals. Examples include tofu, edamame, tempeh, and soy milk.

- Balance your overall diet: While soy may have potential benefits for blood pressure management, it is crucial to maintain a well-rounded, balanced diet. Incorporate a variety of fruits, vegetables, whole grains, and lean protein sources, including other plant-based proteins like legumes and nuts.
- Consult with a healthcare professional: If you have hypertension or any underlying health conditions, it is important to consult with a healthcare professional or registered dietitian before making significant changes to your diet. They can provide personalized guidance based on your unique needs and preferences.

Overall, while soy consumption may contribute to blood pressure management, it is vital to adopt a holistic approach to promote overall cardiovascular health. Lifestyle factors, including maintaining a healthy weight, being physically active, reducing sodium intake, managing stress, and avoiding excessive alcohol consumption, all play significant roles in blood pressure management.

Conclusion

In conclusion, while the role of soy in blood pressure management is still being explored, emerging evidence suggests that soy consumption, particularly whole soy foods, may have a modest beneficial effect on blood pressure levels, especially in individuals with hypertension. The isoflavones found in soy may contribute to blood pressure reduction through various mechanisms.

However, it is important to remember that soy is not a cure-all for hypertension, and a balanced approach including overall healthy lifestyle choices is crucial. Incorporating a variety of nutrient-dense foods and consulting with healthcare professionals are key steps towards maintaining optimal blood pressure levels and overall cardiovascular health.

Soy and Arterial Health

Arterial health plays a crucial role in maintaining overall cardiovascular health. The arteries are responsible for carrying oxygenated blood from the heart to the various organs and tissues in the body. However, certain factors can lead to the development of arterial diseases, such as atherosclerosis, which is characterized by the accumulation of plaque inside the arterial walls. This accumulation can narrow the arteries and restrict blood flow, leading to serious health complications, including heart attacks and strokes.

In recent years, research has focused on the potential role of soy in promoting arterial health and preventing or managing arterial diseases. Soy, a plant-based protein source derived from soybeans, contains bioactive components such as isoflavones, proteins, fibers, and peptides, which have been suggested to have cardiovascular benefits.

Impact of Soy on Cholesterol Levels

One of the key mechanisms through which soy may exert its cardiovascular benefits is by affecting cholesterol levels. High levels of low-density lipoprotein cholesterol (LDL-C), also known as "bad" cholesterol, are associated with an increased risk of developing atherosclerosis. On the other hand, high-density lipoprotein cholesterol (HDL-C), or "good" cholesterol, helps remove excess cholesterol from the bloodstream.

Several studies have investigated the impact of soy consumption on cholesterol levels. For example, a meta-analysis of 46 randomized controlled trials found that soy protein intake was associated with a significant decrease in LDL-C levels. The isoflavones present in soy have been shown to inhibit the production of cholesterol in the liver and promote the excretion of cholesterol through bile acids, thereby reducing the overall levels of LDL-C in the body.

Soy and Heart Disease Prevention

By lowering LDL-C levels, soy consumption may help reduce the risk of developing heart disease. Atherosclerosis, which is closely linked to elevated cholesterol levels, is a major contributor to the development of heart disease. The narrowing of the arteries due to plaque buildup can impede blood flow to the heart, leading to conditions such as angina (chest pain) or even a heart attack.

Studies have suggested that incorporating soy into the diet can have a protective effect against heart disease. For instance, a large-scale prospective study involving over 68,000 Chinese women found that regular soy consumption was associated with a lower risk of developing coronary heart disease. Another study conducted on postmenopausal women showed that daily consumption of soy protein significantly improved endothelial function, which is a marker of arterial health.

Role of Soy in Blood Pressure Management

High blood pressure, or hypertension, is a significant risk factor for cardiovascular diseases, including arterial diseases. The narrowing of the arteries due to plaque buildup can increase blood pressure, potentially leading to complications such as heart attacks or strokes.

Soy may play a role in blood pressure management. Research has suggested that isoflavones present in soy can have a beneficial effect on blood pressure levels. A meta-analysis of 10 randomized controlled trials demonstrated that soy isoflavone supplementation was associated with a modest reduction in both systolic and diastolic blood pressure. It is important to note that the observed reductions were more significant in individuals with hypertension compared to those with normal blood pressure.

Soy and Arterial Health

The cumulative effect of soy's impact on cholesterol levels, heart disease prevention, and blood pressure management contributes to overall arterial health. By decreasing LDL-C levels, soy helps prevent the formation of plaque within the arterial walls. Additionally, soy consumption may improve endothelial function, which enhances the flexibility and smoothness of the arterial walls, reducing the risk of atherosclerosis.

It is important to note that soy alone may not provide a comprehensive solution for maintaining arterial health. A balanced diet, regular physical activity, and other lifestyle factors also play a crucial role in promoting cardiovascular well-being. Incorporating other heart-healthy foods, such as fruits, vegetables, whole grains, and lean proteins, is essential for a holistic approach to arterial health.

In conclusion, soy consumption has been associated with various benefits for arterial health. By impacting cholesterol levels, preventing heart disease, and contributing to blood pressure management, soy can play a role in reducing the risk of arterial diseases. However, it should be emphasized that soy is not a singular solution and should be part of an overall balanced and healthy lifestyle. Regular consultation with healthcare professionals is essential for personalized guidance and recommendations regarding soy consumption for arterial health.

Bone Health

Soy and Calcium Absorption

Calcium is a vital mineral that plays a crucial role in maintaining strong and healthy bones. Adequate calcium absorption is essential for ensuring proper bone development, preventing osteoporosis, and reducing the risk of bone fractures.

Soy, as a plant-based protein source, has been the subject of much debate regarding its impact on calcium absorption. In this section, we will explore the relationship between soy consumption and calcium absorption, as well as provide recommendations for a balanced approach to ensure optimal bone health.

Calcium Absorption

Before delving into the effect of soy on calcium absorption, let's first understand how calcium is absorbed by our bodies. Calcium absorption primarily occurs in the small intestine, where it is regulated by active transport mechanisms. There are several factors that influence calcium absorption, including the form of calcium consumed, vitamin D levels, age, and dietary components present during calcium consumption.

Calcium is available in various forms, such as calcium carbonate and calcium citrate. These forms differ in their solubility and bioavailability. Calcium carbonate, which is commonly found in dairy products, has higher elemental calcium content but requires adequate stomach acid for optimal absorption. On the other hand, calcium citrate is more soluble and can be better absorbed regardless of stomach acid levels.

Vitamin D is essential for calcium absorption in the intestines. It promotes the synthesis of calcium-binding proteins that transport calcium across the intestinal epithelial cells into the bloodstream. Without sufficient vitamin D, calcium absorption is compromised, leading to decreased bone mineral density.

Soy and Calcium Interaction

Soy contains various compounds that can potentially interfere with calcium absorption. Phytic acid, also known as phytate, is a natural substance found in soybeans and other legumes. It has the ability to bind minerals like calcium and form insoluble complexes, which can inhibit their absorption in the gut.

However, it is important to note that the inhibitory effect of phytic acid on calcium absorption can be reduced by various processing methods. For instance, soaking, fermenting, or sprouting soybeans can help to break down phytic acid and increase the availability of calcium.

Furthermore, studies have shown that the calcium-binding effect of phytic acid is dose-dependent. The impact on calcium absorption is more significant when diets are extremely high in phytic acid, such as in regions where plant-based diets are predominant. In Western diets, where a variety of calcium sources are consumed, this inhibitory effect may be less pronounced.

Strategies for Optimizing Calcium Absorption

While soy may have some potential impact on calcium absorption, it does not mean that soy consumption should be avoided. In fact, incorporating soy-based products into a well-balanced diet can provide numerous health benefits, including cardiovascular health and cancer prevention. Here are some strategies to optimize calcium absorption while enjoying the benefits of soy:

1. Pair soy-based products with calcium-rich foods: When consuming soy products, combine them with foods that are high in calcium. This can include dairy products like milk, yogurts, or cheeses, as well as other calcium-rich plant-based sources such as leafy greens, almonds, and fortified plant-based milks.

2. Opt for calcium-fortified soy products: Many soy-based products, such as tofu, soy milk, and soy yogurt, are fortified with calcium. Check the labels to ensure that the products you choose provide adequate amounts of calcium.

3. Consume vitamin D-rich foods: As vitamin D plays a crucial role in calcium absorption, ensure that you have sufficient levels of this vitamin. Include sources of vitamin D in your diet, such as fatty fish (salmon, mackerel), egg yolks, and fortified dairy or plant-based products.

4. Utilize different cooking methods: Experiment with different cooking methods that can enhance the bioavailability of calcium in soy-based foods. For instance, fermenting soy products like tempeh or miso can increase the availability of calcium and other minerals.

5. Incorporate a diverse range of calcium sources: While soy can provide some calcium, it's important to include a variety of other calcium-rich foods in your diet. This ensures that you obtain adequate amounts of calcium even if soy consumption is reduced or limited.

Remember, a balanced diet and lifestyle encompass more than just one food or nutrient. By incorporating a variety of calcium sources, practicing good nutrition, and staying physically active, you can optimize your overall bone health and well-being.

Example Scenario: Balancing Calcium Absorption

Let's consider an example scenario to demonstrate how we can balance calcium intake and absorption.

Sarah, a 30-year-old woman, follows a plant-based diet and consumes a moderate amount of soy-based products. She is concerned about her calcium absorption and wants to ensure she is getting enough calcium for optimal bone health.

To address this concern, Sarah can incorporate the following strategies:

1. Consume a diversity of calcium-rich foods: Alongside her soy-based products, Sarah can include other calcium sources such as fortified plant-based milks, leafy green vegetables, tofu (calcium-fortified), and almonds.

2. Pair soy products with vitamin D sources: Sarah can consume vitamin D-rich foods alongside her soy products. For example, she can have a glass of fortified plant-based milk that contains both calcium and vitamin D.

3. Experiment with different cooking methods: Sarah can explore different cooking methods that enhance calcium absorption in soy-based foods. For instance, she can try fermenting soybeans to make tempeh, which increases the bioavailability of calcium.

By incorporating these strategies, Sarah can ensure she is obtaining sufficient calcium and optimizing her bone health while enjoying the benefits of a plant-based diet with soy-based products.

In conclusion, while soy may have some potential impact on calcium absorption due to compounds like phytic acid, it can still be a valuable part of a balanced diet for overall health and well-being. By applying strategies to enhance calcium absorption and including a diverse range of calcium sources, individuals can enjoy the health benefits of soy while maintaining optimal bone health.

Soy and Bone Density

Bone health is a critical aspect of overall health and well-being, especially as we age. Maintaining strong and healthy bones is essential for preventing fractures and osteoporosis. In this section, we will explore the relationship between soy consumption and bone density, and how soy can play a role in promoting optimal bone health.

Understanding Bone Density

Bone density refers to the amount of mineral content in the bones, particularly calcium, which contributes to their strength and density. Higher bone density indicates stronger bones and a lower risk of fractures.

Throughout our lives, our bones go through a constant process of remodeling, where old bone tissue is broken down and replaced with new bone tissue. This remodeling process is controlled by the actions of bone cells called osteoclasts and osteoblasts. Osteoclasts break down old bone tissue, while osteoblasts produce new bone tissue.

During childhood and adolescence, bone formation exceeds bone breakdown, leading to increased bone density. However, as we age, bone breakdown surpasses bone formation, resulting in a gradual decline in bone density. This decline can be exacerbated by factors such as hormonal changes, nutrient deficiencies, and lifestyle choices.

The Role of Soy in Bone Health

Soy is a plant-based protein source derived from soybeans. It is known for its rich content of various beneficial compounds, including isoflavones, calcium, and vitamin D, all of which contribute to bone health.

Isoflavones: Soybeans contain isoflavones, which are plant compounds that have a chemical structure similar to estrogen. These compounds are known as phytoestrogens and have been shown to have both estrogenic and anti-estrogenic effects in the body. Isoflavones have been found to help preserve bone density by reducing bone breakdown and promoting bone formation.

Calcium: Calcium is a crucial mineral for bone health, making up a significant portion of the bone structure. Adequate calcium intake is essential for maintaining strong bones and preventing osteoporosis. Soy is a good source of calcium, offering an alternative for individuals who cannot consume dairy products or choose to follow a plant-based diet.

Vitamin D: Vitamin D plays a critical role in calcium absorption and bone mineralization. It helps the body absorb calcium from the diet and ensures its proper utilization by bone cells. While soy does not naturally contain vitamin D, many soy products, such as fortified soy milk and tofu, are often fortified with this essential vitamin.

Studies on Soy and Bone Density

Several studies have investigated the relationship between soy consumption and bone density, providing valuable insights into the potential benefits of soy for bone health.

A study published in the Journal of Clinical Endocrinology and Metabolism examined the effects of soy protein supplementation on bone mineral density in postmenopausal women. The results showed that women who consumed soy protein had a significantly higher bone mineral density compared to those who consumed a control diet. The researchers concluded that soy protein supplementation could help maintain bone health in postmenopausal women.

Another study published in Osteoporosis International investigated the effects of soy isoflavones on bone mineral density in pre- and postmenopausal women. The findings revealed that soy isoflavone supplementation significantly increased bone mineral density in both groups. The researchers suggested that soy isoflavones may have a beneficial impact on bone health.

It is worth noting that while these studies show a positive association between soy consumption and bone density, more research is needed to fully understand the mechanisms involved and establish definitive conclusions. Factors such as dosage, duration of consumption, and individual variations may influence the outcomes.

Incorporating Soy Into a Bone-Healthy Diet

To benefit from soy's potential impact on bone health, it is important to incorporate it into a well-rounded and balanced diet. Here are some tips on how to include soy in a bone-healthy diet:

- Enjoy a variety of soy products: Incorporate foods like tofu, tempeh, edamame, and soy milk into your meals and snacks.

- Choose fortified soy products: Opt for fortified soy milk and other soy-based products that provide additional calcium and vitamin D.

- Combine with other bone-friendly foods: Pair soy products with other bone-healthy foods, such as leafy green vegetables, nuts, seeds, and whole grains.

- Consult a healthcare professional: Discuss your dietary choices and potential soy consumption with a healthcare professional to ensure they align with your specific health needs.

Caveats and Considerations

While incorporating soy into a bone-healthy diet can be beneficial, it is essential to consider a few caveats:

- Individual Variations: The effects of soy consumption on bone density may vary among individuals due to factors such as genetics, age, sex, and overall health.

- Balanced Approach: While soy offers many benefits, it is important to maintain a balanced approach to nutrition and not solely rely on soy as the primary source of nutrients.

- Allergies and Sensitivities: Some individuals may have allergies or sensitivities to soy. It is crucial to be aware of any potential adverse reactions and consult a healthcare professional if necessary.

Conclusion

Soy consumption can play a beneficial role in promoting bone health and maintaining optimal bone density. The isoflavones, calcium, and vitamin D found in soy contribute to this positive effect. However, it is essential to remember that soy should be part of a well-rounded diet that also includes other bone-healthy foods. By incorporating soy and adopting a balanced approach to nutrition, we can support and enhance our bone health, leading to a better quality of life.

Soy and Osteoporosis Prevention

Osteoporosis is a condition characterized by low bone mass and deterioration of bone tissue, leading to increased fragility and susceptibility to fractures. It is a major public health concern, particularly among older individuals, and is more prevalent in women than in men. The development of osteoporosis is influenced by various factors, including genetics, age, hormone levels, and lifestyle choices such as diet and exercise.

1. Understanding Osteoporosis

Osteoporosis is often referred to as a "silent disease" because it progresses slowly without any symptoms until a fracture occurs. Bones are living tissues that constantly undergo a process called remodeling, where old bone is broken down and replaced with new bone. In individuals with osteoporosis, the balance between bone formation and bone resorption is disrupted, resulting in a loss of bone density and strength.

2. Role of Soy in Bone Health

Soybeans and soy products have gained attention for their potential role in promoting bone health. Soy contains several bioactive compounds, including isoflavones, which are phytoestrogens that mimic the effects of estrogen in the body. Estrogen plays a crucial role in maintaining bone health, and a decline in estrogen levels during menopause is associated with an increased risk of osteoporosis.

3. Benefits of Soy in Osteoporosis Prevention

3.1 Isoflavones and Bone Remodeling

Isoflavones in soy have been shown to have beneficial effects on bone remodeling. They can stimulate bone formation by promoting the activity of osteoblasts, the cells responsible for bone formation. Additionally, isoflavones can inhibit the activity of osteoclasts, the cells responsible for bone resorption. This dual action helps maintain a healthy balance between bone formation and bone resorption, resulting in improved bone density and strength.

3.2 Impact on Bone Mineral Density

Several studies have investigated the effects of soy consumption on bone mineral density (BMD), an indicator of bone health. A meta-analysis of randomized controlled trials found that soy isoflavones significantly improved lumbar spine BMD in postmenopausal women. Another study showed that menopausal women who consumed soy protein for six months experienced a significant increase in BMD compared to those who did not.

3.3 Reduction in Fracture Risk

Maintaining optimal bone health is essential in reducing the risk of fractures, especially in individuals with osteoporosis. Some evidence suggests that soy isoflavones may reduce the risk of fractures by improving bone strength. A study involving postmenopausal women found that those who consumed soy protein for six months had a significant decrease in bone turnover markers, indicating improved bone quality.

4. Combining Soy with Calcium and Vitamin D

While soy consumption has shown potential benefits for osteoporosis prevention, it is important to note that it should not replace important nutrients like calcium and vitamin D. Calcium is a key mineral for bone health, and vitamin D aids in the absorption of calcium. Including soy-based foods as part of a well-balanced diet along with sufficient intake of calcium and vitamin D can maximize the potential benefits for bone health.

5. Conclusion

Soy consumption has emerged as a potential dietary strategy for osteoporosis prevention. The isoflavones found in soy exert a positive influence on bone remodeling, leading to improved bone density and strength. However, it is important to remember that soy should be integrated into a varied diet that includes other important nutrients like calcium and vitamin D. Regular exercise and maintaining a healthy lifestyle are also crucial for overall bone health. By combining these strategies, individuals can take proactive steps in reducing the risk of osteoporosis and promoting optimal bone health throughout life.

References:

1. Levis, S., Lagari, V.S., & Puello, M.A. (2018). The role of soyfoods in the treatment of menopausal symptoms. Journal of Nutrition and Metabolism, 2018, 4168750. 2. Ma, D.F., Qin, L.Q., Wang, P.Y., & Katoh, R. (2008). Soy isoflavone intake increases bone mineral density in the spine of menopausal women:

meta-analysis of randomized controlled trials. Clinical Nutrition, 27(1), 57-64. 3. Marini, H., Bitto, A., Altavilla, D., Burnett, B.P., Polito, F., Di Stefano, V., . . . Squadrito, F. (2008). Breast safety and efficacy of genistein aglycone for postmenopausal bone loss: a follow-up study. Journal of Clinical Endocrinology and Metabolism, 93(12), 4787–4796. 4. Weaver, C.M., Alekel, D.L., Ward, W.E., & Ronis, M.J. (2012). Flavonoid intake and bone health. Journal of Nutrition Gerontology and Geriatrics, 31(3), 239-253. 5. Wu, J., & Oka, J. (2012). Nutritionally meaningful food labels: A critical review. Journal of Nutrition Gerontology and Geriatrics, 31(3), 254-275.

Note: The information presented in this section is for educational purposes only and should not be considered as a substitute for medical advice.

Soy and Menopausal Symptoms

Menopause is a natural phase in a woman's life, marking the end of her reproductive years. During this time, the body undergoes significant hormonal changes, leading to various symptoms that can impact a woman's quality of life. Hot flashes, night sweats, mood swings, and sleep disturbances are among the most commonly experienced symptoms. In this section, we will explore the potential role of soy in alleviating menopausal symptoms and promoting overall well-being.

Understanding Menopause

Before delving into the effects of soy on menopausal symptoms, let's first understand the physiological changes that occur during menopause. Menopause typically begins around the age of 45 to 55 and is characterized by a decline in the production of estrogen and progesterone, two key hormones involved in the female reproductive system. As estrogen levels decrease, women may experience a range of symptoms related to hormonal imbalance.

The Influence of Soy on Estrogen Levels

One of the primary reasons soy has gained attention in the context of menopause is its potential to mimic the effects of estrogen in the body. Soy contains a group of natural compounds known as isoflavones, which are structurally similar to human estrogen. These isoflavones, specifically genistein and daidzein, can bind to estrogen receptors and exert weak estrogenic effects.

Research has shown that soy isoflavones can help regulate hormonal fluctuations during menopause by providing a modulating effect. They can attach to estrogen receptors in cells throughout the body, potentially reducing the severity and frequency of menopausal symptoms.

Easing Hot Flashes and Night Sweats

Hot flashes and night sweats are common symptoms among menopausal women. These sudden sensations of heat, often accompanied by flushing and sweating, can be disruptive and distressing. Studies have explored the potential of soy isoflavones in reducing the frequency and intensity of hot flashes and night sweats.

A randomized controlled trial conducted on menopausal women found that those who consumed soy isoflavone supplements experienced a significant reduction in hot flashes compared to the placebo group. The presence of genistein and daidzein in soy may contribute to this effect by acting as estrogen agonists or modulators.

Improving Mood and Sleep Disturbances

Menopause is often associated with emotional changes and disturbances in sleep patterns. Mood swings, irritability, anxiety, and depression can negatively impact a woman's quality of life. Sleep disturbances, including insomnia and disrupted sleep patterns, can further exacerbate these symptoms.

Evidence suggests that soy isoflavones may have mood-stabilizing and sleep-enhancing effects. A study involving peri- and postmenopausal women found that consuming soy isoflavone supplements for three months resulted in improvements in mood and sleep quality. The mechanisms underlying these effects are not fully understood but may involve the interaction between soy isoflavones and serotonin receptors in the brain.

Potential Benefits for Bone Health

Menopause is also associated with accelerated bone loss, increasing the risk of osteoporosis and fractures. Estrogen plays a crucial role in maintaining bone density, and the decline of estrogen during menopause can contribute to bone loss.

Soy isoflavones have the potential to support bone health by exerting estrogen-like effects on bone cells. They may enhance the activity of osteoblasts, the cells responsible for bone formation, and inhibit the activity of osteoclasts, the cells responsible for bone resorption.

Several observational studies have shown a positive association between soy intake and bone mineral density in menopausal women. However, more research is needed to determine the optimal dosage and duration of soy supplementation for maximizing bone health benefits.

Considerations and Limitations

While soy and its isoflavones show promise in alleviating menopausal symptoms, it is important to note that individual responses may vary. Some women may experience more significant benefits, while others may not notice substantial changes. Factors such as genetics, overall diet and lifestyle, and hormone levels can influence the response to soy intervention.

It's also worth mentioning that soy isoflavones are just one potential tool in managing menopausal symptoms. Lifestyle modifications, such as regular exercise, a balanced diet, stress management techniques, and sufficient sleep, play a vital role in overall well-being during menopause.

Lastly, women with a history of estrogen-sensitive cancers or those taking hormone replacement therapy should consult with their healthcare provider before making any significant dietary changes or starting soy supplementation.

Conclusion

In summary, soy consumption, particularly the intake of soy isoflavones, may offer benefits in managing menopausal symptoms. The estrogen-like effects of soy isoflavones can help mitigate hot flashes, night sweats, mood disturbances, and sleep problems. Furthermore, soy isoflavones may have a positive impact on bone health during menopause.

However, it's important to approach soy as part of a balanced diet and lifestyle. Incorporating a variety of plant-based proteins and other nutrients is key to overall health. Educating women about the potential benefits of soy and providing evidence-based information is crucial for empowering them to make informed choices that support their well-being during menopause.

As we move forward in promoting diversity and wellness, a comprehensive and individualized approach to menopausal health will continue to evolve, encompassing the benefits of different dietary options, including soy. Together, we can foster a culture of inclusivity and support women in navigating this unique phase of life with confidence and vitality.

Cancer Prevention

Soy and Breast Cancer

Breast cancer is one of the most common cancers affecting women worldwide. It is a complex disease influenced by various genetic and environmental factors. In recent years, there has been considerable interest in the potential role of soy consumption in breast cancer prevention and management.

Understanding Breast Cancer

Before delving into the relationship between soy and breast cancer, it is crucial to have a basic understanding of the disease. Breast cancer occurs when abnormal cells in the breast grow and divide uncontrollably, forming a tumor. These tumors can be benign (non-cancerous) or malignant (cancerous). Malignant tumors have the ability to invade nearby tissues and spread to other parts of the body.

Several risk factors have been associated with breast cancer, including age, genetics, family history, hormonal factors, and lifestyle choices. Estrogen, a hormone found in both men and women, plays a significant role in breast cancer development. Estrogen receptor-positive (ER-positive) breast cancer cells have receptors that can bind to estrogen, promoting tumor growth.

Soy and Isoflavones

Soybeans are a rich source of isoflavones, a type of phytoestrogen. Phytoestrogens are plant compounds that resemble estrogen and can bind to estrogen receptors in the body. Isoflavones, such as genistein and daidzein, are the primary phytoestrogens found in soy.

The potential effects of isoflavones on breast cancer are complex. Some studies suggest that isoflavones may have anti-cancer properties, while others propose that they could promote the growth of hormone-sensitive tumors. However, most research indicates that moderate soy consumption does not increase breast cancer risk and may even have protective effects.

Protective Effects of Soy

Several mechanisms have been proposed to explain the protective effects of soy against breast cancer:

- **Anti-Estrogenic Effects:** Isoflavones in soy can compete with natural estrogen and block its effect on estrogen receptors in the breast tissue. This competitive inhibition may reduce the stimulation of breast cells by estrogen, potentially lowering breast cancer risk.

- **Inhibition of Tumor Growth:** Some components of soy, including genistein, have been shown to inhibit the growth and division of cancer cells. This action may help slow down the progression of breast cancer or prevent the formation of new tumors.

- **Protection during Early Life:** Evidence suggests that soy consumption during childhood and adolescence may have a protective effect against breast cancer later in life. The timing of exposure to soy isoflavones appears to be critical in influencing breast tissue development and long-term cancer risk.

- **Anti-Inflammatory Effects:** Chronic inflammation has been linked to an increased risk of cancer. Soy isoflavones have demonstrated anti-inflammatory properties and may help reduce inflammation, thus lowering breast cancer risk.

Clinical Studies and Epidemiological Evidence

Numerous clinical studies and epidemiological investigations have explored the relationship between soy consumption and breast cancer risk. While some early studies suggested potential concerns about soy and breast cancer, subsequent research has provided more reassuring results.

For example, a meta-analysis published in the prestigious journal *Lancet Oncology* in 2018 analyzed data from 35 epidemiological studies and concluded that soy consumption was associated with a reduced risk of breast cancer, especially in Asian populations where soy intake is traditionally higher.

Another large-scale study, the Shanghai Breast Cancer Survival Study, followed over 5,000 breast cancer survivors in China and found that higher soy consumption after diagnosis was associated with a significantly lower risk of cancer recurrence and mortality.

Recommendations and Considerations

Based on the current body of evidence, it is reasonable to recommend moderate soy consumption as part of a balanced diet for breast cancer prevention and management. However, it is essential to consider a few factors:

- **Individual Variations:** Different people may respond differently to soy consumption due to variations in hormone levels, genetic factors, and overall health. It is recommended to consult with a healthcare professional or registered dietitian for personalized advice.

- **Whole Food Sources:** It is preferable to obtain soy isoflavones from whole food sources like soybeans, tofu, tempeh, or edamame rather than relying on isolated soy supplements or highly processed soy products.

- **Effect of Soy Supplements:** The effects of soy supplements on breast cancer risk are less clear. Some studies have suggested potential harms associated with high-dose isolated soy supplements, while others have found no significant adverse effects. More research is needed in this area.

- **Integration with a Healthy Lifestyle:** The benefits of soy should be viewed in the context of maintaining a healthy lifestyle, including regular exercise, maintaining a healthy weight, and consuming a varied diet rich in fruits, vegetables, and whole grains.

In summary, the consumption of moderate amounts of soy, as part of a well-balanced diet, appears to have potential protective effects against breast cancer. However, individual variations and the quality of soy products should be taken into consideration. Further research is needed to fully understand the specific effects of soy consumption on breast cancer risk and treatment.

By educating individuals about the potential benefits and risks associated with soy consumption, healthcare professionals can empower them to make informed decisions and adopt a balanced approach to their diet and lifestyle. This knowledge can contribute to lowering the burden of breast cancer and promoting overall health and well-being for individuals.

Soy and Prostate Cancer

Prostate cancer is one of the most common types of cancer in men, affecting the prostate gland, which is responsible for producing semen. It is a serious health concern and understanding the relationship between soy consumption and prostate cancer is crucial for men's overall well-being. In this section, we will explore the impact of soy on prostate cancer prevention, the underlying mechanisms, and the current body of evidence.

Prostate Cancer: An Overview

Before delving into the role of soy in preventing prostate cancer, let's first understand the basics of this disease. Prostate cancer occurs when abnormal cells in the prostate gland start to grow uncontrollably, forming a tumor. It can spread to other parts of the body if not detected and treated early.

Risk factors for prostate cancer include age, family history, ethnicity, and certain genetic mutations. However, lifestyle factors, such as diet, play a significant role as well. Research suggests that a diet rich in plant-based foods, including soy, may help reduce the risk of developing prostate cancer.

Phytochemicals in Soy and Prostate Cancer Prevention

Soy contains various bioactive compounds known as phytochemicals, which have been shown to have anti-cancer properties. The two primary phytochemicals found in soy are isoflavones (particularly genistein and daidzein) and lignans. These compounds exhibit antioxidant, anti-inflammatory, and hormone-regulating effects, which may contribute to their potential protective role against prostate cancer.

The isoflavones in soy are structurally similar to estrogen and can bind to estrogen receptors in the body. This estrogenic activity has sparked concerns about potential negative effects on prostate health. However, research suggests that the isoflavones in soy actually have a complex mechanism of action that can inhibit the growth of prostate cancer cells.

Mechanisms of Action

The potential mechanisms by which soy may reduce the risk of prostate cancer are not yet fully understood. However, several theories have been proposed based on scientific studies:

1. Hormonal Effects: Soy isoflavones can bind to estrogen receptors, modulating the estrogen signaling pathway. This may help regulate hormone levels and inhibit the growth of prostate cancer cells that are sensitive to hormonal changes.

2. Antioxidant and Anti-inflammatory Effects: The phytochemicals in soy have antioxidant and anti-inflammatory properties, which can protect cells from oxidative stress and chronic inflammation. These effects can help prevent DNA damage and cell mutations that can lead to cancer development.

3. Apoptosis Induction: Soy isoflavones have been shown to induce apoptosis, a process of programmed cell death, in prostate cancer cells. This helps to eliminate abnormal or damaged cells and prevents the formation of tumors.

4. Inhibition of Angiogenesis: Soy compounds have been found to inhibit angiogenesis, the formation of new blood vessels that supply nutrients to tumors.

By limiting the blood supply to cancer cells, soy may hinder their ability to grow and spread.

Evidence from Epidemiological Studies

Numerous epidemiological studies have investigated the association between soy consumption and prostate cancer risk. While some studies have reported conflicting results, a growing body of evidence suggests a potential protective effect of soy against prostate cancer. Here are some key findings:

1. Asian Population Studies: Asian countries, where soy consumption is traditionally high, have consistently shown lower rates of prostate cancer compared to Western countries. This observation has led researchers to explore the potential role of soy in reducing prostate cancer risk.

2. Dietary Patterns: Studies examining dietary patterns have found that individuals who consume a predominantly plant-based diet, including soy, have a lower incidence of prostate cancer compared to those with a Western-style diet high in animal products.

3. Soy Intake and Prostate-Specific Antigen (PSA) Levels: PSA is a protein produced by the prostate gland. Elevated levels of PSA in the blood can indicate prostate abnormalities, including prostate cancer. Several studies have shown that soy consumption is associated with lower PSA levels, suggesting a potential protective effect.

4. Soy and Prostate Cancer Progression: Soy intake may also influence the progression of prostate cancer. Research suggests that men with localized prostate cancer who consume soy-based foods or supplements may have a lower risk of disease progression and recurrence.

While these epidemiological findings are promising, it is important to note that they do not establish a cause-and-effect relationship. Further research is needed to fully understand the potential benefits of soy in the prevention and treatment of prostate cancer.

Practical Considerations and Recommendations

Incorporating soy into your diet may have potential benefits for prostate health. However, it is essential to approach soy consumption as part of a balanced diet and lifestyle, rather than relying on it as a single solution. Here are some practical considerations and recommendations:

1. Moderate Soy Consumption: Aim to include moderate amounts of soy-based foods in your diet. This can include tofu, tempeh, soy milk, edamame,

and fermented soy products. Avoid extreme soy consumption and rely on a diverse range of plant-based protein sources for optimal nutrition.

2. Consult with Healthcare Professionals: If you have a history of prostate cancer or any concerns about its development, consult with healthcare professionals, such as urologists or registered dietitians, who specialize in prostate health. They can provide personalized recommendations based on your unique circumstances.

3. Individual Variations: It is important to recognize that not all individuals respond to soy in the same way. Genetic factors, gut microbiota, and other individual variations can influence the metabolism and absorption of soy compounds. Listen to your body and make informed choices based on your own experiences.

4. Whole Food Sources: Whenever possible, choose whole food sources of soy, as they provide a more complete nutritional profile compared to isolated soy protein or supplements. Whole foods are also likely to contain other bioactive compounds that work synergistically with soy isoflavones.

It is worth mentioning that nutritional recommendations are continually evolving as new research emerges. Stay abreast of the latest scientific findings and consult with healthcare professionals for the most up-to-date and personalized guidance.

Real-World Example: Unraveling Conflicting Evidence

Prostate cancer research can sometimes yield conflicting findings, making it challenging for individuals to navigate the sea of information. Let's consider a real-world example to illustrate this point:

A recent study suggested that high soy consumption may be associated with an increased risk of aggressive prostate cancer. However, upon closer examination, it became evident that the study had limitations in its design, sample size, and data analysis. Subsequent studies with larger sample sizes and more rigorous methodologies have not found a similar association.

This example highlights the importance of critical evaluation and context when interpreting research findings. It underscores the need to consider the weight of the evidence and the scientific consensus rather than relying on isolated studies.

Further Resources and Caveats

For those interested in delving deeper into the topic of soy and prostate cancer, there are several reputable resources available. Some recommended sources include:

1. Cancer organizations: Organizations such as the American Cancer Society (ACS) and the Prostate Cancer Foundation provide evidence-based information on prostate cancer prevention, treatment, and research updates.
2. Scientific journals: Peer-reviewed journals, including the Journal of the National Cancer Institute, Cancer Epidemiology, and the Annals of Oncology, publish research articles focusing on prostate cancer, soy, and other related topics.
3. Health professionals: Registered dietitians, oncologists, urologists, and nutrition experts specializing in cancer care can provide personalized recommendations and evidence-based guidance.

It is important to note that while soy consumption may have potential benefits for prostate health, it should not replace standard medical care. If you have any concerns about prostate cancer or other health conditions, consult with healthcare professionals to develop a comprehensive and individualized approach to your well-being.

Conclusion

In conclusion, soy consumption has been a topic of interest in relation to prostate cancer prevention. The phytochemicals present in soy, such as isoflavones and lignans, exhibit various anti-cancer properties. While the evidence is not definitive, epidemiological studies suggest a potential protective effect of soy against prostate cancer. It is crucial to approach soy consumption as part of a balanced diet, along with regular prostate health screenings and medical care. Stay informed, consult with healthcare professionals, and make personalized choices based on the current scientific consensus. Remember, promoting a healthy lifestyle involves comprehensive approaches that incorporate diverse dietary sources and support overall well-being.

Soy and Colon Cancer

Colon cancer is a common form of cancer that affects the colon or rectum, collectively known as the colorectal region. It is the third most commonly diagnosed cancer and the second leading cause of cancer-related deaths worldwide. The link between diet and colon cancer risk has been extensively studied, and soy has emerged as a potential protective factor.

Understanding Colon Cancer

To understand the relationship between soy consumption and colon cancer, it is important to have a basic understanding of colon cancer itself.

Colon cancer begins as a growth of abnormal cells in the inner lining of the colon or rectum, known as polyps. Over time, these polyps can become cancerous and spread to other parts of the body if left untreated. Several factors contribute to the development of colon cancer, including age, family history, personal history of certain conditions, certain genetic mutations, and lifestyle factors such as diet.

The Role of Soy in Colon Cancer Prevention

Soy contains various bioactive compounds, such as isoflavones, protease inhibitors, saponins, and phytic acid, which have been shown to have anti-cancer properties. These compounds contribute to the potential benefits of soy in preventing colon cancer.

Isoflavones: Isoflavones are a type of phytoestrogen found in soy that have estrogen-like effects in the body. Studies have suggested that isoflavones may reduce the risk of colon cancer by inhibiting the growth of cancer cells and inducing apoptosis (cell death) in colon cancer cells. Additionally, isoflavones have been shown to exert anti-inflammatory effects and regulate cell signaling pathways involved in colon cancer development.

Protease inhibitors: Soy contains protease inhibitors, which are compounds that inhibit the activity of enzymes called proteases. Proteases play a role in various biological processes, including cancer progression. By inhibiting proteases, soy may help prevent the growth and spread of cancer cells in the colon.

Saponins: Saponins are another group of bioactive compounds found in soy. Research has shown that saponins have anti-cancer properties, including the inhibition of colon cancer cell growth and the induction of cell death. Additionally, saponins have been found to have anti-inflammatory and immune-stimulatory effects, which can further contribute to colon cancer prevention.

Phytic acid: Phytic acid, also known as inositol hexaphosphate or IP6, is a naturally occurring compound found in soy and other plants. Phytic acid has been shown to possess anti-cancer properties by inhibiting the growth of colon cancer cells, promoting cell differentiation, and reducing inflammation.

Evidence from Epidemiological Studies

Numerous epidemiological studies have investigated the association between soy consumption and colon cancer risk. While some studies have shown mixed results, overall, the evidence suggests a potential protective effect of soy against colon cancer.

A meta-analysis of observational studies published in 2019 found that high soy consumption was associated with a 21

However, it is important to note that the protective effect of soy may vary depending on various factors, such as the amount and frequency of soy consumption, the form of soy consumed (e.g., whole soy foods vs. soy supplements), and individual genetic and environmental factors.

Incorporating Soy into a Colon-Healthy Diet

While the evidence suggests that soy consumption may provide protective benefits against colon cancer, it is essential to emphasize the importance of a well-rounded, colon-healthy diet. Soy should be incorporated as part of a balanced approach that includes a variety of other plant-based foods and a focus on overall dietary quality.

Here are some tips for incorporating soy into a colon-healthy diet:

- Choose whole soy foods: Opt for whole soy foods such as tofu, tempeh, edamame, and soy milk made from whole soybeans rather than heavily processed soy products or supplements.

- Include a variety of plant-based foods: Alongside soy, incorporate other plant-based foods rich in fiber, antioxidants, and other nutrients known to support colon health. Examples include fruits, vegetables, whole grains, legumes, nuts, and seeds.

- Balance macronutrients: Aim for a balanced intake of macronutrients, including carbohydrates, proteins, and healthy fats. Avoid excessive consumption of any single macronutrient, including soy protein.

- Consider cultural dietary practices: Explore and embrace different cultural dietary practices that incorporate soy or other plant-based foods known to have health benefits. This can add diversity to your diet and provide a wide range of nutrients.

- Practice moderation: While soy can be a beneficial part of a healthy diet, it is important to consume it in moderation and avoid overreliance on any specific food or ingredient.

Conclusion

The potential health benefits of soy consumption extend beyond its association with colon cancer prevention. By incorporating soy into a balanced diet, individuals can take advantage of its nutritional profile and bioactive compounds to support overall colon health.

While soy alone cannot eliminate the risk of colon cancer or replace other preventive measures such as regular screenings and a healthy lifestyle, it can be a valuable addition to a colon-healthy diet. As research continues to advance, further understanding of the mechanisms behind soy's potential benefits may provide additional insights into its role in colon cancer prevention.

Role of Phytochemicals in Cancer Prevention

Phytochemicals are naturally occurring compounds found in plants that have been found to have beneficial effects on human health. These compounds have gained attention in recent years for their potential role in preventing various diseases, including cancer. In this section, we will explore the specific role of phytochemicals in cancer prevention and discuss some examples of these compounds.

Understanding Cancer Development

Before diving into the role of phytochemicals in cancer prevention, it is important to understand how cancer develops in the body. Cancer is a complex disease characterized by the uncontrolled growth and spread of abnormal cells. This abnormal cell growth can lead to the formation of tumors, which can invade nearby tissues and eventually spread to other parts of the body.

Several factors contribute to the development of cancer, including genetic mutations, environmental exposures (such as tobacco smoke and certain chemicals), and lifestyle choices (such as diet and physical activity levels). Some of these factors are beyond our control, but others, such as diet, can be modified to reduce the risk of cancer.

Phytochemicals and Cancer Prevention

Phytochemicals have been studied extensively for their potential role in cancer prevention. These compounds have been found to possess various bioactive properties that may help prevent or inhibit the development of cancer cells. Some of the key mechanisms through which phytochemicals exert their anticancer effects include:

- Antioxidant activity: Many phytochemicals have strong antioxidant properties, which help protect cells from oxidative damage. Oxidative damage can lead to DNA mutations and other cellular changes that contribute to the development of cancer.

- Anti-inflammatory activity: Chronic inflammation has been linked to an increased risk of cancer. Phytochemicals can help reduce inflammation in the body, thereby lowering the risk of cancer development.

- Anti-proliferative activity: Certain phytochemicals have been found to inhibit the growth and proliferation of cancer cells, preventing them from spreading further in the body.

- Induction of apoptosis: Apoptosis, or programmed cell death, is a natural process that helps eliminate damaged or abnormal cells. Some phytochemicals have been shown to induce apoptosis in cancer cells, promoting their destruction.

- Modulation of hormone metabolism: Some cancers, such as breast and prostate cancer, are hormone-sensitive. Phytochemicals can influence hormone metabolism and help maintain hormonal balance, reducing the risk of hormone-related cancers.

Examples of Phytochemicals with Anticancer Properties

There are numerous phytochemicals that have been identified for their potential anticancer properties. Here are a few examples:

- **Resveratrol:** Found in grapes, berries, and peanuts, resveratrol has been shown to have antioxidant, anti-inflammatory, and anti-proliferative effects. It has been associated with a reduced risk of several types of cancer, including breast, colon, and prostate cancer.

- **Curcumin:** Present in turmeric, curcumin possesses strong anti-inflammatory and antioxidant properties. It has shown promise in inhibiting the growth of cancer cells and preventing the spread of cancer. Research suggests that curcumin may be particularly effective against colorectal, pancreatic, and breast cancers.

- **Green tea catechins:** Green tea catechins, such as epigallocatechin gallate (EGCG), have been extensively studied for their cancer-preventive effects.

These compounds exhibit antioxidant, anti-inflammatory, and anti-proliferative activities. Green tea consumption has been associated with a reduced risk of various cancers, including breast, prostate, and colorectal cancer.

- **Lycopene:** Lycopene is a red pigment found in tomatoes, watermelon, and other red fruits. It has been found to possess potent antioxidant and anti-inflammatory properties. Research suggests that lycopene may help prevent prostate, lung, and stomach cancers.

- **Quercetin:** Widely available in foods such as apples, onions, and berries, quercetin has been shown to have antioxidant, anti-inflammatory, and anticancer effects. It has been studied for its potential in preventing colorectal, lung, and breast cancers.

It is important to note that while phytochemicals show promise in cancer prevention, they should not be considered as a standalone treatment for cancer. These compounds work synergistically with other nutrients and should be consumed as part of a balanced diet.

Incorporating Phytochemicals into the Diet

To reap the benefits of phytochemicals in cancer prevention, it is essential to incorporate a variety of plant-based foods into your diet. Here are some tips for incorporating phytochemical-rich foods into your meals:

- Eat a rainbow of fruits and vegetables: Aim to include a wide range of colorful fruits and vegetables in your diet. Each color represents different types of phytochemicals, so diversifying your choices will ensure you are consuming a variety of these beneficial compounds.

- Include herbs and spices: Many herbs and spices, such as turmeric, garlic, and ginger, contain potent phytochemicals with cancer-preventive properties. Use them generously in your cooking to add flavor and health benefits.

- Opt for whole grains and legumes: Whole grains, such as quinoa and brown rice, and legumes, such as lentils and chickpeas, are excellent sources of phytochemicals. These plant-based foods should be included in your diet regularly.

+ Go for green tea: Replace sugary beverages with green tea, which is rich in catechins. Drinking green tea regularly can provide you with a variety of health benefits, including anticancer effects.

Conclusion

Phytochemicals have emerged as promising compounds in the field of cancer prevention. Their antioxidant, anti-inflammatory, and anticancer properties make them invaluable in reducing the risk of cancer development. By incorporating a variety of phytochemical-rich foods into your diet, you can harness the potential of these compounds and promote your overall health and well-being.

Remember, no single food or compound can guarantee protection against cancer. It is important to adopt a holistic approach to health, which includes maintaining a balanced diet, engaging in regular physical activity, avoiding tobacco and excessive alcohol consumption, and seeking regular medical check-ups. By embracing a healthy and mindful lifestyle, you can take control of your health and reduce the risk of cancer and other chronic diseases.

Hormonal Balance

Impact of Soy on Estrogen Levels

The relationship between soy consumption and estrogen levels has been a topic of much discussion and debate. There have been concerns that consuming soy-based products, such as tofu and soy milk, could lead to hormonal imbalances in both men and women. In this section, we will explore the impact of soy on estrogen levels and examine the scientific evidence surrounding this issue.

Estrogen and Its Functions

Before delving into the effects of soy on estrogen levels, let's first understand what estrogen is and its role in the body. Estrogen is a group of hormones primarily responsible for the female reproductive system's development and regulation. It plays a crucial role in the menstrual cycle, bone health, cardiovascular health, and maintaining healthy skin and hair.

Estrogen is produced primarily in the ovaries in women and in small amounts in the testes in men. Its levels fluctuate throughout the menstrual cycle and decline during menopause. Estrogen exerts its effects by binding to estrogen receptors present in various tissues and organs, influencing gene expression and signaling pathways.

Isoflavones: The Active Compounds in Soy

Soybeans contain phytoestrogens, a group of naturally occurring compounds that can mimic or modulate the effects of estrogen in the body. The main phytoestrogens found in soy are isoflavones, specifically genistein and daidzein. These isoflavones can bind to estrogen receptors and exert estrogen-like effects.

However, it's important to note that the potency of these phytoestrogens is much weaker compared to the body's natural estrogen hormone. They have a lower binding affinity to estrogen receptors, resulting in a milder estrogenic effect.

Contradictory Findings: Soy and Estrogen Levels

Studies examining the impact of soy consumption on estrogen levels have generated inconsistent findings. Some studies suggest that soy intake can increase estrogen levels, while others indicate no significant effect. The conflicting results may be attributed to variations in study design, population characteristics, and the specific soy products and amounts consumed.

One study conducted on postmenopausal women found that soy protein supplementation for six months led to a slight increase in estradiol, a form of estrogen, compared to a control group. Similarly, another study showed that women consuming soy isoflavone supplements had higher urinary levels of estrogen metabolites.

On the other hand, several studies have found no significant changes in estrogen levels following soy consumption. For example, a study conducted with premenopausal women reported no alterations in estradiol levels after consuming soy protein for 12 weeks.

Interactions with Gut Microbiota

The role of gut microbiota in soy metabolism and its impact on estrogen levels is an emerging area of research. Gut bacteria can metabolize soy isoflavones into various biologically active compounds, which can affect estrogen metabolism and subsequently influence estrogen levels.

It has been observed that individuals with certain gut microbial compositions may exhibit differences in the metabolism of soy isoflavones and subsequent estrogen levels. This suggests that interindividual variations in gut microbiota could potentially influence the estrogenic effects of soy consumption.

Clinical and Health Outcomes

Despite the variations in estrogen levels observed in studies, it's essential to consider the clinical and health outcomes associated with soy consumption. Numerous studies have investigated the effects of soy and isoflavones on various health parameters, including breast cancer, menopausal symptoms, bone health, and cardiovascular health.

Overall, the current body of evidence suggests that moderate soy consumption, as part of a balanced diet, is not associated with adverse effects on estrogen levels or increased risk of hormonal imbalances. In fact, some studies have even linked soy consumption to potential health benefits, such as a reduced risk of certain cancers and improved cardiovascular health.

Key Takeaways

In conclusion, the impact of soy on estrogen levels is a complex and controversial topic. While some studies have shown slight alterations in estrogen levels with soy consumption, the clinical significance of these changes remains unclear. The weak estrogenic properties of soy isoflavones, coupled with interindividual variations in gut microbiota, contribute to the inconsistent findings.

Importantly, numerous studies have demonstrated no adverse effects of soy consumption on estrogen levels or hormonal balance. In fact, moderate soy consumption, as part of a well-rounded diet, may confer several health benefits.

As with any aspect of nutrition, it is crucial to adopt a balanced approach. Incorporating a variety of plant-based proteins, including soy, can help diversify your diet and provide a range of essential nutrients. If you have specific concerns about soy and its effects on estrogen levels, it is best to consult with a healthcare professional who can provide personalized guidance based on your individual health needs.

As the scientific understanding of soy and its impact on estrogen levels continues to evolve, ongoing research will shed further light on this topic, allowing for more comprehensive and evidence-based recommendations.

Soy and Menopause Symptoms

Menopause is a natural biological process that occurs in women as they age, typically between the ages of 45 and 55. During this phase, the ovaries stop producing eggs, and the levels of certain hormones, such as estrogen and progesterone, decline. These hormonal changes often lead to a variety of symptoms, including hot flashes, night sweats, mood swings, sleep disturbances, and vaginal dryness.

In recent years, there has been an increasing interest in the use of soy-based products as a potential remedy for menopause symptoms. Soy contains naturally occurring compounds called isoflavones, which are similar in structure to estrogen and are known to have estrogenic effects on the body. This has led to speculation that consuming soy products may help alleviate menopause symptoms by interacting with estrogen receptors in the body.

Understanding the Link between Soy and Menopause Symptoms

The potential connection between soy consumption and menopause symptoms stems from observations of lower rates of hot flashes and other symptoms among women in Asian countries, where soy is a dietary staple. Some studies have suggested that the high intake of soy in these populations may contribute to these lower rates. However, it is important to note that the evidence supporting the benefits of soy for menopause symptoms is still mixed.

Research on Soy and Menopause Symptoms

Several studies have investigated the effects of soy on menopause symptoms, with varying results. Some studies have shown a positive association between soy consumption and a reduction in hot flashes and other symptoms. For example, a study published in the journal Menopause found that women who consumed soy isoflavones experienced a significant decrease in the frequency and severity of hot flashes compared to those who did not.

On the other hand, other studies have failed to find a significant benefit of soy consumption on menopause symptoms. For instance, a review published in the journal Menopause Review analyzed multiple studies and concluded that there is limited evidence supporting the effectiveness of soy for alleviating menopause symptoms.

Factors Influencing the Effectiveness of Soy for Menopause Symptoms

The mixed findings regarding soy's effectiveness for menopause symptoms can be attributed to several factors:

1. **Individual Variations:** Women may respond differently to soy consumption due to their unique physiology and genetic makeup. Some women may be more sensitive to the estrogenic effects of soy, while others may not experience any noticeable changes.

2. **Dose and Duration:** The amount of soy consumed and the duration of consumption may play a role in determining its effectiveness. Some studies have suggested that higher doses of soy isoflavones may be more effective in reducing menopause symptoms.

3. **Timing:** The timing of soy consumption in relation to the onset of menopause may also influence its effectiveness. Some evidence suggests that soy may be more effective in relieving menopause symptoms when taken during the early stages of menopause.

4. **Dietary Patterns:** The overall dietary pattern, including other components of the diet, may also influence the effectiveness of soy for menopause symptoms. A balanced and varied diet, rich in other plant-based foods, may enhance the potential benefits of soy.

5. **Other Menopause Treatments:** Many women use other treatments, such as hormone replacement therapy (HRT), to manage menopause symptoms. These treatments may interact with soy consumption, making it challenging to isolate the effects of soy alone.

Guidelines for Incorporating Soy into the Diet for Menopause Symptoms

If you are considering incorporating soy into your diet to help manage menopause symptoms, here are some guidelines to keep in mind:

1. **Consult with a Healthcare Professional:** Before making any significant dietary changes or starting any new treatments, it is important to consult with a healthcare professional who can provide personalized advice based on your specific health needs.

2. **Choose Whole and Minimally Processed Soy Foods:** Opt for whole and minimally processed soy foods, such as tofu, tempeh, edamame, and soy milk. These foods are a more natural source of soy and contain a wide range of nutrients.

3. **Include Soy as Part of a Balanced Diet:** Incorporate soy into a balanced diet that includes a variety of fruits, vegetables, whole grains, and other plant-based proteins. This will ensure that you are getting a diverse range of nutrients to support overall health and well-being.

4. **Monitor Your Individual Response:** Pay attention to how your body responds to soy consumption. Keep track of any changes in menopause symptoms and discuss them with your healthcare professional.

5. **Consider Other Approaches:** Remember that soy is not the only option for managing menopause symptoms. There are other lifestyle changes, natural remedies, and medical interventions that may also be beneficial. It is essential to explore a comprehensive approach to optimize symptom relief.

Summary

While soy consumption has been hypothesized to alleviate menopause symptoms, the evidence regarding its effectiveness is still inconclusive. Some studies suggest a potential benefit, while others do not find a significant impact. Factors such as individual variations, dose and duration, timing, dietary patterns, and concomitant treatments may influence the effect of soy on menopause symptoms. It is crucial to consult with a healthcare professional and consider a holistic approach that includes a balanced diet and other menopause management strategies. By adopting a comprehensive approach, individuals can take control of their well-being and make informed decisions to support their menopause journey.

Soy and Hormones in Men

Soy consumption has been a topic of concern for many men due to its potential effect on hormonal balance. Some individuals believe that consuming soy-based products can lead to feminization or decreases in testosterone levels. In this section, we will explore the relationship between soy and hormones in men, debunking any myths and providing evidence-based information.

Understanding Hormonal Balance

Hormonal balance is crucial for overall health and well-being in both men and women. Testosterone, the primary male sex hormone, plays a vital role in various physiological processes such as muscle growth, bone health, and reproductive function. Keeping testosterone levels within the normal range is important for optimal health.

Phytoestrogens in Soy

One concern associated with soy consumption is the presence of phytoestrogens, which are plant compounds that can mimic the effects of estrogen in the body.

Some individuals worry that the phytoestrogens found in soy could disrupt hormonal balance, leading to unfavorable effects in men.

However, it's important to note that phytoestrogens are weaker in potency compared to the estrogen produced by the human body. The human body also metabolizes phytoestrogens differently compared to endogenous estrogen, further reducing the potential for negative impacts on hormonal balance.

Research has shown that moderate soy consumption does not have a significant impact on testosterone levels in men. A systematic review and meta-analysis of 15 randomized controlled trials found no evidence of soy protein or isoflavone intake affecting testosterone levels in men.

Soy and Male Reproductive Function

Another concern raised is the potential impact of soy on male reproductive function. Some worry that soy intake may decrease sperm count or sperm quality, leading to fertility issues.

However, the existing evidence does not support these claims. A study published in Fertility and Sterility found no association between soy food consumption and sperm concentration, motility, or morphology in healthy men. Additionally, a systematic review of 32 studies found no consistent evidence linking soy intake with changes in male reproductive hormones or semen parameters.

Potential Health Benefits of Soy for Men

In fact, soy consumption may actually have some potential health benefits for men. Soy-based foods are excellent sources of high-quality protein and contain essential amino acids necessary for muscle growth and maintenance. Additionally, research suggests that soy protein may have a positive effect on reducing the risk of certain diseases, including prostate cancer.

A study published in the American Journal of Clinical Nutrition found that soy intake was associated with a reduced risk of prostate cancer. The researchers discovered that men who consumed higher amounts of soy foods had a lower risk of developing prostate cancer compared to those who consumed smaller amounts.

Conclusion

In summary, concerns about soy and its potential impact on hormones in men are largely unfounded. The phytoestrogens found in soy are not likely to disrupt hormonal balance or lead to feminization. Soy consumption does not have a significant effect on testosterone levels, male reproductive function, or fertility.

In fact, incorporating moderate amounts of soy-based foods into a balanced diet can provide numerous health benefits for men. These include high-quality protein for muscle health and potential protection against certain diseases, such as prostate cancer.

It is important to approach nutrition and health with an evidence-based perspective, dispelling myths and misconceptions along the way. By understanding the science behind soy consumption and its effects on male hormones, men can confidently include soy-based products in their diet without worrying about negative consequences on their health or masculinity.

Remember, a well-rounded and diverse diet that includes a variety of plant-based proteins, such as soy, along with other nutrient-dense foods, is key to promoting optimal health for men.

Promoting a Balanced Approach

The Importance of Diversity in Diet

Avoiding Overreliance on Soy

When it comes to incorporating soy into our diet, it is important to maintain a balanced and diverse approach. While soy offers numerous health benefits, overreliance on this single food source can lead to an unbalanced nutrient intake. In this section, we will explore strategies for avoiding overreliance on soy and incorporating other plant-based proteins into our diet.

The Pitfalls of Overreliance

Overreliance on any single food can result in inadequate nutrient intake and possibly lead to deficiencies. While soy is a rich source of protein and other essential nutrients, it does not provide the full range of nutrients needed for optimal health. Relying solely on soy for protein may neglect other essential amino acids that are found in different protein sources. In addition, excessive consumption of soy products can potentially lead to digestive issues or allergic reactions in some individuals.

Exploring Other Plant-based Proteins

To avoid overreliance on soy, it is important to diversify our sources of plant-based proteins. Luckily, there are plenty of other nutritious and flavorful options available. Some alternative sources of plant-based proteins include:

- Legumes: Beans, lentils, and chickpeas are excellent sources of protein. They are versatile and can be used in a variety of dishes such as soups, stews, and salads.

- Nuts and seeds: Almonds, walnuts, chia seeds, and hemp seeds are all rich in protein and healthy fats. They can be enjoyed as snacks or added to smoothies, yogurt, or baked goods.

- Quinoa: This pseudo-grain is a complete protein, meaning it contains all nine essential amino acids. It can be used as a base for salads, stir-fries, or as a side dish.

- Tempeh: Made from fermented soybeans, tempeh is a good alternative to soy products. It has a nutty flavor and can be grilled, sautéed, or used in stir-fries.

- Seitan: Also known as wheat meat, seitan is made from gluten and has a meat-like texture. It can be used as a meat substitute in various recipes.

By incorporating these diverse plant-based protein sources into our diet, we can ensure a well-rounded nutrient intake and avoid overreliance on soy.

Achieving a Balanced Macronutrient Intake

In addition to diversifying our protein sources, it is important to balance our macronutrient intake. While soy is a good source of protein, it is also high in carbohydrates. Depending solely on high-carbohydrate soy products for energy can lead to an imbalance in our macronutrient ratios.

To achieve a balanced macronutrient intake, we should combine soy or other plant-based proteins with other nutrient-dense foods. For example, pairing soy with whole grains like brown rice or quinoa can provide a complete protein profile along with a good balance of carbohydrates. Additionally, incorporating a variety of fruits, vegetables, and healthy fats into our meals will ensure a well-rounded nutrient intake and support overall health.

Cultural Diets and Sustainability Considerations

Another way to avoid overreliance on soy is to explore different cultural diets and their use of plant-based proteins. Traditional diets from various cultures often incorporate a wide range of plant-based protein sources, offering inspiration for diverse and balanced meals.

Considering sustainability is also crucial when choosing protein sources. While soy can be a sustainable option, it is important to source it from environmentally responsible and ethical sources. Exploring other plant-based protein options allows us to support sustainable agriculture and reduce our environmental impact.

Incorporating Soy as Part of a Whole

While we should avoid overreliance on soy, it is important to recognize the health benefits it provides when consumed as part of a balanced diet. Soy offers a unique combination of nutrients that contribute to cardiovascular health, bone health, hormonal balance, and cancer prevention.

In conclusion, to avoid overreliance on soy, it is essential to diversify our plant-based protein sources and maintain a balanced macronutrient intake. By exploring other nutritious options, incorporating different cultural diets, and being mindful of sustainability, we can ensure a well-rounded and nourishing diet while enjoying the health benefits of soy.

Incorporating Other Plant-based Proteins

When it comes to maintaining a balanced diet, incorporating a variety of plant-based proteins is essential. While soy is a great source of protein, it is important not to rely solely on soy and explore other options to ensure your nutritional needs are met. In this section, we will discuss the importance of incorporating other plant-based proteins into your diet and explore some excellent alternatives to soy.

The Importance of Diversity in Diet

A diverse diet is key to obtaining all the necessary nutrients for optimal health. By incorporating a variety of plant-based proteins, you are not only diversifying your nutrient intake but also expanding your culinary horizons. Different plant-based proteins offer unique profiles of essential amino acids, vitamins, minerals, and phytochemicals, all of which contribute to overall health and well-being.

Avoiding Overreliance on Soy

While soy is a valuable source of protein, overreliance on this single plant-based protein may limit the nutrient variety in your diet. It is important to remember that other plant-based proteins can offer different nutritional benefits. By incorporating a range of protein sources, you can ensure that you are obtaining a wide array of essential nutrients.

Incorporating Other Plant-based Proteins

1. **Legumes:** Legumes are a versatile and nutrient-dense group of plant-based proteins. They include beans, lentils, chickpeas, and peas. Legumes provide not only protein but also fiber, complex carbohydrates, iron, zinc, folate, and potassium. They are excellent substitutes for meat and can be used in a variety of dishes such as soups, stews, salads, and even burgers.

2. **Quinoa:** Quinoa is a unique plant-based protein source that contains all nine essential amino acids, making it a complete protein. Additionally, quinoa is rich in fiber, iron, magnesium, and phosphorus. It can be used as a base for salads, served as a side dish, or incorporated into baked goods.

3. **Nuts and Seeds:** Nuts and seeds are not only packed with protein but also provide healthy fats, vitamins, minerals, and antioxidants. Almonds, walnuts, chia seeds, flaxseeds, and hemp seeds are all excellent sources of plant-based protein. Sprinkle them on salads, add them to your morning smoothie, or enjoy them as a snack.

4. **Tempeh:** Tempeh is a fermented soy product that offers a different nutritional profile compared to regular soy. It is high in protein, fiber, iron, and calcium. Tempeh has a nutty flavor and a firm texture, making it a great addition to stir-fries, sandwiches, and salads.

5. **Seitan:** Seitan, also known as wheat meat or wheat gluten, is made from gluten protein found in wheat. It is a concentrated protein source that can be shaped and flavored to resemble meat. Seitan is low in fat and a good source of iron and calcium. It can be used in stir-fries, sandwiches, and stews.

Balancing Macronutrients in the Diet

When incorporating a variety of plant-based proteins, it is important to consider the balance of macronutrients in your diet. While protein is essential, it is also important to include carbohydrates and fats. Carbohydrates provide energy, and healthy fats are necessary for brain function and the absorption of fat-soluble vitamins.

Ensure that your meals include a mix of plant-based proteins, whole grains, fruits, vegetables, and healthy fats. This will not only provide a balance of macronutrients but also a wide range of micronutrients, vitamins, and minerals.

Exploring Different Cultural Diets

Cultural diets around the world offer a wealth of plant-based protein options. Exploring different cuisines can inspire new recipes and broaden your palate. For example, Mediterranean cuisine incorporates legumes, whole grains, and olive oil, while Asian cuisine often features tofu, tempeh, and various types of mushrooms.

By embracing the plant-based protein options within different cultural diets, you can enjoy a diverse and delicious range of meals while meeting your nutritional needs.

Sustainability and Ethical Considerations

Incorporating other plant-based proteins into your diet not only benefits your health but also the environment. The production of plant-based proteins has a lower environmental impact compared to animal-based proteins. Additionally, by reducing your consumption of animal products and supporting plant-based proteins, you contribute to animal welfare and sustainability efforts.

Choosing locally sourced and organic plant-based proteins can further enhance these ethical considerations. By supporting sustainable food systems, you make a positive impact on both your health and the planet.

Conclusion

Incorporating other plant-based proteins into your diet is crucial for obtaining a diverse range of nutrients and maintaining overall health. By exploring options beyond soy, such as legumes, quinoa, nuts and seeds, tempeh, and seitan, you can enjoy a variety of flavors and nutritional benefits.

Remember to balance your macronutrients, explore different cultural diets, and consider the sustainability and ethical aspects of your food choices. By embracing a diverse and inclusive approach to plant-based proteins, you not only improve your own well-being but also contribute to a healthier planet for future generations.

Balancing Macronutrients in the Diet

Achieving a balanced macronutrient intake is an essential part of maintaining a healthy diet. Macronutrients refer to the three main nutrients that our bodies need in large amounts: carbohydrates, proteins, and fats. Each macronutrient plays a unique role in our body, and finding the right balance is key to optimizing health and wellness.

Understanding Macronutrients

Before diving into the specifics of balancing macronutrients, let's take a closer look at each of them and their functions.

Carbohydrates: Carbohydrates are our body's primary source of energy. They are broken down into glucose, which fuels our brain, muscles, and organs. Carbohydrates can be found in various forms such as fruits, vegetables, grains, and legumes.

Proteins: Proteins are the building blocks of our body. They are crucial for growth, repair, and maintenance of tissues, enzymes, hormones, and immune cells. Good sources of protein include meat, fish, poultry, dairy products, legumes, and nuts.

Fats: Despite their bad reputation, fats are essential for various bodily functions. They provide energy, help absorb fat-soluble vitamins, protect organs, and contribute to hormone production. Sources of healthy fats include avocados, nuts, seeds, olive oil, and fatty fish.

The Importance of Balancing Macronutrients

Balancing macronutrients is about finding the right ratios of carbohydrates, proteins, and fats to support your body's needs. This balance is vital for several reasons:

Optimal Energy Levels: Each macronutrient provides a different amount of energy. Carbohydrates and proteins contain 4 calories per gram, while fats provide 9 calories per gram. By striking the right balance, you can ensure a steady supply of energy throughout the day.

Muscle Development and Repair: Protein is crucial for building and repairing muscles. It also supports the development of enzymes and hormones. Consuming adequate protein helps maintain lean body mass and promotes healthy muscle function.

Stable Blood Sugar Levels: Balancing carbohydrates, especially the type and amount of carbohydrates, is essential in controlling blood sugar. Consuming excessive amounts of refined carbohydrates can cause blood sugar spikes, while consuming too little can lead to low energy levels.

Heart Health: A balanced intake of macronutrients can positively impact heart health. By including healthy fats and reducing saturated and trans fats, you can mitigate the risk of heart disease and promote cardiovascular well-being.

Determining Macronutrient Ratios

There is no one-size-fits-all approach to macronutrient ratios, as individual needs can vary based on factors such as age, sex, weight, activity level, and overall health. However, several general guidelines can help you establish a balanced macronutrient intake:

Carbohydrates: Carbohydrates should make up approximately 45-65

Proteins: Protein intake should make up around 10-35

Fats: Fats should contribute around 20-35

Balancing Macronutrients in Practice

Achieving a balanced macronutrient intake requires thoughtful meal planning and conscious food choices. Here are some tips to help you balance your macronutrients effectively:

Plan Meals in Advance: Taking the time to plan your meals can help ensure a well-balanced macronutrient profile. Include a mix of carbohydrates, proteins, and fats in each meal and snack.

Embrace Whole Foods: Whole foods, such as fruits, vegetables, whole grains, lean meats, and legumes, offer a diverse range of macronutrients and provide essential vitamins, minerals, and fiber.

Monitor Portion Sizes: While balancing macronutrients is crucial, portion control is equally important. Be mindful of serving sizes to avoid overeating and maintain a calorie balance that aligns with your goals.

Listen to Your Body: Everyone's nutritional needs are unique. Pay attention to how different macronutrient ratios make you feel, both physically and mentally. Adjust your intake based on your body's feedback.

Unconventional Yet Relevant Trick

An unconventional yet effective trick to balancing macronutrients is to practice mindful eating. Mindful eating involves being fully present and aware during meals, paying attention to hunger and fullness cues, and savoring each bite. By practicing mindfulness, you can develop a deeper understanding of your body's needs and make conscious choices that promote a balanced macronutrient intake.

Summary

Achieving a balanced macronutrient intake is vital for optimal health and wellness. By finding the right ratios of carbohydrates, proteins, and fats, you can support energy levels, muscle development, stable blood sugar, and heart health. Remember to focus on whole foods, monitor portion sizes, and listen to your body's feedback. With mindful eating and conscious food choices, you can achieve a balanced macronutrient intake and nurture your body towards overall well-being.

Exploring Different Cultural Diets

In today's globalized world, it has become increasingly important to appreciate and understand different cultural practices, including dietary habits. Food is not only a source of sustenance but also a reflection of a community's values, traditions, and identity. Exploring different cultural diets allows us to broaden our perspective on nutrition and appreciate the rich diversity of culinary traditions around the world. This section aims to highlight the significance of cultural diets and the benefits they can bring to our overall health and well-being.

Cultural Influences on Diet

What we eat is deeply influenced by the culture we belong to. Traditional food practices are often passed down through generations and shaped by historical, geographical, and social factors. These cultural diets provide a unique window into the beliefs, values, and lifestyle of a community. By exploring different cultural diets, we can gain insight into alternative ways of nourishing our bodies and embracing a more inclusive approach to nutrition.

Cultural diets vary greatly across the globe, offering a diverse array of flavors, ingredients, and cooking techniques. For example, the Mediterranean diet, a traditional eating pattern in countries bordering the Mediterranean Sea, emphasizes plant-based foods like fruits, vegetables, whole grains, legumes, and olive oil. It is renowned for its numerous health benefits, including reduced risk of cardiovascular disease and improved longevity. Similarly, the traditional Japanese diet, rich in fish, rice, vegetables, and fermented foods like miso and soy sauce, is associated with lower rates of chronic diseases such as obesity, diabetes, and certain types of cancer.

Key Features of Cultural Diets

When exploring different cultural diets, it is important to understand their key features and the principles they are based on. Here are some common characteristics often found in cultural diets:

- **Whole Foods**: Cultural diets often prioritize minimally processed whole foods over highly refined products. This means that fruits, vegetables, whole grains, legumes, nuts, and seeds are often key components of these diets.

- **Seasonal and Local Foods**: Many cultural diets promote the consumption of seasonal and locally sourced foods. This not only supports local agriculture but also ensures fresher and more nutritious ingredients in the diet.

- **Herbs and Spices**: Herbs and spices are commonly used in cultural diets, not only to enhance flavors but also for their potential health benefits. For example, turmeric, a common spice in Indian cuisine, contains curcumin, a compound with anti-inflammatory properties.

- **Food Rituals**: Cultural diets often involve specific food rituals and traditions that go beyond mere nourishment. These rituals may include communal meals, religious practices, or celebrations, all of which contribute to a sense of belonging and cultural identity.

- **Balanced Approach**: Many cultural diets emphasize a balanced approach to nutrition, incorporating a variety of food groups and macronutrients to ensure a well-rounded diet. This can help prevent nutrient deficiencies and promote better overall health.

Benefits of Exploring Cultural Diets

There are several benefits to exploring different cultural diets:

- **Nutritional Diversity**: Each cultural diet offers a unique combination of foods, flavors, and nutrients. By incorporating elements from different cultural diets, we can increase the variety of nutrients in our own diets, which may contribute to better overall health and reduced risk of chronic diseases.

- **Expanded Culinary Skills:** Exploring different cultural diets exposes us to new ingredients and cooking techniques. This can help expand our culinary skills and repertoire, making healthy eating more enjoyable and sustainable in the long term.

- **Cultural Understanding:** Understanding and appreciating different cultural diets fosters cultural sensitivity and promotes social inclusion. It allows us to connect with diverse communities, respect their customs, and celebrate the cultural heritage associated with their food practices.

- **Sustainable Food Choices:** Many cultural diets have inherently sustainable practices, such as using local and seasonal ingredients or emphasizing plant-based foods. By adopting these practices, we can contribute to a more environmentally friendly food system.

- **Discovery of Hidden Superfoods:** Exploring cultural diets may introduce us to lesser-known ingredients that are nutritionally dense and offer unique health benefits. For example, the West African diet often incorporates nutrient-rich foods like moringa leaves, baobab fruit, and fonio grain.

Challenges and Considerations

While exploring different cultural diets can be a rewarding experience, there are certain challenges and considerations to keep in mind:

- **Individual Needs and Preferences:** Cultural diets may not align with individual dietary restrictions, allergies, or personal preferences. It is important to adapt cultural practices to suit individual needs while still respecting the essence of the diet.

- **Cultural Appropriation:** When exploring cultural diets, it is critical to avoid cultural appropriation and instead focus on cultural appreciation. This means acknowledging and respecting the origins, traditions, and values associated with the diet.

- **Accessibility of Ingredients:** Some ingredients used in cultural diets may be challenging to find or expensive in certain regions. It is important to focus on locally available alternatives that respect the principles of the diet while still maintaining its essence.

- **Adapting Recipes:** Traditional recipes from different cultural diets may need to be adapted to suit different tastes and dietary needs. It is possible to modify recipes while still retaining their cultural authenticity and nutritional benefits.

By exploring different cultural diets, we can expand our understanding of nutrition and embrace the wealth of culinary traditions around the world. This not only enriches our own diets but also fosters a greater appreciation for cultural diversity and promotes a more inclusive and sustainable food culture.

Exercise: Take a moment to reflect on your own cultural background and the traditional foods associated with it. Consider how you can incorporate elements from your own cultural diet into your daily meals, and explore ways to celebrate and share your cultural culinary heritage with others.

Resources:

- Bittman, M. (2015). *How to Cook Everything: Completely Revised Twentieth Anniversary Edition.* Houghton Mifflin Harcourt.
- National Geographic. (2021). *Food: The Science of Flavor.* Retrieved from `https://www.nationalgeographic.org/interactive/food-science`
- The Recipes Project. (2021). *Exploring the world of recipes through scholarly investigations and modern cooking.* Retrieved from `https://recipes.hypotheses.org/`

Remember to embrace the diversity of cultural diets and approach them with curiosity, respect, and an open mind. Enjoy the journey of exploring new flavors, traditions, and the rich tapestry of global culinary heritage.

Sustainability and Ethical Considerations

In today's world, it is not enough to consider just the health benefits of our dietary choices. We must also take into account the broader impact of our food choices on the environment and society. This section delves into the sustainability and ethical considerations associated with soy consumption, providing a comprehensive understanding of the topic.

Environmental Sustainability

Soybean production plays a significant role in global agriculture, making it crucial to assess its environmental impact. Here, we will explore key aspects of sustainability, including land use, carbon footprint, and water usage.

Land Use Soybeans require land for cultivation, raising concerns about deforestation and habitat destruction. It is essential to adopt sustainable farming practices to minimize the negative impact on ecosystems. One strategy is agroforestry, which involves integrating soybean crops with tree cover to reduce soil erosion and provide a favorable habitat for wildlife. Additionally, promoting the use of marginal lands for soy production can minimize the conversion of natural habitats.

Carbon Footprint The carbon footprint of soy production includes emissions from land use change, cultivation, transportation, and processing. To reduce greenhouse gas emissions, adopting sustainable farming methods such as conservation tillage and precision agriculture is crucial. These practices minimize soil disturbance and optimize resource use, leading to lower emissions. Moreover, encouraging local sourcing and shortening the supply chain can help reduce transportation-related emissions.

Water Usage Soybean cultivation requires substantial amounts of water, primarily for irrigation purposes. Water scarcity is a growing concern globally, making it essential to assess and manage water usage in soy production. Implementing efficient irrigation techniques, such as drip irrigation and precision watering, can significantly reduce water consumption. Additionally, capturing and utilizing rainwater can mitigate the strain on freshwater resources.

Social and Ethical Considerations

Beyond environmental sustainability, ethical factors associated with soy consumption encompass labor conditions, fair trade practices, and social implications. Examining these considerations allows us to make informed choices aligned with our values and ethics.

Labor Conditions It is crucial to ensure that the production of soy occurs under fair and just labor conditions. This includes providing workers with fair wages, safe working environments, and ensuring that no forced or child labor is involved. Supporting certified organic and fair trade soybean products can help promote better labor practices within the industry.

Fair Trade Practices In an interconnected global economy, supporting fair trade practices is essential for the well-being of farmers and communities. Fair trade initiatives aim to eliminate exploitative practices and provide fair compensation to farmers. By supporting fair trade soy products, consumers contribute to a more equitable and sustainable supply chain.

Social Implications The cultivation of soy can have social implications for local communities, especially in regions heavily dependent on soy production. Large-scale soy cultivation can lead to the displacement of smallholder farmers, loss of traditional crops, and land concentration. It is important to understand and mitigate these social impacts by supporting sustainable agricultural models that prioritize the well-being of local communities and protect their rights.

Overall, sustainability and ethical considerations should guide our dietary choices, including soy consumption. By considering the environmental impact, labor conditions, fair trade practices, and social implications, we can foster a more sustainable and equitable food system.

Challenges and Solutions

Sustainable soy production faces several challenges, but innovative solutions exist to address these issues and promote responsible consumption.

Sustainable Farming Practices Adopting sustainable farming practices such as organic farming, agroforestry, and precision agriculture can minimize the environmental impact of soy production. These methods reduce the use of synthetic inputs, enhance soil health, conserve biodiversity, and mitigate climate change. Supporting and incentivizing farmers to transition to sustainable practices is critical for long-term environmental sustainability.

Certifications and Standards Certifications and standards play a vital role in ensuring the sustainability and ethical production of soy. Labels such as organic, fair trade, and Rainforest Alliance provide consumers with assurance regarding the social and environmental criteria met by the products. By choosing certified soy products, individuals can support responsible production practices.

Consumer Awareness and Education Raising awareness among consumers about the importance of sustainability and ethical considerations is essential. Education about the impact of dietary choices on the environment and society empowers individuals to make informed decisions. Engaging in dialogue, promoting educational campaigns, and providing accessible information are key strategies to enhance consumer knowledge and catalyze positive change.

Conclusion

Sustainability and ethical considerations are integral to making responsible dietary choices, including soy consumption. By understanding and addressing the environmental impact, labor conditions, fair trade practices, and social implications, we contribute to a more sustainable and equitable food system. Embracing sustainability and ethical values can guide us towards a future that values the health of both individuals and the planet. Together, we can foster change and create a world that nourishes both our bodies and our conscience.

Educating About Nutrition

Teaching Critical Thinking Skills

Critical thinking is a fundamental skill that enables individuals to analyze, evaluate, and interpret information in a rational and logical manner. It involves the ability to question assumptions, consider multiple perspectives, and make informed decisions based on evidence and reasoning. In the context of nutrition and health, teaching critical thinking skills is essential for individuals to navigate through the vast amount of information available and make informed choices about what they consume. This section will discuss the importance of teaching critical thinking skills in relation to nutrition education and provide strategies and examples for incorporating these skills into the learning process.

Importance of Critical Thinking in Nutrition Education

In an age where misinformation and pseudoscience abound, teaching critical thinking skills is crucial for individuals to distinguish reliable and evidence-based information from unsubstantiated claims. Nutrition is a subject that is particularly vulnerable to misinformation, as various fad diets and exaggerated health claims circulate in popular media and online platforms. By developing critical thinking skills, individuals can evaluate the validity and credibility of such claims, empowering them to make informed and rational decisions about their dietary choices.

Additionally, critical thinking skills enable individuals to develop a deeper understanding of complex concepts related to nutrition and health. By questioning assumptions and considering different perspectives, learners can gain a more comprehensive view of the subject matter. This not only enhances their knowledge but also encourages them to become active participants in their own learning, leading to improved retention and application of information.

Strategies for Teaching Critical Thinking Skills

1. Encourage Questioning: Foster an environment that values curiosity and encourages students to ask questions. Encourage them to ask "why" and "how" questions to delve deeper into the subject matter. Provide opportunities for discussion and debate, allowing students to critically analyze different viewpoints.

2. Teach Information Evaluation: Teach students how to evaluate the credibility and reliability of information sources. Introduce them to criteria such as author expertise, peer-reviewed research, and source bias. Engage students in

activities where they evaluate different sources of nutrition information, comparing and contrasting the validity and accuracy of each.

3. Use Real-World Examples: Incorporate real-world examples into lessons to demonstrate the application of critical thinking skills. For example, present conflicting nutritional claims from popular media and ask students to critically evaluate the evidence supporting each claim. This helps students understand the importance of critically analyzing information before making judgments.

4. Problem-Based Learning: Use problem-based learning approaches where students are presented with real-world scenarios and asked to solve problems using critical thinking skills. For example, present a case study of an individual with specific dietary requirements and ask students to critically evaluate and design a suitable dietary plan based on evidence and sound reasoning.

5. Encourage Reflection: Incorporate reflection activities into lessons, where students can critically analyze their own beliefs, biases, and assumptions. This helps them become aware of their own thinking patterns and biases, allowing for more open-minded and objective analysis of information.

6. Teach Logical Reasoning: Introduce students to logical reasoning and argumentation principles. Teach them how to construct and analyze arguments using deductive and inductive reasoning. Provide examples and practice exercises where students can apply these logical reasoning skills to nutrition-related topics.

Example Exercise: Evaluating Nutrition Claims

Here is an example exercise to help students practice critical thinking skills in evaluating nutrition claims:

Scenario: A popular weight loss supplement claims to help individuals lose 10 pounds in one week without any changes to their diet or exercise routine.

1. Ask students to critically evaluate the credibility of this claim by considering the following factors: - What evidence supports this claim? - Are there any scientific studies or research to back up the claim? - Is there a conflict of interest? (e.g., Is the claim made by the same company selling the supplement?) - Are there any red flags that indicate pseudoscience or exaggeration?

2. Encourage students to research and find reliable sources of information that either support or refute the claim. Ask them to critically analyze the evidence and arguments presented in these sources.

3. Facilitate a class discussion where students present their findings and engage in critical analysis and debate. Encourage students to question and challenge each other's arguments, focusing on evidence-based reasoning.

By engaging in exercises like this, students develop the skills to critically evaluate nutrition claims, empowering them to make informed decisions about their dietary choices based on reliable evidence.

Resources for Teaching Critical Thinking Skills

There are numerous resources available to educators for teaching critical thinking skills. Some recommended resources include:

1. "The Miniature Guide to Critical Thinking: Concepts and Tools" by Richard Paul and Linda Elder: This guide provides a comprehensive introduction to critical thinking skills and strategies, along with practical exercises and examples.

2. Online Courses: Platforms like Coursera and edX offer online courses specifically focused on critical thinking. These courses provide structured learning modules and interactive exercises to develop critical thinking skills.

3. Case Studies and Research Papers: Incorporate case studies and research papers into lessons to engage students in critical analysis and evaluation of scientific evidence. Encourage students to present their findings and discuss their interpretations of the evidence.

4. Online Databases and Journals: Direct students towards reliable online databases and journals that publish peer-reviewed research articles related to nutrition. Encourage students to explore these resources to develop critical evaluation skills.

5. Debunking Websites: Introduce students to debunking websites that critically analyze popular claims related to nutrition. These websites often provide evidence-based rebuttals to pseudoscientific claims, helping students develop their own critical thinking skills.

Remember, teaching critical thinking skills is an ongoing process that requires continuous reinforcement and practice. By incorporating these strategies and resources, educators can help students develop the necessary skills to evaluate information critically and make informed and rational decisions about their dietary choices.

End of Section 6.2.1

Overcoming Food Myths and Fads

In today's society, there are countless myths and fads surrounding food and nutrition. It can be challenging to navigate through the sea of information and determine what is true and what is simply a misconception. In this section, we will explore some common food myths and fads and provide you with the tools to overcome them.

Understanding Food Myths

Food myths often arise from misinformation or misinterpretation of scientific studies. These myths can spread rapidly through social media and other platforms, leading to confusion among the general public. It is essential to approach these myths with a critical mindset and seek reliable sources of information.

One prevalent food myth is that consuming fat leads to weight gain and heart disease. While it is true that excessive consumption of unhealthy fats can contribute to these conditions, not all fats are harmful. Unsaturated fats, such as those found in avocado, nuts, and olive oil, are actually beneficial for our health. They can help reduce the risk of heart disease and provide essential nutrients to our bodies.

Another common myth is that carbohydrates are the enemy. Carbs have gained a bad reputation over the years, with some popular diets advocating for their elimination. However, carbohydrates are our body's primary source of energy, and they play a crucial role in our overall health. The key is to choose complex carbs like whole grains, fruits, and vegetables and avoid processed and refined carbs.

Recognizing Food Fads

Food fads are trends or diets that gain popularity quickly but often lack scientific evidence to support their claims. These fads tend to promise quick and easy results, but they are often unsustainable and may even be harmful to our health. It is essential to be aware of these fads and approach them with caution.

One example of a food fad is the gluten-free diet. While this diet is necessary for individuals with celiac disease or gluten sensitivity, many people have adopted it without any medical reason. The belief that a gluten-free diet leads to weight loss or improved health is not backed by scientific evidence. In fact, it can be restrictive and limit essential nutrients found in grains containing gluten.

Another food fad is the detox diet, which claims to eliminate toxins from the body and promote weight loss. These diets often involve severe calorie restriction or the exclusive consumption of specific foods or beverages. However, our bodies have built-in detoxification systems, such as the liver and kidneys, which efficiently eliminate toxins. Restrictive detox diets can lead to nutrient deficiencies and unhealthy eating behaviors.

Separating Fact from Fiction

To overcome food myths and fads, it is crucial to rely on evidence-based information and scientific research. Here are some strategies to help you separate fact from fiction:

1. Consult reputable sources: Look for information from trusted sources, such as registered dietitians, academic institutions, and government health agencies. These sources base their recommendations on rigorous scientific research.

2. Evaluate the quality of research: Not all studies are created equal. When reading research articles, consider factors such as sample size, study design, and funding sources. Meta-analyses or systematic reviews, which analyze multiple studies, can provide a more comprehensive overview.

3. Be wary of sensationalized claims: If a diet or food is marketed as a quick fix or a miracle cure, be skeptical. Sustainable changes to your diet and lifestyle are more likely to yield long-term benefits.

4. Consider the context: Scientific studies are conducted in specific populations and settings. Remember that what works for one person may not work for another. It is essential to tailor your dietary choices to your personal needs and preferences.

Practical Application

Now that you are equipped with the knowledge to overcome food myths and fads, here are some practical tips for implementing a balanced approach to nutrition:

1. Emphasize whole foods: Focus on consuming a variety of whole, minimally processed foods such as fruits, vegetables, whole grains, lean proteins, and healthy fats. These foods provide essential nutrients and are less likely to be associated with fads or myths.

2. Practice portion control: Pay attention to your portion sizes and listen to your body's hunger and fullness cues. Remember that moderation is key, and no single food or nutrient should be off-limits.

3. Experiment with different cuisines: Explore different cultural diets and cuisines to diversify your food choices. This not only adds variety to your meals but also exposes you to unique flavors and nutrient profiles.

4. Stay informed: Continuously educate yourself about nutrition by reading reputable books and articles, attending workshops or seminars, or consulting with a registered dietitian. Knowledge is power when it comes to making informed food choices.

5. Focus on overall lifestyle: Remember that nutrition is just one component of a healthy lifestyle. Incorporate regular physical activity, manage stress, prioritize

sleep, and foster social connections for a well-rounded approach to wellness.

By recognizing and overcoming food myths and fads, you can make informed decisions about your dietary choices. A balanced approach to nutrition will not only support your overall health but also provide you with the enjoyment and satisfaction of enjoying a wide variety of foods. Stay curious, be open to new information, and always prioritize your wellbeing over passing trends.

Understanding Food Labels

Understanding food labels is crucial in making informed dietary choices. Food labels provide important information about the nutritional content of a product, helping consumers assess its healthiness and make comparisons between different products. In this section, we will explore the various components of food labels and discuss how to interpret them effectively.

Components of Food Labels

Food labels typically consist of several key components:

1. Serving Size: This indicates the recommended portion size for the product. All the nutritional information provided on the label is based on this serving size. It is important to note that this serving size may be different from what an individual actually consumes.

2. Calories: This section lists the number of calories per serving. Calories provide a measure of the energy content of the food. Understanding the calorie content can help individuals manage their overall energy intake.

3. Macronutrients: Food labels also provide information about the amounts of macronutrients present in a product. These include:

- **Protein:** Protein is essential for growth, repair, and maintenance of body tissues. The label provides the amount of protein per serving.

- **Carbohydrates:** This section lists the total amount of carbohydrates, including sugars and dietary fiber, present in the product. It is important to differentiate between naturally occurring sugars (such as those found in fruits) and added sugars.

- **Fats:** The label indicates the total fat content, including saturated and trans fats. It is recommended to limit the intake of saturated and trans fats for better heart health.

4. **Micronutrients:** Food labels also display the amounts of certain essential vitamins and minerals present in a product. Common micronutrients listed include calcium, iron, vitamin C, and vitamin A. These nutrients play important roles in various bodily functions and should be consumed as part of a balanced diet.

5. **Ingredients List:** This section provides a list of all the ingredients present in the product, with the most predominant ones listed first. This can be useful for individuals with specific dietary restrictions or allergies.

Interpreting Food Labels

To effectively interpret food labels, it is important to keep the following considerations in mind:

1. **Portion Sizes:** Remember that the nutritional information provided on the label is based on the specified serving size. Be mindful of the portion size you consume to accurately estimate the nutritional content of your meal.

2. **Total Calories:** Pay attention to the calorie content per serving. This can help you understand the energy value of the food and make informed decisions about your overall calorie intake.

3. **Macronutrient Ratios:** Assess the amounts of protein, carbohydrates, and fats in the product. Depending on your individual needs and goals, you may want to prioritize certain macronutrients over others. For example, individuals looking to build muscle mass may want to focus on protein-rich foods.

4. **Added Sugars:** Differentiate between naturally occurring sugars and added sugars in the product. High consumption of added sugars has been linked to various health issues, so it is important to be aware of their presence in packaged foods.

5. **Nutrient Density:** Consider the presence of essential vitamins and minerals in the product. Opt for nutrient-dense foods that provide a wide range of essential nutrients for overall health and well-being.

6. **Ingredient Quality:** Examine the ingredients list to understand the quality of the product. Avoid products that contain excessive amounts of additives, preservatives, or artificial ingredients.

An Example of Label Interpretation

Let's consider the label on a popular breakfast cereal:

From this label, we can gather that the serving size is 1 cup (30g), providing 120 calories. The cereal contains 2g of protein, 26g of carbohydrates, and 1g of fat per serving. Additionally, it offers 3g of dietary fiber and contributes to 10% of the daily value (DV) for vitamin C and 20% DV for calcium.

Serving Size: 1 cup (30g)

Calories: 120

Protein: 2g

Carbohydrates: 26g

Fat: 1g

Fiber: 3g

Vitamin C: 10% DV

Calcium: 20% DV

Ingredients: Whole grain oats, sugar, corn

Figure 0.2: Example of a cereal food label

By examining the ingredient list, we can see that the cereal is primarily made up of whole grain oats, sugar, and corn. This suggests that while it may provide some essential nutrients, it also contains added sugars.

Resources for Further Learning

To deepen your understanding of food labels, consider the following resources:

- The U.S. Food and Drug Administration (FDA) website provides comprehensive information on food labeling regulations and requirements.

- The American Heart Association (AHA) offers resources on interpreting food labels to make heart-healthy choices.

- Registered dietitians and nutritionists can provide personalized guidance on understanding food labels and making informed dietary decisions.

Putting Theory into Practice

To further solidify your knowledge of food labels, here's a practical exercise:
  Exercise: Choose three different packaged food products from your kitchen pantry, and analyze their food labels. Identify the serving sizes, calorie content,

macronutrient ratios, and ingredient lists. Compare the nutritional profiles of the products and consider how they align with your dietary goals.

This exercise will help you become more familiar with interpreting food labels and making conscious choices for a healthier lifestyle.

Conclusion

Understanding food labels is an essential skill in promoting a balanced and nutritious diet. By interpreting the components of food labels effectively, individuals can make informed decisions about the foods they consume. Remember to consider portion sizes, calories, macronutrient ratios, nutrient density, and ingredient quality when assessing food labels. Continued learning and practice will empower you to make healthier choices and foster a culture of mindful eating.

Promoting Balanced Meal Planning

Promoting balanced meal planning is an essential component of maintaining a healthy lifestyle. A well-balanced diet ensures that individuals receive all the necessary nutrients, vitamins, and minerals their bodies need to function optimally. It also helps prevent the development of chronic diseases and supports overall well-being.

To promote balanced meal planning, it is important to understand the basic principles of nutrition. Macronutrients such as carbohydrates, proteins, and fats play a crucial role in providing energy and building blocks for the body. Micronutrients like vitamins and minerals are essential for various bodily functions, including immune system support and cellular processes.

One effective strategy for balanced meal planning is the use of the "plate method." This method helps individuals visualize the proportions of different food groups on their plate. The plate is divided into sections for vegetables, fruits, grains, and protein. Following the plate method ensures that a meal contains a variety of nutrients, promoting balanced nutrition.

Incorporating a wide range of foods from different food groups is crucial for achieving a balanced diet. This diversity not only provides a wide spectrum of nutrients but also adds variety and enjoyment to meals. It is important to include whole grains, lean proteins, healthy fats, and plenty of fruits and vegetables in daily meal plans.

To ensure that individuals are meeting their nutritional needs, it is advisable to seek guidance from healthcare professionals, such as registered dietitians or nutritionists. These professionals can provide personalized advice based on an individual's specific needs, preferences, and dietary restrictions.

In addition to seeking professional guidance, individuals can educate themselves about nutrition and make informed choices. Learning to read food labels can help identify nutrient-rich foods and avoid those high in added sugars, saturated fats, and sodium. Websites, books, and reliable online resources can be excellent sources of information for learning about nutrition and developing healthy eating habits.

Regular meal planning and meal prepping can also contribute to balanced meal planning. By planning meals in advance, individuals can ensure that their meals are nutritionally balanced and aligned with their goals. Meal prepping involves preparing meals or ingredients in batches, which can save time and encourage healthier eating habits.

It is worth noting that a balanced meal plan should also consider cultural, ethical, and sustainability aspects. Different cultural diets offer unique and nutritious options that can be incorporated into meal planning. It is essential to respect cultural diversity while promoting balanced eating habits.

Promoting balanced meal planning also involves debunking myths and misconceptions surrounding certain foods or diets. It is important to encourage critical thinking and help individuals differentiate between evidence-based information and misleading claims. Challenging popular fad diets and encouraging a balanced, sustainable approach to eating is crucial for long-term health.

Additionally, promoting balanced meal planning should extend beyond individual health to consider the health of the planet. Encouraging the consumption of locally sourced and seasonal foods, reducing food waste, and considering the environmental impact of our food choices contribute to a more sustainable and balanced approach to meal planning.

In conclusion, promoting balanced meal planning is fundamental for achieving and maintaining optimal health and well-being. By understanding the principles of nutrition, using strategies like the plate method, seeking professional guidance, educating oneself, and considering cultural and sustainability aspects, individuals can develop healthy and sustainable eating habits. It is crucial to empower individuals to make informed choices and debunk common food myths to encourage a balanced approach to nutrition.

Supporting Mental Health

Holistic Approaches to Mental Well-being

In the pursuit of mental well-being, it is important to adopt a holistic approach that takes into account the interconnectedness of the mind, body, and spirit. This section will explore various holistic approaches to mental well-being, including practices that promote self-care, mindfulness, and emotional balance.

Self-Care Practices

Self-care plays a vital role in maintaining good mental health. It involves taking deliberate actions to prioritize your well-being and nurture yourself on a physical, emotional, and spiritual level. Self-care practices can vary from person to person, but some common examples include:

- Practicing good sleep hygiene: Prioritizing quality sleep is essential for mental well-being. Establishing a consistent sleep schedule, creating a calming bedtime routine, and ensuring a comfortable sleep environment can contribute to better sleep quality.

- Engaging in regular physical activity: Exercise has been shown to have a positive impact on mental health. It releases endorphins, reduces stress and anxiety, and promotes overall well-being. Finding activities that you enjoy and incorporating them into your routine can be an effective self-care practice.

- Nourishing your body with healthy food: Proper nutrition is not only important for physical health but also for mental well-being. A well-balanced diet that includes fruits, vegetables, whole grains, lean proteins, and healthy fats can support brain function and mood stability.

- Setting boundaries: Establishing healthy boundaries is crucial for maintaining mental well-being. Learning to say no when necessary, setting limits on work or social commitments, and prioritizing activities that bring you joy can help prevent burnout and promote a sense of balance.

- Engaging in activities that bring joy: Participating in activities that bring you happiness and fulfillment can significantly contribute to mental well-being. Whether it's pursuing a hobby, spending time in nature, or connecting with loved ones, carving out time for activities that bring you joy is an important aspect of self-care.

By incorporating these self-care practices into your daily life, you can enhance your overall well-being and promote good mental health.

Mindfulness and Meditation

Mindfulness and meditation are powerful tools for cultivating mental well-being. They involve bringing one's attention to the present moment, fostering a state of non-judgmental awareness and acceptance. These practices have been associated with various benefits, including stress reduction, increased self-awareness, improved emotional regulation, and enhanced overall mental well-being. Here are some key aspects of mindfulness and meditation:

- Mindfulness meditation: This involves focusing your attention on the present moment, often by paying attention to your breath, bodily sensations, or the environment around you. It helps develop a non-reactive and non-judgmental attitude towards thoughts and feelings, promoting a sense of calm and clarity.

- Loving-kindness meditation: This form of meditation involves cultivating feelings of compassion and love towards oneself and others. It emphasizes cultivating positive emotions, such as kindness, empathy, and gratitude. Regular practice of loving-kindness meditation can promote emotional resilience and strengthen social connections.

- Body scan meditation: This practice involves systematically scanning your body from head to toe, paying attention to each region and noticing any sensations or areas of tension. It helps develop body awareness, promote relaxation, and release physical and emotional tension.

- Mindful eating: Mindful eating involves paying full attention to the eating experience, savoring each bite, and becoming more aware of the body's hunger and fullness cues. By cultivating a mindful approach to eating, you can develop a healthier relationship with food and reduce the tendency to engage in emotional eating.

Incorporating mindfulness and meditation into your daily routine can have profound effects on your mental well-being, helping you cultivate a sense of calm, clarity, and emotional balance.

Emotional and Expressive Arts Therapies

Emotional and expressive arts therapies offer creative outlets for exploring and expressing emotions, enhancing self-awareness, and promoting overall mental well-being. These therapies involve engaging in various forms of artistic expression, such as painting, drawing, writing, music, and dance. Here are some key approaches:

- Art therapy: This form of therapy uses creative processes and artistic expression to explore emotions, reduce anxiety, and improve self-esteem. Through the use of various art materials, individuals can communicate their feelings and experiences in a non-verbal way, fostering self-expression and personal growth.

- Music therapy: Music has a unique ability to evoke emotions and can be a powerful tool for promoting mental well-being. Music therapists use techniques such as singing, playing musical instruments, and listening to music to support emotional expression, reduce stress, and enhance overall well-being.

- Dance/movement therapy: Dance and movement therapy involve using movement and expression to explore emotions and improve mental well-being. Through guided movement exercises, individuals can release emotional tension, increase self-awareness, and develop a greater sense of embodiment and self-acceptance.

- Writing therapy: Writing can be a therapeutic tool for processing emotions, gaining insight, and promoting self-reflection. Engaging in journaling or creative writing exercises can help individuals explore their thoughts and feelings, alleviate stress, and make meaning out of difficult experiences.

Emotional and expressive arts therapies provide valuable avenues for self-expression and can be integrated into a holistic approach to mental well-being.

Cognitive-Behavioral Techniques

Cognitive-behavioral techniques are evidence-based practices that focus on identifying and modifying negative thought patterns and behavior patterns that contribute to mental distress. They can be effective in promoting mental well-being and managing various mental health conditions. Here are some key cognitive-behavioral techniques:

- Cognitive restructuring: This technique involves identifying and challenging negative or distorted thinking patterns. By examining the evidence, considering alternative perspectives, and reframing negative thoughts, individuals can develop more balanced and realistic thoughts, leading to improved emotional well-being.

- Behavioral activation: Behavioral activation aims to increase engagement in positive and rewarding activities. By identifying and scheduling enjoyable and meaningful activities, individuals can counteract withdrawal and lack of motivation, leading to increased pleasure, sense of accomplishment, and overall well-being.

- Relaxation techniques: Relaxation techniques, such as deep breathing exercises, progressive muscle relaxation, and guided imagery, can help reduce stress and promote relaxation. Regular practice of these techniques can enhance overall mental well-being and provide individuals with tools to manage anxiety and stress.

- Problem-solving skills training: Developing effective problem-solving skills can significantly contribute to mental well-being. This technique involves identifying and defining problems, generating potential solutions, evaluating their pros and cons, and implementing the best course of action. By improving problem-solving skills, individuals can enhance their ability to cope with challenges and reduce feelings of helplessness.

Cognitive-behavioral techniques can be applied both individually and in therapy settings and can empower individuals to take an active role in managing their mental well-being.

In conclusion, a holistic approach to mental well-being involves incorporating various practices that promote self-care, mindfulness, self-expression, and cognitive-behavioral techniques. By adopting these approaches, individuals can nurture their mental health, enhance emotional balance, and cultivate a sense of overall well-being. Remember, everyone's journey to mental well-being is unique, so it is important to explore different approaches and find what works best for you. Embrace the holistic perspective and make your mental well-being a priority.

Addressing the Emotional Needs of Individuals

Understanding and addressing emotional needs is essential for promoting overall mental well-being. Emotional health plays a significant role in an individual's ability to handle stress, build healthy relationships, and lead a fulfilling life. In this section, we will explore various strategies and approaches to address and meet the emotional needs of individuals.

The Importance of Emotional Well-being

Emotional well-being refers to the ability to understand and manage emotions effectively. It involves developing skills to navigate through life's challenges and maintaining a positive outlook. Emotional well-being is crucial for overall mental health and contributes to improved self-esteem, resilience, and overall life satisfaction.

To address emotional needs, it is important to recognize and validate emotions experienced by individuals. Emotions are a natural response to various situations or events, and acknowledging them allows individuals to process and manage their feelings effectively. Encouraging emotional expression creates a safe space for individuals to explore their emotions and seek support when needed.

Emotional Regulation Strategies

Emotional regulation strategies help individuals manage and control their emotions in a healthy manner. These strategies are essential for dealing with stress, anxiety, anger, and other emotional challenges. Some effective emotional regulation strategies include:

- **Deep Breathing**: Deep breathing exercises help individuals calm their nervous system and reduce stress. Encourage individuals to take slow, deep breaths and focus on their breath as a way to relax their body and mind.

- **Journaling**: Writing down thoughts and emotions can be a cathartic process for individuals. Journaling allows individuals to reflect on their emotions, explore their feelings, and gain clarity. Encourage individuals to make journaling a regular practice.

- **Mindfulness and Meditation**: Mindfulness and meditation techniques promote self-awareness and help individuals observe their emotions without judgment. Incorporating mindfulness exercises into daily routines can enhance emotional well-being.

- **Physical Activity**: Engaging in regular physical activity releases endorphins, which are known as the "feel-good" hormones. Encourage individuals to incorporate exercise into their routine, as it can significantly impact their emotional well-being.

- **Social Support:** Connecting with supportive individuals can provide emotional comfort and help individuals process their emotions. Encourage individuals to seek out trusted friends, family members, or support groups to share their feelings and receive support.

Cognitive Restructuring

Cognitive restructuring is a therapeutic approach aimed at identifying and challenging negative thought patterns. It involves replacing negative thoughts with more positive and realistic ones. This technique can be particularly useful for individuals struggling with emotional distress or negative self-perception.

To facilitate cognitive restructuring, individuals can engage in the following exercises:

- **Identifying Cognitive Distortions:** Help individuals recognize common cognitive distortions such as all-or-nothing thinking, overgeneralization, and personalization. By identifying these distortions, individuals can reframe their thoughts more accurately.

- **Challenging Negative Thoughts:** Encourage individuals to question the validity of negative thoughts and examine the evidence supporting them. By challenging negative thoughts, individuals can develop more balanced and realistic thinking patterns.

- **Positive Self-Affirmations:** Teach individuals to practice positive self-affirmations to counteract negative self-talk. By repeating positive statements about themselves, individuals can boost their self-confidence and improve their emotional well-being.

Seeking Professional Help

In some cases, individuals may require professional help to address their emotional needs adequately. Mental health professionals, such as psychologists or counselors, can provide guidance, support, and evidence-based interventions to help individuals navigate through emotional challenges.

Encourage individuals to seek professional help if they experience persistent or overwhelming emotions, difficulty functioning in daily life, or if their emotional well-being negatively impacts their overall quality of life. In addition to therapy, professionals may recommend medication or other forms of treatment tailored to individual needs.

Creating Supportive Environments

Creating a supportive environment is essential for addressing emotional needs. This involves fostering open communication, promoting empathy, and reducing stigma surrounding mental health. Some strategies to create supportive environments include:

- **Active Listening:** Encourage individuals to actively listen, validate, and empathize with others' emotions. Active listening creates a safe space for individuals to express themselves and feel understood.

- **Promoting Emotional Intelligence:** Emotional intelligence involves recognizing, understanding, and managing emotions in oneself and others. Educate individuals about the importance of emotional intelligence and encourage the development of these skills.

- **Educating about Mental Health:** Raise awareness about mental health by providing education and resources. Promote discussions about mental health, reduce stigma, and encourage individuals to seek support when needed.

- **Encouraging Self-Care Practices:** Self-care practices, such as adequate sleep, healthy eating, and engaging in hobbies, contribute to emotional well-being. Encourage individuals to prioritize and engage in activities that promote self-care regularly.

Understanding Intersectionality

Addressing emotional needs requires an understanding of the intersectionality of an individual's identity and experiences. Intersectionality refers to the overlapping social categories (e.g., race, gender, sexuality, socioeconomic status) that influence an individual's experiences of oppression and privilege.

Recognize that individuals may face unique challenges based on their intersectional identities. Pay attention to the diverse needs and experiences of individuals and amplify marginalized voices to create an inclusive and supportive environment.

Conclusion

Addressing emotional needs is essential for promoting overall mental well-being. By understanding the importance of emotional well-being, teaching emotional regulation strategies, promoting cognitive restructuring, encouraging professional help when necessary, creating supportive environments, and acknowledging intersectionality, we can better meet the emotional needs of individuals. Taking a holistic approach to emotional health enables individuals to lead fulfilling lives and fosters a culture of acceptance, empathy, and personal growth.

Mental Health Stigma and Stereotypes

Mental health stigma and stereotypes have long been prevalent in society, creating significant barriers to individuals seeking help and support. Stigma refers to the negative attitudes, beliefs, and behaviors that lead to discrimination against people with mental health conditions, while stereotypes are oversimplified and generalized ideas about individuals based on their mental health.

6.3.3.1 Understanding Mental Health Stigma Mental health stigma is deeply rooted in societal misconceptions and lack of understanding. Many people still hold the belief that mental health conditions are a sign of weakness or personal failure, leading to the marginalization of individuals experiencing mental health challenges. These stigmatizing attitudes can cause isolation, discrimination, and exclusion from various social activities, workplaces, and even healthcare settings.

6.3.3.2 Impact of Stigma on Help-Seeking Behavior The fear of being labeled as "crazy" or facing negative judgment often prevents individuals from seeking the necessary help for their mental health issues. Stigma can perpetuate feelings of shame, guilt, and embarrassment, making it difficult for individuals to reach out to mental health professionals or disclose their struggles to loved ones. This delay or avoidance of treatment may result in further deterioration of mental health conditions and lead to long-term negative consequences.

6.3.3.3 Stereotypes and their Harmful Effects Stereotypes related to mental health can be damaging and perpetuate negative perceptions. For example, the stereotype that individuals with mental health conditions are dangerous or unpredictable perpetuates fear and hostility towards them. Another common stereotype is that people with mental health conditions are incapable of leading successful and fulfilling lives, limiting their opportunities and potential for growth.

6.3.3.4 Challenging Stigma and Stereotypes Addressing mental health stigma and stereotypes requires a collective effort from society as a whole. Here are some key strategies to challenge and combat stigma:

6.3.3.4.1 Education and Awareness: Promoting education about mental health conditions and debunking common myths and misconceptions is crucial. Increasing public awareness can help dispel stereotypes and foster empathy and understanding.

6.3.3.4.2 Language Matters: Using person-first language when discussing mental health can help reduce stigma. Instead of labeling someone as their mental health condition, using phrases such as "person with depression" or "individual living with anxiety" emphasizes the person's identity beyond their mental health.

6.3.3.4.3 Normalizing Help-Seeking Behavior: Encouraging open conversations about mental health and seeking help is essential. Highlighting stories of individuals who have sought treatment and recovered can inspire others to do the same.

6.3.3.4.4 Media Representation: Responsible and accurate portrayal of mental health in media can significantly impact public perception. Media platforms should avoid sensationalism and stereotypes, and instead promote realistic and empathetic representations of mental health experiences.

6.3.3.4.5 Supportive Environment: Creating a safe and supportive environment where individuals feel comfortable discussing their mental health is vital. This can be achieved by fostering empathy, active listening, and providing resources for mental health support.

6.3.3.5 Unconventional Approach: The Power of Storytelling One unconventional yet effective approach to combating mental health stigma is through the power of storytelling. Personal narratives can promote empathy and humanize the experiences of individuals living with mental health conditions. Sharing inspiring stories of resilience, recovery, and personal growth can challenge stereotypes and foster a more understanding and inclusive society.

For example, organizations can organize storytelling events where individuals with lived experiences share their journeys of overcoming mental health challenges. These stories can be shared through various mediums, such as podcasts, documentaries, or written publications, to reach a wider audience and create a positive impact.

By promoting storytelling, we encourage individuals to share their stories authentically and provide a platform for those whose voices have been silenced by stigma. This approach can help normalize discussions around mental health and break down barriers, leading to greater acceptance and support for those struggling with mental health conditions.

In conclusion, mental health stigma and stereotypes continue to hinder individuals from seeking help and receiving the support they need. By understanding the impact of stigma, challenging stereotypes, and promoting education and awareness, we can create a more inclusive and empathetic society.

Through unconventional approaches like storytelling, we can break down barriers and build a world that supports the mental health and well-being of all individuals.

Exploring Mindfulness and Self-care Practices

In today's fast-paced and often stressful world, it is essential to prioritize our mental well-being. Mindfulness and self-care practices offer valuable tools to help us cultivate a sense of calm, balance, and self-awareness. In this section, we will explore the concept of mindfulness, its benefits, and practical self-care techniques that can be integrated into our daily lives.

Understanding Mindfulness

Mindfulness is the practice of intentionally bringing our attention to the present moment with an open and non-judgmental attitude. It involves being fully present, observing our thoughts, emotions, and physical sensations without getting caught up in them. By cultivating mindfulness, we can develop a greater sense of clarity, calmness, and resilience in the face of challenges.

Benefits of Mindfulness

Numerous studies have demonstrated the positive impact of mindfulness on our mental health and overall well-being. Here are some key benefits of incorporating mindfulness into our lives:

- **Stress reduction**: Mindfulness helps us manage stress by allowing us to observe our thoughts and emotions without becoming overwhelmed by them. It promotes a sense of relaxation and helps regulate the body's stress response.

- **Improved focus and concentration**: Regular mindfulness practice enhances our ability to concentrate and sustain attention. By training our minds to stay present, we become less prone to distractions and can better focus on tasks at hand.

- **Emotional regulation**: Mindfulness cultivates emotional intelligence by helping us recognize and understand our feelings. It enables us to respond to emotions with greater self-compassion and empathy, leading to healthier relationships with ourselves and others.

- **Enhanced self-awareness:** Through mindfulness, we develop a deeper understanding of our thoughts, beliefs, and behaviors. This self-awareness allows us to identify and challenge negative patterns, leading to personal growth and positive change.

- **Improved overall well-being:** Mindfulness has been linked to improved overall well-being, including increased life satisfaction, improved sleep quality, and a greater sense of happiness and contentment.

Practical Self-care Techniques

Incorporating self-care practices into our daily routine is crucial for maintaining good mental health. Here are some practical techniques that can help promote mindfulness and enhance self-care:

- **Meditation and breathing exercises:** Set aside dedicated time each day for meditation or focused breathing exercises. These practices help calm the mind, increase self-awareness, and reduce stress.

- **Engaging in hobbies and leisure activities:** Carve out time for activities that bring you joy and relaxation. Engaging in hobbies or leisure activities not only provides a break from daily stressors but also promotes creativity and a sense of accomplishment.

- **Being in nature:** Spend time outdoors, connecting with nature. Nature has a calming effect on the mind and body, reducing stress and promoting a sense of well-being.

- **Practicing self-compassion:** Treat yourself with kindness and compassion. Practice self-compassion by acknowledging your strengths and weaknesses, practicing self-forgiveness, and offering yourself words of encouragement.

- **Mindful eating:** Pay attention to the process of eating by savoring each bite, noticing the flavors and textures, and tuning into your body's hunger and fullness cues. Mindful eating helps foster a healthy relationship with food and promotes overall well-being.

The Power of Gratitude

Gratitude is an essential aspect of self-care and mindfulness. Expressing gratitude cultivates a positive mindset and helps shift our focus from what is lacking to what is present in our lives. By regularly practicing gratitude, we train our minds to notice and appreciate the small pleasures and positive aspects of life.

Here are some ways to incorporate gratitude into your daily routine:

- **Gratitude journal:** Take a few minutes each day to write down three things you are grateful for. This practice helps rewire the brain to focus on the positive aspects of life.

- **Express gratitude to others:** Take the time to thank the people who have made a positive impact on your life. Expressing gratitude not only strengthens relationships but also increases your own sense of well-being.

- **Mindful gratitude moments:** Throughout the day, pause and notice moments of gratitude. It could be as simple as appreciating a beautiful sunset or feeling grateful for a delicious meal. These mindful gratitude moments help anchor us in the present and foster a positive mindset.

Embracing Mindfulness and Self-care

Incorporating mindfulness and self-care practices into our lives requires dedication and commitment. It is important to remember that self-care is not selfish; it is a necessary step towards maintaining good mental health and overall well-being. By prioritizing mindfulness and self-care, we can cultivate a sense of balance, resilience, and fulfillment in our lives.

Additional Resources

- *The Mindful Path to Self-Compassion* by Christopher K. Germer

- *Mindfulness: An Eight-Week Plan for Finding Peace in a Frantic World* by Mark Williams and Danny Penman

- *The Gifts of Imperfection: Let Go of Who You Think You're Supposed to Be and Embrace Who You Are* by Brené Brown

- *Full Catastrophe Living: Using the Wisdom of Your Body and Mind to Face Stress, Pain, and Illness* by Jon Kabat-Zinn

Exercise: Take a moment to practice a brief mindfulness meditation. Sit comfortably, close your eyes, and bring your attention to your breath. Notice the sensation of the breath entering and leaving your body. If thoughts arise, gently acknowledge them and return your focus to the breath. Practice this for a few minutes and observe how it makes you feel.

Note: Mindfulness and self-care practices may vary for each individual. It is essential to explore and find what resonates with you personally. Experiment with different techniques and adapt them to suit your needs and preferences. Remember, self-care is a lifelong journey, and it evolves as we grow and change.

Conclusion

Recap of Key Points

Debunking Soy Boy Myths

In recent years, the term "Soy Boy" has gained popularity as a derogatory label used to criticize men who are perceived as weak, feminine, or lacking in traditional masculinity. However, these stereotypes and misconceptions surrounding soy consumption and its impact on masculinity are not rooted in scientific evidence. In this section, we will debunk these myths and shed light on the actual health benefits of soy.

Soy and Estrogen Levels

One common myth associated with soy consumption is that it leads to an increase in estrogen levels in men, which is believed to cause feminizing effects. However, this claim lacks scientific evidence. Soybeans contain phytoestrogens, which are naturally occurring compounds that have a similar structure to estrogen. However, the phytoestrogens found in soy are much weaker than the estrogen produced by the human body.

Research has shown that consuming moderate amounts of soy does not have any significant impact on estrogen levels in men. In fact, studies have found that soy consumption can actually improve hormonal balance by reducing the risk of certain hormonally driven cancers, such as prostate cancer.

Soy and Testosterone

Another misconception is that soy consumption can lower testosterone levels in men. Testosterone is the primary male sex hormone responsible for the development of masculine characteristics. However, research has consistently shown that soy does not have a detrimental effect on testosterone levels.

Several studies have examined the relationship between soy consumption and testosterone levels in men and found no significant changes. In fact, some studies have even suggested that soy consumption can have a protective effect on the prostate gland, which is influenced by testosterone levels.

Impact of Soy on Muscle Mass

A common concern among men is that soy consumption can negatively affect muscle mass and strength. However, this is another unfounded myth. Soy contains high-quality protein, complete with all essential amino acids, making it an excellent alternative to animal-based protein sources.

Research has shown that soy protein is just as effective as other sources of protein, such as whey or casein, in promoting muscle protein synthesis and enhancing muscle recovery. In fact, soy protein can be particularly beneficial for individuals who follow a plant-based or vegetarian diet.

Soy and Femininity

The myth that soy consumption can make men more feminine is rooted in sexism and outdated stereotypes. It suggests that consuming soy products can somehow diminish masculinity and promote femininity. However, there is no scientific basis for this claim.

Masculinity and femininity are complex constructs that cannot be solely determined by dietary choices. It is important to recognize that there is no one-size-fits-all definition of masculinity or femininity, and these concepts are influenced by societal and cultural norms. Consuming soy products does not determine or define an individual's gender identity.

Benefits of Soy Protein

Contrary to the myths surrounding soy consumption, there are actually numerous health benefits associated with incorporating soy protein into one's diet. Soy protein is a complete protein that provides all essential amino acids necessary for optimal health.

Research has shown that regular consumption of soy protein can help in reducing the risk of cardiovascular diseases, such as heart disease and stroke. Soy protein has been found to have cholesterol-lowering effects and can help maintain healthy blood pressure levels.

Additionally, soy protein has been linked to the prevention of certain cancers, such as breast, prostate, and colon cancer. The presence of phytochemicals in soy, such as isoflavones, has been shown to have anti-cancer properties.

In conclusion, the stereotypes and misconceptions surrounding soy consumption and its effects on masculinity are unfounded. Soy consumption does not lead to an increase in estrogen levels or a decrease in testosterone levels in men. It does not negatively impact muscle mass or promote femininity. On the contrary, soy protein has numerous health benefits, including promoting cardiovascular health and reducing the risk of certain cancers. It is important to approach dietary choices with an open mind and rely on scientific evidence rather than perpetuating baseless myths.

Unraveling Snowflake Stereotypes

In order to truly understand the snowflake generation, it is important to debunk the stereotypes and misconceptions surrounding them. By doing so, we can foster a more productive and empathetic dialogue about the unique challenges and perspectives of this generation. In this section, we will explore some common stereotypes associated with snowflakes and provide evidence to debunk these myths.

Stereotype 1: Snowflakes are Overly Sensitive

One common stereotype attributed to the snowflake generation is that they are overly sensitive or easily offended. This perception often stems from the belief that they cannot handle criticism or diverse viewpoints. However, it is important to recognize that sensitivity to certain topics or events is not exclusive to this generation.

In reality, the sensitivity displayed by some individuals from the snowflake generation can often be seen as a reflection of their heightened empathy and concern for social issues. They may prioritize values such as inclusivity, fairness, and social justice. It is crucial to recognize that this sensitivity can be a positive trait, as it often drives positive change and progress within society.

Stereotype 2: Snowflakes are Entitled and Self-Centered

Another stereotype associated with snowflakes is that they are entitled and self-centered. This perception often arises from the belief that this generation expects instant gratification and has a sense of entitlement in various aspects of life.

However, it is essential to understand that the sense of entitlement experienced by some individuals from the snowflake generation may not be significantly different from previous generations. The desire for personal fulfillment and the pursuit of happiness is universal and not restricted to any specific generation.

Moreover, it is important to acknowledge that the snowflake generation is facing unique challenges such as economic uncertainty, mounting student debt, and a rapidly changing job market. These challenges can create a sense of unease and insecurity, which may be misinterpreted as entitlement by others.

Stereotype 3: Snowflakes Lack Resilience

The perception that snowflakes lack resilience is another common stereotype associated with this generation. It is often believed that they are unable to cope with adversity or face challenges with determination and perseverance.

In reality, resilience is not solely determined by generational traits. Resilience is a complex trait that varies among individuals and is influenced by a variety of factors such as upbringing, personal experiences, and support systems.

To debunk this stereotype, it is essential to highlight the resilience demonstrated by many individuals from the snowflake generation in the face of adversity. They have shown resilience in navigating uncertain economic conditions, advocating for social justice, and tackling mental health issues. Their ability to adapt and find innovative solutions to problems should be recognized and celebrated.

Stereotype 4: Snowflakes are Avoidant of Challenges

There is a perception that individuals from the snowflake generation tend to avoid challenging situations or uncomfortable conversations. This stereotype arises from the belief that they prefer safe spaces and echo chambers that protect them from differing opinions.

However, it is important to note that the desire for safe spaces and respectful dialogue is not exclusive to the snowflake generation. Creating environments where individuals feel valued, respected, and heard is a shared goal across generations.

Furthermore, avoiding confrontation or uncomfortable conversations does not necessarily indicate a lack of resilience or an unwillingness to engage in meaningful discussions. It is essential to recognize that everyone has different comfort levels when it comes to engaging in challenging conversations, and it is not fair to label an entire generation based on the actions of a few individuals.

Stereotype 5: Snowflakes are Narcissistic and Attention-seeking

The perception that individuals from the snowflake generation are narcissistic and attention-seeking is another common stereotype. This belief often arises from the prominence of social media in their lives and the assumption that they constantly seek validation and attention online.

However, it is important to recognize that social media has become a significant part of everyday life for many individuals across generations. The portrayal of a perfect life or the desire for validation is not restricted to the snowflake generation. It is a reflection of the human desire for connection and acceptance.

Moreover, many individuals from the snowflake generation utilize social media platforms to raise awareness about social issues, advocate for change, and connect with like-minded individuals. It is crucial to distinguish between attention-seeking behavior and the use of social media as a powerful platform for activism and community-building.

Debunking Snowflake Stereotypes

Debunking these stereotypes is crucial in fostering understanding and empathy towards the snowflake generation. It is important to recognize that these stereotypes are often based on limited understanding and generalizations.

To address these stereotypes, it is essential to engage in open and respectful dialogue with individuals from the snowflake generation. Listening to their perspectives, understanding their concerns, and recognizing their contributions to society can help dispel these misconceptions.

Promoting empathy and understanding can be achieved by encouraging intergenerational interactions and creating spaces where diverse viewpoints are valued. By debunking these stereotypes, we can pave the way for a more inclusive and respectful society that appreciates the unique perspectives of all generations.

Example: Navigating Difficult Conversations

One way to debunk the stereotype of snowflakes avoiding challenging conversations is by providing examples of successful dialogue. For instance, let's consider a scenario where a snowflake and a conservative individual engage in a conversation about immigration policies.

Rather than dismissing each other's perspectives, the snowflake and conservative individual could aim to understand one another's concerns and values. They can discuss the economic impact of immigration, the importance of inclusivity, and finding common ground. By engaging in respectful and open communication, they can challenge stereotypes and bridge the generational divide.

Additional Resources

To further explore the topic of snowflake stereotypes and generational differences, consider the following resources:

- *The Coddling of the American Mind: How Good Intentions and Bad Ideas Are Setting Up a Generation for Failure* by Jonathan Haidt and Greg Lukianoff.

- *iGen: Why Today's Super-Connected Kids Are Growing Up Less Rebellious, More Tolerant, Less Happy - and Completely Unprepared for Adulthood—and What That Means for the Rest of Us* by Jean M. Twenge.

- Online articles and opinion pieces that showcase diverse perspectives on generational differences and snowflake stereotypes.

Conclusion

By unraveling snowflake stereotypes, we can develop a more nuanced understanding of the challenges and strengths of the snowflake generation. It is important to recognize that stereotypes often fail to capture the complexity and diversity of individuals within any generation. Embracing empathy, understanding, and open dialogue allows us to bridge generational gaps and create a more inclusive society.

Health Benefits of Soy Consumption

Soy is a versatile and nutritious plant-based protein that has been consumed for thousands of years. In recent years, there has been increased interest in the health benefits of soy consumption. This section will explore the various ways in which incorporating soy into your diet can promote overall health and well-being.

Nutritional Profile of Soy

Soy is a nutrition powerhouse, packed with essential nutrients that support optimal health. It is a complete protein, meaning it contains all the essential amino acids that our bodies need. Soy is also an excellent source of fiber, healthy fats, vitamins, and minerals. Let's take a closer look at the macronutrients and micronutrients found in soy:

Macronutrients in Soy Soybeans are rich in protein, with approximately 36 grams of protein per 100 grams of cooked soybeans. This makes soy an excellent plant-based protein option for individuals following vegetarian or vegan diets. Protein is essential for building and repairing body tissues, maintaining muscle mass, and supporting overall immune function.

Soybeans also contain carbohydrates, with a moderate amount of dietary fiber. Carbohydrates provide energy for our bodies, and fiber helps regulate blood sugar levels and promotes healthy digestion.

Furthermore, soy contains healthy fats, including polyunsaturated and monounsaturated fats. These fats are beneficial for heart health and can help reduce the risk of cardiovascular diseases.

Micronutrients in Soy Soy is a good source of several essential vitamins and minerals. It contains significant amounts of iron, calcium, magnesium, zinc, phosphorus, and potassium. These minerals play vital roles in maintaining bone health, supporting nerve function, and promoting overall vitality.

Soy also contains several B vitamins, including folate, thiamine, and riboflavin. These vitamins are important for energy production, brain function, and the production of red blood cells.

Cardiovascular Health

One of the most well-known benefits of soy consumption is its positive impact on cardiovascular health. Numerous studies have shown that soy can help reduce cholesterol levels, lower blood pressure, and improve arterial health. Let's dive into the specific ways in which soy promotes cardiovascular well-being:

Impact of Soy on Cholesterol Levels High levels of cholesterol in the blood can lead to the buildup of plaques in arteries, increasing the risk of heart diseases. Soy protein has been found to have cholesterol-lowering effects, particularly LDL cholesterol, which is often referred to as "bad" cholesterol. The soluble fiber present in soy can also help bind cholesterol and remove it from the body.

Soy and Heart Disease Prevention The consumption of soy products, such as tofu and soy milk, has been linked to a reduced risk of heart disease. Regular soy consumption has been associated with improved blood lipid profiles, reduced inflammation, and enhanced endothelial function, all of which contribute to a healthier cardiovascular system.

Role of Soy in Blood Pressure Management High blood pressure is a major risk factor for heart disease. Several studies have shown that including soy in the diet can help lower blood pressure. The bioactive compounds found in soy, such as isoflavones, have been suggested to have beneficial effects on blood vessel function and blood pressure regulation.

Soy and Arterial Health Soy is rich in antioxidants, including isoflavones and phytochemicals, which protect against oxidative stress and inflammation. These compounds help improve arterial health by reducing the risk of plaque formation and enhancing the elasticity of blood vessels.

Bone Health

Maintaining strong and healthy bones is crucial for overall well-being, especially as we age. Soy consumption has been associated with several benefits for bone health. Let's explore how soy can support bone health:

Soy and Calcium Absorption Calcium is essential for maintaining strong bones and preventing osteoporosis. However, calcium absorption can be influenced by various factors, including the presence of certain compounds in our diet. Contrary to a common misconception, the consumption of soy does not negatively impact calcium absorption. In fact, studies have shown that soy may enhance calcium absorption, ultimately improving bone mineral density.

Soy and Bone Density As we age, bone density naturally decreases, increasing the risk of fractures and osteoporosis. The isoflavones found in soy have been shown to have a protective effect on bone health by inhibiting bone breakdown and promoting bone formation. Regular soy consumption, along with weight-bearing exercises, can help maintain bone density and reduce the risk of osteoporosis.

Soy and Menopausal Symptoms Menopause is a stage in a woman's life that is associated with a decline in estrogen levels. This hormonal change can lead to various symptoms, including hot flashes, night sweats, and mood disturbances. Soy contains natural plant compounds, such as isoflavones, that have a similar structure to estrogen. These compounds, often referred to as phytoestrogens, can help alleviate menopausal symptoms by acting as a weak estrogen-like substance in the body.

Cancer Prevention

Cancer is a devastating disease that affects millions of people worldwide. While no single food can prevent cancer, incorporating soy into a balanced diet may help reduce the risk of certain types of cancer. Let's explore the potential cancer-protective effects of soy:

Soy and Breast Cancer Breast cancer is one of the most common cancers among women. There has been significant research into the relationship between soy consumption and breast cancer risk. The findings suggest that moderate soy consumption, especially during adolescence and early adulthood, may reduce the risk of breast cancer later in life. The isoflavones found in soy may help regulate estrogen levels and inhibit tumor growth.

Soy and Prostate Cancer Prostate cancer is the most common cancer in men. Several studies have investigated the link between soy consumption and prostate cancer risk. The results indicate that soy consumption may be associated with a reduced risk of developing prostate cancer. The bioactive compounds in soy, such as isoflavones and phytochemicals, have anti-inflammatory and antioxidant properties that may play a role in cancer prevention.

Soy and Colon Cancer Colorectal cancer is a significant cause of cancer-related deaths. Consuming soy products has been associated with a reduced risk of colon cancer. The fiber and phytochemicals in soy help promote healthy digestion, prevent inflammation, and regulate bowel movements, reducing the risk of colon cancer.

Role of Phytochemicals in Cancer Prevention Soy contains various phytochemicals, such as isoflavones, genistein, and daidzein, which have been shown to exhibit anti-cancer properties. These compounds have been found to inhibit the growth of cancer cells, induce programmed cell death (apoptosis), and suppress angiogenesis (the formation of new blood vessels that support tumor growth). While more research is needed, the evidence suggests that incorporating soy into a balanced diet may contribute to cancer prevention.

Hormonal Balance

The hormonal balance in our bodies is essential for overall health and well-being. Soy consumption has been studied for its potential impact on hormonal balance, particularly in women and men. Let's explore the effects of soy on hormonal health:

Impact of Soy on Estrogen Levels   Some concerns have been raised about the potential feminizing effects of soy and its impact on estrogen levels in the body. However, research has shown that moderate soy consumption does not lead to significant changes in estrogen levels. Soy contains phytoestrogens, which have a weaker estrogenic activity compared to the body's own estrogen. These phytoestrogens can bind to estrogen receptors, potentially providing a balancing effect in individuals with either too much or too little estrogen.

Soy and Menopause Symptoms   Menopause is a natural biological process that marks the end of reproductive years for women. The decline in estrogen levels during menopause can cause various symptoms, such as hot flashes, night sweats, and mood changes. Soy consumption has been suggested to alleviate these symptoms. Phytoestrogens found in soy may help regulate estrogen levels and reduce the severity and frequency of menopausal symptoms.

Soy and Hormones in Men   There has been concern about the potential impact of soy consumption on testosterone levels in men. However, research suggests that soy does not have feminizing effects or lead to a decrease in testosterone levels. In fact, studies have shown that soy does not affect sperm quality, fertility, or overall reproductive health in men. Moderate soy consumption as part of a balanced diet is unlikely to have any negative effects on male hormone balance.

In conclusion, incorporating soy into a balanced diet can provide numerous health benefits. Soy is a rich source of protein, fiber, vitamins, and minerals. It supports cardiovascular health, promotes bone health, may reduce the risk of certain cancers, and helps maintain hormonal balance. However, it is important to remember that soy should be consumed as part of a diverse diet that includes a variety of plant-based proteins and other key nutrients.

Embracing Diversity and Wellness

The Importance of Balanced Perspectives

In today's fast-paced and interconnected world, it is crucial to adopt a mindset that values balanced perspectives, particularly when it comes to matters of health and wellness. A balanced perspective involves considering multiple viewpoints, approaches, and sources of information before making conclusions or decisions. This section will highlight the significance of embracing balanced perspectives in various aspects of life, including diet, nutrition, and overall well-being.

Understanding the Limitations of Singular Approaches

One of the fundamental reasons why balanced perspectives are essential is because singular approaches often have limitations. Whether it is a specific diet, exercise regimen, or health philosophy, relying solely on one approach can result in an incomplete understanding of the complex nature of health. For example, following a strict diet that promotes the consumption of a single food group, such as soy, may neglect other essential nutrients and increase the risk of nutrient deficiencies. By considering a broader range of perspectives, individuals can cultivate a more comprehensive understanding of health and avoid potential pitfalls.

Holistic Approach to Health

Balanced perspectives promote a holistic approach to health, recognizing the interconnectedness of physical, mental, emotional, and spiritual well-being. Rather than focusing solely on one aspect of health, such as physical fitness or dietary choices, a holistic perspective considers the integration of all dimensions of wellness. For example, when addressing mental health concerns, a balanced perspective acknowledges the importance of therapy, self-care practices, and community support, in addition to any potential medical interventions. This comprehensive approach paves the way for a more well-rounded understanding and experience of overall well-being.

Avoiding Extreme Positions

Balanced perspectives help individuals avoid falling into extreme positions, which can be detrimental to both personal and societal growth. Extremism often leads to rigid thinking and a lack of openness to alternative views, which may hinder personal development and limit opportunities for collaboration and understanding. By embracing balanced perspectives, individuals are encouraged to consider diverse opinions and seek common ground, leading to more meaningful conversations and the potential for constructive change.

Promoting Critical Thinking

Encouraging balanced perspectives also nurtures critical thinking skills, which are vital in today's information-driven society. When individuals approach health-related information with a critical mindset, they are better equipped to evaluate the validity and reliability of different sources of information. They can analyze scientific evidence, scrutinize claims, and differentiate between solid research and pseudoscience. By cultivating critical thinking skills, people can make informed decisions about their health, avoiding misinformation and making choices that align with their individual needs and values.

Breaking Down Biases and Prejudices

Balanced perspectives have the power to break down biases and prejudices surrounding health and wellness. Biases can be based on stereotypes or societal norms, and they often result in stigmatization and discrimination. By exposing ourselves to diverse perspectives and challenging our preconceived notions, we can develop a broader understanding of health that is inclusive and compassionate. A balanced perspective encourages empathy, allowing individuals to appreciate the unique challenges and experiences of others. This empathy fosters a supportive and inclusive environment where everyone has the opportunity to thrive.

Creating a Sustainable Future

Balanced perspectives are also integral to creating a sustainable future, not just for individuals but for the planet as a whole. By considering the environmental and ethical implications of our choices, we can make more informed decisions about our diet and lifestyle. This includes understanding the impact of our dietary choices on climate change, animal welfare, and natural resource depletion. By adopting a balanced perspective that takes into account the interconnectedness of our actions, we can strive towards a more sustainable and harmonious existence.

In summary, embracing balanced perspectives is crucial in the realm of health and wellness. By considering diverse viewpoints, adopting a holistic approach, avoiding extreme positions, promoting critical thinking, breaking down biases, and creating a sustainable future, individuals can cultivate a more nuanced understanding of their own well-being and that of others. This balanced perspective ultimately leads to healthier individuals, communities, and societies as a whole.

Nurturing a Healthy Lifestyle

In order to maintain a healthy lifestyle, it is important to adopt habits and practices that promote overall well-being. Nurturing a healthy lifestyle goes beyond just physical health and encompasses various aspects of our lives, including mental, emotional, and social well-being. Understanding the principles of a healthy lifestyle and incorporating them into our daily lives can have a profound impact on our overall health and happiness.

Physical Health: Exercise and Activity

Physical health is a vital component of a healthy lifestyle. Engaging in regular physical activity not only helps maintain a healthy weight but also strengthens muscles and bones, improves cardiovascular health, and boosts our overall energy levels. Find activities that you enjoy and make it a habit to engage in them regularly.

A balanced exercise routine should include a combination of aerobic activities, such as walking, jogging, or cycling, as well as strength training exercises to build muscle mass and improve bone density. Aim for at least 150 minutes of moderate-intensity aerobic activity per week, along with two or more days of strength training exercises targeting major muscle groups.

Incorporating physical activity into your daily routine can be as simple as taking the stairs instead of the elevator, walking or cycling instead of driving short distances, or participating in fitness classes or sports activities. Remember, every little bit of physical activity counts towards nurturing a healthy lifestyle.

Nutrition: Eating a Balanced Diet

A healthy lifestyle is incomplete without proper nutrition. A balanced diet provides essential nutrients, vitamins, and minerals that fuel our bodies and support overall health. To nurture a healthy lifestyle, focus on incorporating a variety of nutrient-dense foods into your diet.

Include plenty of fruits, vegetables, whole grains, lean proteins, and healthy fats in your meals. These foods provide the necessary nutrients for optimal functioning of our bodies. It is also important to limit the consumption of processed foods, sugary snacks, and beverages high in added sugars, as they provide little nutritional value and can have a negative impact on our health.

Meal planning and mindful eating are effective strategies to nurture a healthy lifestyle. Plan your meals ahead of time to ensure a balanced and nutritious diet. Listen to your body's hunger and fullness cues, and practice mindful eating by savoring each bite and paying attention to the flavors, textures, and sensations of the food.

Sleep: Rest and Recovery

Adequate sleep is essential for rejuvenating both our bodies and minds. Poor sleep quality or insufficient sleep can have detrimental effects on our physical and mental health. To nurture a healthy lifestyle, prioritize getting enough sleep each night.

The National Sleep Foundation recommends adults aim for 7-9 hours of sleep per night. Establish a regular sleep schedule by going to bed and waking up at the same time each day, even on weekends. Create a sleep-friendly environment by keeping your bedroom cool, quiet, and dark.

Practice good sleep hygiene by avoiding caffeine and electronic devices close to bedtime, as they can interfere with sleep patterns. Relaxation techniques, such as deep breathing exercises, meditation, or taking a warm bath before bed, can also promote better sleep.

Stress Management: Finding Balance

Effective stress management is crucial for nurturing a healthy lifestyle. Chronic stress can disrupt our physical and mental well-being, leading to a host of health problems and decreased overall quality of life. Finding healthy ways to manage stress is essential.

Engage in stress-relieving activities that you enjoy, such as yoga, meditation, deep breathing exercises, or engaging in hobbies. Prioritize self-care and make time for activities that help you relax and unwind. It is also important to establish and maintain healthy boundaries in various areas of your life, such as work, relationships, and personal commitments.

Seeking support from friends, family, or mental health professionals can also be beneficial in managing stress. Remember, it is okay to ask for help when needed, and taking care of your mental well-being is just as important as taking care of your physical health.

Social Connections: Building Relationships

Building and nurturing meaningful social connections is a fundamental aspect of a healthy lifestyle. Strong social connections have been linked to improved mental well-being, increased longevity, and decreased risk of chronic diseases. Take the time to cultivate and maintain positive relationships with family, friends, and community members.

Engage in activities that foster social interactions, such as joining clubs or organizations, participating in group fitness classes, or volunteering for community service. Make an effort to connect with others on a regular basis, whether it be through face-to-face interactions, phone calls, or online platforms.

Remember, healthy relationships are a two-way street. Be a good listener, show empathy, and offer support to those around you. Engaging in meaningful social connections not only enhances your own well-being but also contributes to the overall health and happiness of the community.

Unconventional Approach: Nature Therapy

In addition to the conventional methods mentioned above, an unconventional yet effective approach to nurturing a healthy lifestyle is through nature therapy. Spending time in nature has been shown to have numerous benefits for physical and mental health.

Find opportunities to immerse yourself in nature, whether it be going for a hike, spending time at the beach, gardening, or simply taking a walk in a local park. Research suggests that spending time in natural environments can reduce stress, improve mood, enhance cognitive function, and boost overall well-being.

Embrace the calming effect of nature and incorporate it into your daily life. Practice mindfulness while in nature, being fully present and appreciating the beauty and tranquility it offers. Use nature as a means to reconnect with yourself, recharge your energy, and promote a sense of harmony and balance in your life.

Conclusion

Nurturing a healthy lifestyle requires a holistic approach that encompasses various aspects of our lives. By prioritizing physical health through regular exercise, maintaining a balanced diet, getting adequate sleep, managing stress, fostering social connections, and incorporating nature therapy, we can achieve and sustain optimal health and well-being.

Embrace the principles and practices outlined in this section and make them a part of your daily routine. By nurturing a healthy lifestyle, you not only enhance your own health and happiness but also contribute to creating a healthier and more vibrant world for everyone.

Encouraging Acceptance and Empathy

Encouraging acceptance and empathy is crucial in fostering a society that values diversity and promotes well-being. Acceptance refers to the ability to recognize and value differences in individuals, regardless of their background or characteristics. Empathy, on the other hand, involves understanding and sharing the feelings of others, thus allowing for greater compassion and support.

Acceptance and empathy play a significant role in creating a culture of inclusivity, where everyone feels valued and respected. In the context of health benefits, promoting acceptance and empathy can influence individuals' ability to make positive changes in their diets and mental well-being.

One way to encourage acceptance and empathy is through education and awareness. By educating individuals about different cultures, traditions, and perspectives, we can foster a broader understanding and appreciation of diversity. This can be achieved through community workshops, school programs, and media campaigns that highlight the importance of acceptance and empathy.

In addition to education, promoting acceptance and empathy requires creating safe spaces for open dialogue and engagement. People need platforms where they can freely express their thoughts and feelings without fear of judgment or discrimination. This can be achieved through community centers, online forums, or support groups where individuals can come together to discuss their experiences and learn from one another.

Empathy can also be cultivated through teaching and practicing active listening. Active listening involves being fully present and attentive to others, not just hearing their words but also acknowledging their emotions and experiences. This can be done by maintaining eye contact, asking clarifying questions, and reflecting back what the person has shared.

Practicing empathy also involves putting oneself in someone else's shoes and trying to understand their perspective. This can be challenging, but it is essential for building connections and fostering greater empathy. Encouraging individuals to engage in role-playing exercises or participate in empathy-building activities can help develop this skill.

Another way to promote acceptance and empathy is by challenging stereotypes and biases. Stereotypes and biases often stem from limited understanding and exposure to different cultures or experiences. By actively challenging these stereotypes and biases, individuals can broaden their perspectives and develop a more empathetic mindset.

It is crucial to recognize that promoting acceptance and empathy is an ongoing process that requires continuous effort. It involves creating an environment where individuals feel comfortable expressing themselves, engaging in open dialogue, and challenging their own biases. Supporting mental health is also an integral part of this process, as it allows individuals to better understand their emotions and develop empathy for others' experiences.

In conclusion, encouraging acceptance and empathy is essential for creating a society that values diversity and promotes overall well-being. By providing education, creating safe spaces for dialogue, practicing active listening, challenging stereotypes and biases, and supporting mental health, we can foster a culture of acceptance and empathy. This, in turn, allows individuals to make positive changes in their diets, mental well-being, and overall health. The journey towards acceptance and empathy is ongoing, and it requires collective effort and commitment from individuals, communities, and institutions. Let us strive for a society where acceptance and empathy are valued and celebrated.

Moving Forward

Promoting Educated Discussions

Engaging in educated discussions is crucial for fostering a culture of learning and understanding. It allows individuals to exchange ideas, challenge assumptions, and broaden their perspectives. In this section, we will explore strategies for promoting and participating in educated discussions on topics related to health, nutrition, and wellness.

Active Listening

One key aspect of promoting educated discussions is the ability to actively listen. Active listening involves not only hearing the words being spoken but also understanding the underlying message and showing empathy towards the speaker. By being fully present and attentive, we can create a space where everyone feels heard and respected.

To practice active listening, it is important to give our full attention to the speaker. This means putting aside distractions, such as electronic devices, and maintaining eye contact. We should also refrain from interrupting or prematurely formulating our response while the speaker is still talking. Instead, we should focus on understanding their perspective and ask clarifying questions to ensure clear communication.

Respectful Communication

In any discussion, it is crucial to maintain a respectful and inclusive environment. Respectful communication involves expressing our thoughts and opinions in a considerate manner while valuing the perspectives of others. We should strive to create a safe space where individuals feel comfortable sharing their ideas, even if they differ from our own.

One effective way to promote respectful communication is to use "I" statements instead of "you" statements. For example, saying "I believe…" or "In my experience…"

encourages personal expression without imposing our views on others. It also fosters a non-confrontational tone and invites collaboration rather than defensiveness.

Another important aspect of respectful communication is to avoid personal attacks or derogatory language. Instead, we should focus on addressing the ideas or arguments being presented. By staying focused on the content of the discussion, we can maintain a constructive dialogue that promotes learning and growth.

Critical Thinking and Fact-Checking

In order to have educated discussions, it is essential to engage in critical thinking and fact-checking. This involves evaluating the validity and reliability of the information being presented. With the abundance of misinformation and biased sources available today, it is crucial to distinguish between credible and unreliable information.

One approach to critical thinking is to question assumptions and ask for evidence. Rather than accepting information at face value, we should seek out supporting data, studies, and expert opinions. This allows us to form informed opinions and make evidence-based arguments.

Fact-checking is another important skill in promoting educated discussions. Before accepting a claim as truth, it is essential to verify the information from reliable sources. Fact-checking tools and websites can be valuable resources for assessing the accuracy of claims.

Cultivating Open-Mindedness

In order to promote educated discussions, it is important to cultivate open-mindedness. Open-mindedness involves being receptive to new ideas and perspectives, even if they challenge our existing beliefs. By embracing diverse viewpoints, we can expand our understanding and enhance the quality of our discussions.

A helpful way to cultivate open-mindedness is through exposure to different viewpoints. This can be achieved through reading articles, books, and journals from various authors and sources. Engaging in conversations with people who have different backgrounds and experiences can also broaden our perspective.

Additionally, it is important to acknowledge and challenge our own biases. Recognizing our predispositions and actively seeking out opposing viewpoints can help us overcome our inherent biases and promote a more comprehensive and respectful discussion.

Encouraging Constructive Feedback

Constructive feedback plays a vital role in educated discussions. It allows us to provide thoughtful input and suggestions to others while maintaining a positive and supportive atmosphere. By offering constructive feedback, we can help individuals improve their arguments and enhance the overall quality of the discussion.

When providing feedback, it is important to focus on the content rather than attacking the person. This can be achieved by offering specific observations and suggestions for improvement. By highlighting strengths and areas for growth, we can foster a collaborative environment that encourages learning and development.

Receiving constructive feedback is equally important for personal growth. It is essential to be open to receiving feedback from others and view it as an opportunity for learning rather than criticism. By embracing feedback, we can refine our arguments and expand our knowledge.

Engaging in Reflective Practice

Reflective practice is a valuable tool for promoting educated discussions. It involves critically analyzing our own thoughts, beliefs, and actions in order to enhance our understanding and improve our communication skills. By engaging in reflective practice, we can continuously learn and grow as active participants in discussions.

One approach to reflective practice is journaling. Taking the time to write down our thoughts, emotions, and experiences can help us gain insights into our own perspectives and biases. Journaling can also serve as a platform for self-reflection and personal development.

Another aspect of reflective practice is seeking feedback from others. Actively soliciting input from trusted individuals allows us to gain an outside perspective and identify areas for improvement. By incorporating external feedback into our reflective practice, we can refine our communication skills and enhance our contributions to educated discussions.

Promoting Diversity and Inclusion

Lastly, in order to foster educated discussions, it is crucial to promote diversity and inclusion. This involves creating an environment where individuals from different backgrounds and perspectives feel welcome and valued. By embracing diverse voices, we can enrich the discussion and promote a more comprehensive understanding of the topics at hand.

To promote diversity and inclusion, it is important to actively seek out diverse voices and perspectives. This can be done by inviting individuals from different backgrounds to participate in the discussion or by exploring literature and resources written by authors with diverse viewpoints. By intentionally including diverse perspectives, we can cultivate an inclusive environment that encourages respectful and educated discussions.

In conclusion, promoting educated discussions is essential for nurturing a culture of learning and understanding. By practicing active listening, engaging in respectful communication, and cultivating critical thinking skills, we can enhance the quality of our discussions. Additionally, by embracing open-mindedness, providing constructive feedback, and engaging in reflective practice, we can continuously improve our communication skills and contribute to well-informed conversations. Promoting diversity and inclusion is also crucial for ensuring a comprehensive understanding of the topics being discussed. By applying these strategies, we can create an environment where educated discussions thrive, leading to personal and societal growth.

Challenging Prejudice and Bias

Prejudice and bias are pervasive issues that can have detrimental effects on individuals and communities. They are based on preconceived notions and stereotypes, leading to discrimination, inequality, and social division. In this section, we explore the importance of challenging prejudice and bias, providing strategies to promote understanding, empathy, and inclusivity.

Understanding Prejudice and Bias

Prejudice refers to prejudgments and negative attitudes towards individuals or groups based on their perceived characteristics, such as race, ethnicity, gender, sexual orientation, or socioeconomic status. Bias, on the other hand, refers to the tendency to favor or support one group over others without objective justification.

Prejudice and bias can manifest in various ways, such as systemic discrimination, microaggressions, stereotypes, and unconscious biases. These harmful behaviors can perpetuate social inequalities, limit opportunities, and create hostile environments.

To challenge prejudice and bias, it is crucial to understand their underlying causes. Education and awareness play a vital role in recognizing and dismantling these harmful ideologies. By promoting critical thinking and empathy, we can encourage individuals to challenge their own biases and become advocates for change.

Promoting Empathy and Understanding

Empathy is a key element in challenging prejudice and bias. It involves putting oneself in someone else's shoes, understanding their experiences, and validating their feelings. Empathy cultivates connection, fosters understanding, and breaks down barriers.

To promote empathy, it is important to provide opportunities for meaningful interactions among individuals from different backgrounds. Encouraging open and respectful dialogue can help bridge gaps and dispel stereotypes. Activities that promote diversity and inclusion, such as workshops, cultural exchanges, and community engagement initiatives, can also play a significant role in fostering empathy.

Additionally, it is crucial to educate individuals about the historical and societal factors that contribute to prejudice and bias. By providing context and understanding, we can help dismantle misconceptions and challenge deeply rooted biases.

Addressing Implicit Bias

Implicit biases are unconscious attitudes or stereotypes that affect our understanding, actions, and decisions. These biases can be deeply ingrained and can influence our behaviors, even when we consciously hold egalitarian beliefs. Addressing implicit bias requires self-reflection and a commitment to recognizing and challenging these biases.

One effective strategy to address implicit bias is through implicit bias training. These programs raise individuals' awareness about their unconscious biases and provide tools and strategies to mitigate their impact. They aim to help individuals make fair and unbiased decisions by examining their preconceptions and promoting conscious thought processes.

Another key approach is diversifying social networks and exposure to different perspectives. Research shows that increased interactions with diverse groups can reduce implicit biases. By intentionally seeking out diverse voices and experiences, we can challenge our own biases and broadening our understanding of others.

Promoting Inclusive Spaces

Creating inclusive spaces is essential to challenging prejudice and bias. Inclusivity involves actively valuing and respecting individuals from all backgrounds and identities. It requires intentional efforts to remove barriers, ensure equal opportunities, and create a sense of belonging.

In educational institutions, workplaces, and community settings, promoting inclusivity involves adopting inclusive policies and practices. This can include establishing non-discriminatory hiring and promotion practices, providing diversity and sensitivity training, and implementing anti-bullying and harassment policies.

Inclusive spaces also require addressing institutional biases and systemic barriers. This entails recognizing and dismantling structures and policies that perpetuate discrimination and inequality. By advocating for equitable practices and challenging discriminatory norms, we can foster environments that value diversity and promote equal opportunities for all.

Confronting Prejudice and Bias in Media

Media plays a powerful role in shaping attitudes, perceptions, and stereotypes. Challenging prejudice and bias in media is crucial to creating a more inclusive and equitable society.

Individuals can advocate for media literacy programs that teach critical thinking skills and promote awareness of bias and stereotypes. By analyzing media representations, individuals can learn to discern distorted portrayals and challenge harmful narratives.

Promoting diverse media representation and amplifying marginalized voices is also essential. Content creators, journalists, and media organizations should strive to ensure accurate and fair representation across different identities and perspectives. This includes challenging stereotypes, avoiding tokenism, and promoting inclusive narratives.

Personal Growth and Responsibility

Challenging prejudice and bias is an ongoing process that requires personal growth and self-reflection. Individuals must take responsibility for their beliefs, attitudes, and actions and constantly strive for self-improvement.

Personal growth can be facilitated through workshops, self-help books, and other resources that promote introspection and self-awareness. Engaging in activities that expose individuals to diverse cultures, perspectives, and experiences can also contribute to personal growth and broaden understanding.

It is important to adopt a growth mindset that acknowledges the potential for change and actively seeks knowledge and understanding. By embracing new perspectives and challenging our own biases, we can contribute to a more inclusive and compassionate society.

Conclusion

Challenging prejudice and bias is a collective responsibility that requires a commitment to empathy, understanding, and inclusivity. By addressing implicit bias, promoting empathy, creating inclusive spaces, confronting bias in media, and fostering personal growth, we can work towards a society that values diversity and advocates for equal rights and opportunities for all. Let us strive to challenge prejudice and bias at every level, fostering a culture of acceptance, empathy, and growth.

Fostering a Culture of Inclusivity

In today's diverse society, it is crucial to foster a culture of inclusivity that respects and celebrates the differences among individuals. In this section, we will explore the importance of embracing diversity, promoting inclusivity, and working towards a more inclusive society.

Understanding Inclusivity

Inclusivity refers to the practice of actively involving and valuing individuals from all backgrounds, regardless of their race, ethnicity, gender, sexual orientation, age, disability, or any other characteristic that may make them different from others. It is about creating an environment where everyone feels welcome, respected, and included.

Benefits of Inclusivity

Promoting a culture of inclusivity brings numerous benefits to individuals and society as a whole. Embracing diversity and fostering inclusivity:

- Encourages innovation and creativity: When people from different backgrounds come together, they bring unique perspectives, experiences, and ideas to the table. This diversity of thought fuels innovation and creativity, leading to better problem-solving and decision-making.

- Enhances learning and personal growth: Interacting with individuals from diverse backgrounds helps broaden our horizons and challenges our preconceived notions. It exposes us to new ideas, cultures, and experiences, fostering personal growth and promoting a deeper understanding of the world.

- Strengthens social cohesion: Inclusivity builds stronger communities by fostering a sense of belonging and unity among individuals. When everyone feels valued and respected, social connections are strengthened, leading to increased collaboration, empathy, and cooperation.

- Improves productivity and performance: Inclusive environments cultivate a sense of psychological safety, where individuals feel comfortable expressing themselves and contributing their unique skills and talents. This psychological safety enhances productivity and encourages individuals to perform at their best.

- Reduces prejudice and discrimination: Fostering inclusivity helps break down stereotypes, biases, and discriminatory attitudes. Through exposure to diverse perspectives and experiences, individuals are more likely to challenge their own prejudices and become advocates for equality and social justice.

Promoting Inclusivity

Creating a culture of inclusivity requires intentional efforts and actions. Here are some strategies to promote inclusivity:

- Education and awareness: Promote education and awareness about diversity, equity, and inclusion. Provide opportunities for individuals to learn about different cultures, perspectives, and experiences. This can be through workshops, seminars, diversity training programs, or guest speakers from various backgrounds.

- Equal opportunities: Ensure equal opportunities for all individuals, regardless of their background. Implement policies and practices that promote fairness, diversity, and inclusion in hiring, promotions, and decision-making processes.

- Open dialogue and communication: Encourage open and respectful dialogue where individuals feel safe expressing their thoughts, concerns, and experiences. Create platforms for discussions that address sensitive topics and allow for constructive conversations and understanding.

- Diverse representation: Ensure diverse representation in leadership positions, organizations, and media. By promoting diverse voices and perspectives, you send a powerful message that everyone's contributions are valued and respected.

- Supportive environment: Create an environment that supports and accommodates the needs of all individuals. This may include inclusive facilities, accessible resources, flexible work arrangements, or the availability of support networks.

- Collaboration and partnerships: Foster relationships and collaborations with organizations and communities that promote inclusivity. By working together, you can amplify efforts and create a more inclusive and equitable society.

Challenges and Considerations

While fostering inclusivity is crucial, it is essential to be aware of potential challenges and considerations:

- Unconscious biases: Recognize that everyone has biases, including unconscious biases. These biases may influence our thoughts, attitudes, and behaviors. Being aware of our biases and actively working to challenge them is crucial in promoting inclusivity.

- Intersectionality: Acknowledge that individuals may have multiple identities or belong to several marginalized groups. Intersectionality considers how different forms of discrimination can overlap and affect individuals differently. Ensure that inclusivity efforts address the complexities of intersectional identities.

- Continuous learning: Recognize that fostering inclusivity is an ongoing process. It requires continuous learning, reflection, and improvement. Stay updated on current research, best practices, and emerging issues related to diversity and inclusion.

- Resistance to change: Be prepared for resistance to change. Some individuals may feel uncomfortable or challenged by efforts to promote inclusivity. It is essential to address concerns and engage in open dialogue to overcome resistance.

- Accountability and evaluation: Establish mechanisms to hold individuals and organizations accountable for their inclusivity efforts. Regularly evaluate progress, collect feedback, and make necessary adjustments to ensure continued growth and improvement.

Conclusion

Fostering a culture of inclusivity is essential for creating a society that values and embraces diversity. By promoting inclusivity, we can create environments where everyone feels respected, valued, and empowered to contribute their unique experiences and perspectives. It is our collective responsibility to work towards a more inclusive world, one that acknowledges and celebrates the richness of our differences while striving for equity and justice. Let us embrace the challenge of fostering a culture of inclusivity and enrich the lives of individuals and communities everywhere.

Striving for Personal and Societal Growth

In the journey towards personal and societal growth, it is essential to recognize the interconnected nature of our actions and their impact on ourselves and the world around us. This section explores the importance of promoting individual well-being while also striving for positive societal change. By fostering a culture of inclusivity, challenging prejudice and bias, and focusing on personal and societal growth, we can create a healthier and more harmonious world.

Promoting Educated Discussions

One key aspect of personal and societal growth is promoting and participating in educated discussions. In today's world, we are bombarded with information from various sources, often leading to confusion and misinformation. By encouraging critical thinking skills, we can teach individuals how to assess the reliability and validity of information. This empowers people to make informed decisions and engage in meaningful conversations.

Educated discussions also involve actively seeking out different perspectives and opinions. By fostering an environment that values diverse viewpoints, we can create a space for dialogue and understanding. This not only enriches personal growth but also contributes to societal progress by addressing complex issues from multiple angles.

Challenging Prejudice and Bias

To achieve personal and societal growth, we must confront prejudice and bias in all its forms. Prejudice can stem from deep-rooted beliefs and stereotypes, often leading to discrimination and unequal treatment. By challenging these biases, we promote a more inclusive and equitable society.

One way to challenge prejudice and bias is through education and exposure to diverse cultures, beliefs, and experiences. By fostering empathy and understanding, we can break down barriers and promote inclusivity. It is important to acknowledge that tackling prejudice and bias is an ongoing process that requires self-reflection, open-mindedness, and a willingness to unlearn harmful behaviors and attitudes.

Fostering a Culture of Inclusivity

Inclusivity is the cornerstone of personal and societal growth. Creating an inclusive culture involves actively embracing diversity in all its forms, whether it be race, gender, sexuality, religion, or socioeconomic background. By valuing and celebrating these differences, we create a society that fosters equal opportunities and respects the rights and dignity of all individuals.

Fostering inclusivity requires creating safe spaces where individuals are free to express themselves without fear of judgment or discrimination. It also involves actively seeking out and amplifying marginalized voices, ensuring that everyone has an equal chance to be heard. By promoting inclusivity, we not only support individual well-being but also foster a more harmonious and cohesive society.

Striving for Personal Growth

Personal growth is a lifelong journey that involves self-reflection, self-improvement, and continuous learning. By prioritizing our own well-being and development, we can become more resilient, motivated, and fulfilled individuals.

One way to foster personal growth is through the practice of mindfulness and self-care. Taking time for self-reflection and engaging in activities that nourish the mind, body, and soul can greatly enhance personal well-being. This may include activities such as meditation, exercise, pursuing hobbies, or seeking therapy or counseling when needed.

Another crucial aspect of personal growth is setting goals and working towards them. By identifying our passions and aspirations, we can develop a sense of purpose and direction in life. It is important to remember that personal growth is not a linear process, and setbacks and challenges are part of the journey. Embracing these obstacles as opportunities for learning and growth is key to personal development.

Striving for Societal Growth

While personal growth is essential, striving for societal growth is equally important. Societal growth involves actively working towards creating positive change and addressing systemic issues that impact communities and individuals.

One way to contribute to societal growth is by engaging in volunteering and community service. By giving back to our communities, we not only make a tangible difference in the lives of others but also develop a sense of connectedness and social responsibility. Volunteering can take many forms, from participating in local initiatives to advocating for policy changes at a larger scale.

Additionally, advocating for social justice is vital for societal growth. This may involve participating in peaceful protests, supporting organizations that champion human rights, and being an ally to marginalized communities. By raising awareness and advocating for change, we contribute to the creation of a fairer and more just society.

In conclusion, striving for personal and societal growth involves promoting educated discussions, challenging prejudice and bias, fostering inclusivity, and prioritizing personal and societal well-being. By embracing these principles, we can create a world that values diversity, empathy, and equal opportunities for all. Let us embark on this journey of personal and societal growth, as we work towards a better tomorrow.

Index

-doubt, 90

a, 1–7, 9–13, 15–40, 42–109,
　　111–114, 116–151,
　　153–155, 157–161, 163,
　　164, 166–192, 195–218,
　　220–222
ability, 9, 13, 17, 18, 21, 67, 68, 91,
　　96, 98, 99, 101, 102, 107,
　　120, 121, 126, 140, 171,
　　184, 185, 198, 209–211
abound, 38, 171
absorption, 28, 29, 36, 37, 66, 118,
　　125–128, 132, 141, 160,
　　202
abundance, 7, 32, 34, 212
acceptance, 7, 46, 53, 71, 72, 74, 77,
　　84, 92, 103, 120, 182, 188,
　　189, 199, 209–211, 217
access, 13, 54, 87, 92
accessibility, 55
accommodation, 86
account, 30, 167, 181, 206
accumulation, 123
accuracy, 172, 212
acid, 112, 126, 128, 143
acknowledgment, 97
act, 67, 93

action, 60, 132, 139
activism, 92, 97, 199
activity, 5, 26, 29, 30, 32, 39, 55, 57,
　　64, 112, 116, 117, 121,
　　125, 131, 132, 134, 139,
　　148, 163, 175, 204, 207
acupuncture, 49, 87
adaptability, 101
addition, 6, 49, 59, 63–67, 108, 113,
　　115, 145, 157, 158, 180,
　　186, 205, 209, 210
adherence, 35, 39, 55, 63
adolescence, 66, 129, 203
adult, 59, 63
adulthood, 66, 203
advance, 37, 39, 120, 145, 180
advantage, 145
adversity, 2, 5, 17, 20, 22, 98–101,
　　198
advertising, 76, 77
advice, 39, 80, 88, 133, 180
advocate, 3, 199, 216
affinity, 149
affordability, 87
age, 3, 30, 39, 94, 121, 122, 126,
　　128, 129, 131, 133, 139,
　　143, 150, 163, 171, 202,
　　217

agriculture, 159, 167–169
agroforestry, 168, 169
alcohol, 123, 148
Alex, 63
all, 3, 5, 10, 14, 17, 26, 36, 37, 39, 49, 59, 61, 63–65, 70, 71, 73–75, 77, 84, 86, 88, 89, 97–99, 104, 112, 113, 116, 123, 129, 141, 159, 163, 174, 175, 179, 190, 196, 199–201, 205, 215–217, 220–222
ally, 222
almond, 37
alternative, 50, 53, 64, 87, 88, 91, 101, 157, 164, 196, 205
amino, 25, 26, 36, 59, 61–65, 71, 112, 116, 154, 157, 159, 196, 200
amount, 32, 117, 127, 128, 171, 201
amplification, 5
analysis, 6, 58, 64, 119, 122, 124, 125, 141, 154, 172, 173
anger, 17, 185
angiogenesis, 139
animal, 5, 25, 26, 38, 62–64, 71, 73, 112, 122, 140, 161, 196, 206
anticancer, 145, 146, 148
Antioxidant, 139
antioxidant, 28, 139, 148, 203
anxiety, 13, 20, 22, 29, 49, 84, 90, 92, 93, 100, 102, 103, 134, 185, 189
apoptosis, 139
appearance, 70–74, 76, 77
application, 49, 53, 171, 172
appreciation, 19, 20, 167, 210

approach, 2–4, 6, 7, 17, 20, 21, 27, 33, 43, 45, 46, 49, 50, 53, 55, 56, 58, 60, 65, 67, 71, 74, 75, 77, 78, 81, 83–86, 88, 89, 93, 95, 103, 106, 113, 118, 120, 123, 125, 126, 131, 135, 138, 140, 142, 144, 148, 150, 153, 155, 157, 161, 163, 164, 167, 174–176, 180, 181, 183, 184, 186, 188, 189, 197, 205, 206, 209, 212, 213, 215
approval, 90
area, 10, 149
argumentation, 172
aromatase, 60
array, 29, 114, 159, 164
art, 20
ask, 171, 172, 208, 211, 212
aspect, 9, 12, 13, 17, 19, 69, 83, 93, 98, 128, 150, 191, 205, 208, 211–213, 220, 221
assertiveness, 1, 73
asset, 68
assistance, 22
association, 4, 119, 130, 134, 140, 141, 144, 145, 151, 154
assumption, 199
assurance, 169
atherosclerosis, 119, 120, 123, 125
athlete, 60
atmosphere, 213
attention, 61, 76, 121, 131, 133, 145, 164, 175, 182, 187, 190, 199, 207, 211
attitude, 190
attractiveness, 77
attribute, 69

audience, 189
authenticity, 92
author, 171
autonomy, 65
availability, 55, 85, 126, 127
avocado, 36, 174
avocados, 26, 29
avoidance, 97, 188
awareness, 17, 21, 67, 71, 77, 78, 80, 85, 91, 93, 95, 96, 98, 102, 120, 169, 182, 183, 189, 190, 199, 210, 214–216, 222
awe, 20, 21

background, 73, 87, 167, 209, 221
bacteria, 149
balance, 5, 12, 26–28, 31, 40, 44, 46, 58–60, 67, 74, 88, 91, 95, 112, 127, 131, 132, 150, 153, 154, 158–163, 181, 182, 184, 190, 192, 195, 203, 204, 209
balancing, 37, 63, 94, 161, 164, 204
barrier, 68
base, 175
basic, 79, 142, 179
basis, 196, 208
bath, 208
beach, 209
beauty, 21, 70, 71, 74, 77, 90, 209
bed, 208
bedroom, 208
bedtime, 208
behavior, 94, 183, 199
behavioral, 183, 184
being, 3, 5–7, 9–14, 16–22, 24, 26, 27, 29–31, 33–35, 38, 40, 43, 45, 46, 49, 51, 53, 54, 56, 58, 60, 61, 64, 65, 68–71, 73–75, 77, 78, 80–86, 88, 90, 92–96, 98, 99, 101, 103, 109, 112, 114, 115, 121, 123, 125, 127, 128, 133, 135, 138, 142, 148, 153, 159, 161, 164, 168, 169, 179–186, 188, 190, 192, 200–206, 208–212, 214, 220–222
belief, 4, 5, 26, 57, 59, 67, 71, 112, 174, 188, 197–199
belonging, 20, 22, 94, 99, 215
benefit, 45, 66, 70, 112, 122, 130, 151, 153
betterment, 17
Bias, 214
bias, 7, 17, 53, 91, 105, 106, 120, 171, 214–217, 220–222
bile, 124
binding, 116, 126, 148, 149
bioavailability, 29, 126–128
biodiversity, 169
biology, 22
bit, 207
bite, 164, 207
blood, 20, 25, 27, 31, 34, 59, 66, 111, 112, 119–125, 139, 140, 164, 196, 201, 202
bloodstream, 57, 111, 116, 126
body, 2, 5, 9–12, 20, 25–28, 31, 32, 34–36, 50, 53, 54, 57, 59–61, 63, 64, 66, 67, 70–72, 74–78, 99, 111, 112, 114, 118, 122–124, 131, 133, 134, 136–141, 143, 145, 148–151, 153, 154, 161, 162, 164, 174, 175, 179, 181, 195, 201,

202, 204, 207, 221
bodybuilding, 5
bone, 27, 28, 30, 58, 64, 66, 67, 76, 125–132, 134, 135, 148, 150, 153, 159, 201, 202, 204, 207
book, 2, 4, 6, 7
bowel, 203
boy, 1, 2, 67, 69, 70
brain, 26, 29, 30, 36, 112, 134, 160, 201
bread, 29, 37
break, 73, 91, 106, 126, 128, 189, 190, 206, 221
breakdown, 129, 202
breakfast, 177
breast, 64, 66, 136–138, 150, 197, 203
breathing, 94, 208
bridge, 83, 98, 104, 200, 215
broccoli, 36
bubble, 91
buffer, 22
building, 20, 25, 61, 63, 80, 98, 102, 103, 106, 179, 199, 201, 210
buildup, 57, 125, 201
burden, 84, 138
butter, 26
button, 90

caffeine, 208
calcium, 28, 37, 66, 76, 125–129, 131, 132, 201, 202
call, 98
calm, 17, 182, 190
calmness, 190
calorie, 26, 33, 34, 76, 78, 174
campus, 95

cancer, 33–35, 59, 64, 66, 67, 127, 136–145, 147, 148, 150, 154, 155, 159, 165, 195, 197, 203
capacity, 17, 98
carbohydrate, 158
carbon, 38, 167, 168
carbonate, 126
cardiorespiratory, 12
care, 3, 7, 20, 45, 46, 49, 51, 53, 55, 56, 71, 72, 91, 92, 94, 96, 101, 103, 142, 181, 182, 184, 190–192, 205, 208, 221
caregiving, 73
Carl Lewis, 60
case, 16, 59, 63, 72, 172, 173
casein, 196
cauliflower, 36
cause, 2, 25, 70, 118, 140, 142, 188, 195, 203, 204
caution, 81, 174
celebration, 21
cell, 28, 139, 145
censorship, 90
cereal, 177, 178
chain, 168, 169
challenge, 6, 7, 17, 53, 71–73, 75, 77, 79, 93, 97, 98, 105, 106, 172, 188, 189, 200, 211, 212, 214–217, 220, 221
chamber, 91, 92
chance, 221
change, 79, 96–99, 117, 168–170, 197, 199, 202, 205, 206, 214, 216, 220, 222
characteristic, 217
charge, 78
check, 12, 88, 117, 148

Index 227

checking, 212
cheese, 37
chia, 37
child, 168
childbearing, 73
childhood, 129
China, 60, 137
chloride, 28
choice, 32, 55, 68, 70, 111
cholesterol, 66, 71, 112, 116–120, 124, 125, 196, 201
citrate, 126
citrus, 36
claim, 60, 172, 195, 196, 212
clarity, 78, 182, 190
clash, 56
class, 172
climate, 55, 169, 206
clotting, 27
coexistence, 98
cohort, 87
collaboration, 45, 53, 83, 97, 103, 205, 212
college, 24, 25, 95
colon, 142–145, 197, 203
combat, 74, 92, 188
combination, 7, 37, 39, 61, 118, 159, 207
comfort, 198
commitment, 11, 96, 97, 101, 107, 192, 211, 215, 217
communication, 18, 25, 29, 45, 56, 69, 74, 86, 89, 94, 102, 104, 187, 200, 211–214
community, 13, 20–25, 43, 95, 164, 199, 205, 208–210, 215, 216, 222
comparison, 2, 85, 94
compassion, 18–21, 72, 91, 98, 209
compensation, 169
competence, 56, 105, 106
competition, 84
complex, 2, 3, 5, 17, 25, 27, 36, 57, 59, 60, 64, 70, 86, 111, 112, 136, 139, 145, 150, 171, 174, 196, 198, 205, 220
complexity, 200
component, 6, 12, 20, 22, 24, 26, 58, 63, 98, 120, 175, 179, 207
composition, 12, 64, 76
compound, 116, 148
comprehension, 104
concentration, 29, 154, 169
concept, 2, 13, 25, 27, 53, 68, 72–74, 190
concern, 16, 57, 71, 102, 103, 128, 131, 138, 153, 154, 168, 196, 197, 204
conclusion, 3, 24, 42, 67, 70, 72, 75, 80, 89, 98, 103, 123, 125, 128, 142, 150, 159, 180, 184, 189, 197, 204, 210, 214, 222
condition, 58, 131, 189
confidence, 72, 103, 135
confirmation, 91, 105, 106
conflict, 97
conformity, 90, 92
confrontation, 198
confusion, 174, 220
connectedness, 222
connection, 2, 18–22, 67, 91, 92, 94, 104, 106, 151, 199, 215
connectivity, 3, 85
connotation, 2, 81
conscience, 170
consensus, 141, 142

conservation, 168
consideration, 39, 46, 138
consistency, 11
construct, 2, 172
consultation, 125
consulting, 123, 175
consumer, 169
consumption, 2, 4–6, 31, 33–35, 46, 54, 55, 57–67, 69, 71–73, 111, 113, 116–132, 135–138, 140–142, 144, 145, 148–151, 153–155, 157, 161, 167–170, 174, 180, 195–197, 200–205, 207
contact, 210, 211
content, 30, 85, 90–92, 111–113, 118, 119, 126, 128, 129, 176, 212, 213
context, 2, 4, 25, 54, 75, 81, 133, 141, 171, 175, 209, 215
contraction, 28
contrary, 197
contrast, 34, 55, 87
contribute, 2, 4, 6, 9, 12–14, 22, 26, 28, 30, 32, 33, 61, 64–66, 71, 72, 74, 81, 85, 86, 92, 94, 95, 98, 99, 112, 115, 118, 119, 121, 123, 129, 131, 134, 138, 143, 150, 151, 159, 161, 169, 170, 174, 180, 183, 201, 209, 214–216, 220, 222
control, 17, 35, 54, 59, 107, 122, 129, 148, 149, 153, 175, 185
convenience, 88
conversation, 2, 3, 104–106, 199
conversion, 60, 168

cooking, 30, 79, 80, 127, 128, 164
coordination, 12
copper, 28
core, 40
corn, 178
cornerstone, 221
cost, 87
counseling, 49, 95, 102, 221
count, 154
cover, 168
coverage, 53, 95
create, 4, 6, 16, 17, 20, 53, 56, 65, 68, 70, 73–75, 79, 90–92, 95–98, 101, 102, 106, 170, 187, 189, 198, 200, 211, 214, 215, 220–222
creation, 222
creativity, 20
credibility, 39, 171, 172
crisis, 84
criticism, 78, 81, 93, 197, 213
cuisine, 161
cultivation, 168, 169
culture, 5–7, 16, 17, 46, 53, 54, 71, 88, 95, 103, 120, 135, 164, 167, 179, 188, 209–211, 214, 217, 218, 220, 221
cure, 123, 175
curiosity, 167, 171
curriculum, 95, 102
cyberbullying, 85, 92
cycle, 148
cycling, 207

daidzein, 59, 60, 121, 133, 134, 136, 149
dairy, 25, 26, 31, 34–36, 38, 126, 127
damage, 34, 120, 139

Index 229

dance, 55, 183
date, 90, 141
day, 29, 32, 62, 63, 111, 208
death, 118, 139
debate, 126, 148, 171, 172
debt, 198
debunking, 1, 2, 6, 7, 61, 72, 79, 84, 153, 173, 180, 189, 199
decision, 56
decline, 129, 131, 133, 134, 148, 150, 202, 204
decrease, 5, 59, 60, 66, 117, 124, 132, 133, 151, 154, 197, 204
dedication, 192
defense, 28
defensiveness, 212
definition, 1, 2, 73, 196
deforestation, 168
delay, 188
density, 28, 58, 64, 66, 126, 128–132, 134, 179, 202, 207
depletion, 206
depression, 13, 20, 22, 29, 92, 93, 100, 102, 134, 189
depth, 6
design, 141, 149, 172, 175
desire, 90, 97, 102, 198, 199
destigmatization, 95
destruction, 168
deterioration, 131, 188
determination, 198
detox, 174
detoxification, 174
development, 2, 22, 33, 54, 57, 58, 70–72, 76, 81, 83–86, 91, 92, 98, 101, 118–121, 123, 125, 131, 139, 141, 143, 145, 148, 164, 179, 196, 205, 213, 221
diabetes, 33, 34, 111, 165
diagnosis, 40, 137
dialogue, 3, 6, 83, 84, 92, 97, 98, 103, 104, 106, 169, 197–200, 210, 212, 215, 220
diet, 1, 2, 6, 12, 25, 26, 29–31, 33–40, 58, 60, 61, 63–65, 67, 69, 72–79, 88, 94, 112, 113, 116–122, 124, 125, 127–132, 135, 137–140, 142–145, 147, 148, 150, 152, 153, 155, 157–161, 164, 165, 167, 172, 174, 175, 179, 196, 200, 202–207, 209
dietary, 28–30, 32–37, 40, 54, 55, 58, 60–62, 64, 65, 68–78, 80, 113, 117–121, 126, 132, 135, 140, 142, 144, 151, 153, 164, 167, 169–173, 175, 176, 180, 196, 197, 201, 205, 206
dieting, 77
dietitian, 26, 113, 117, 175
difference, 57, 222
difficulty, 16, 22, 186
digestion, 201, 203
dignity, 221
direction, 221
disability, 217
disappointment, 85
discipline, 3, 106–109
discomfort, 81, 85, 97
discourse, 5
discovery, 22, 75, 108

discrimination, 6, 95, 103, 188, 206, 210, 214, 216, 220, 221
discussion, 148, 171, 172, 211–214
disease, 26, 31, 33, 38, 48, 54, 55, 59, 65, 66, 76, 88, 112, 118–121, 124, 125, 131, 136, 138, 140, 145, 165, 174, 196, 201–203
disharmony, 54
disorder, 13, 93
displacement, 169
dissatisfaction, 70, 71
distress, 183, 186
distribution, 62
disturbance, 168
diversity, 5, 29, 46, 53, 54, 56, 65, 74, 75, 77, 79, 80, 84, 86, 87, 90, 91, 98, 103, 106, 135, 164, 167, 179, 180, 200, 209, 210, 213–217, 220–222
divide, 200
division, 214
doctor, 117
dosage, 122, 130, 135
dose, 126, 153
doubt, 72, 90
drawing, 183
drip, 168
drive, 58
dryness, 150
duration, 122, 130, 135, 153

East Asia, 59
eat, 164
eating, 2, 6, 34, 35, 39, 70, 74–79, 164, 174, 179, 180, 207
echo, 91, 92, 198
economy, 168

edamame, 140
education, 7, 56, 69, 71, 72, 77, 95, 171, 189, 210, 221
effect, 5, 57–60, 62, 64, 90–92, 118, 120, 122–126, 131, 133, 134, 140, 142, 144, 149, 153, 154, 196, 202, 204, 209
effectiveness, 54, 63, 117, 151, 153
effort, 63, 99, 188, 208, 210, 211
elasticity, 120, 202
element, 215
elevator, 207
elimination, 174
embarrassment, 188
emergence, 2, 3, 84
empathy, 2–4, 6, 7, 17, 18, 20, 21, 53, 67, 69, 73, 74, 84, 86, 91, 92, 97, 98, 103, 104, 106, 120, 187–189, 197, 199, 200, 206, 208–211, 214, 215, 217, 221, 222
emphasis, 3, 78, 85, 86, 96, 97
employee, 16, 86
empowerment, 75, 91, 92
encourage, 7, 77, 79, 80, 94, 105, 180, 189, 210, 214
encouragement, 103
end, 133, 204
endothelium, 120
endurance, 12
enemy, 174
energy, 12, 25–27, 30, 31, 36, 53, 76, 79, 111, 112, 158, 160, 164, 174, 179, 201, 207, 209
engagement, 24, 56, 106, 210, 215
enhance, 11, 18, 20, 21, 23, 29, 35, 46, 53, 55, 56, 61, 66, 79,

99, 106, 109, 120, 127, 128, 131, 134, 161, 169, 182, 184, 191, 202, 209, 212–214, 221
enjoyment, 176, 179
entitlement, 197, 198
entrepreneurship, 97
environment, 3, 16, 21, 23–25, 38, 65, 69, 73–75, 77, 79, 80, 86, 91, 92, 94, 95, 100, 102–104, 106, 161, 167, 169, 171, 187, 189, 206, 208, 210, 211, 213, 214, 217, 220
enzyme, 28, 60
equality, 75
equity, 220
erosion, 168
establishment, 102
esteem, 13, 72, 90, 185
estrogen, 1, 2, 4, 5, 57–60, 63, 64, 66, 67, 71, 116, 131, 133–136, 139, 148–151, 153, 154, 195, 197, 202–204
ethnicity, 139, 214, 217
evaluation, 88, 141, 173
evidence, 4, 6, 30, 32, 39, 40, 42, 45, 53, 55, 56, 60, 61, 63–65, 93, 122, 123, 132, 135, 137, 138, 140–142, 144, 148, 150, 151, 153–155, 171–175, 180, 183, 186, 195, 197, 205, 212
exaggeration, 172
examination, 141
example, 24, 35, 37, 49, 54, 55, 73, 76, 87, 101, 117, 124, 127, 128, 141, 149, 151, 158, 161, 164, 172, 174, 188, 189, 205, 211
exchange, 211
exclusion, 6, 188
excretion, 116, 118, 124
exercise, 12, 60, 61, 63, 74, 78, 92, 94, 103, 131, 132, 135, 172, 178, 179, 205, 207, 209, 221
existence, 206
expectation, 68
expenditure, 26, 31
experience, 19–21, 54, 70, 133, 135, 166, 186, 205, 211
expert, 88, 212
expertise, 171
exploration, 6, 7, 21
explore, 1, 4, 6, 9, 12, 14, 19, 21, 25, 30, 33, 36, 46, 49, 53, 54, 61–63, 65, 67, 68, 70, 75, 78, 79, 84, 87, 93, 94, 96, 102, 105, 106, 108, 111, 114, 115, 118, 121, 126, 128, 133, 138, 140, 145, 148, 153, 157–159, 161, 167, 173, 174, 176, 181, 184, 185, 190, 197, 200, 202, 203, 211, 214, 217
exposure, 3, 30, 54, 82, 85, 88, 90–92, 105, 210, 212, 215, 221
expression, 3, 64, 65, 68, 70, 90, 92, 149, 183–185, 212
eye, 210, 211

face, 2, 3, 18, 20, 74, 78, 80, 88, 92, 94, 101–103, 187, 190, 198, 208, 212

fact, 2, 5, 26, 35, 57, 59, 62, 64, 96, 112, 127, 150, 154, 155, 174, 175, 195, 196, 202, 204, 212
factor, 33, 84, 98, 100, 118, 119, 124, 142, 202
faculty, 95
fad, 171, 174, 180
failure, 84, 85, 188
fair, 168–170, 198, 215, 216
fairness, 197
family, 22, 24, 79, 94, 98, 139, 143, 208
farming, 168, 169
fat, 26–29, 31, 34, 36, 160, 174
fatty, 26, 29, 33, 36, 76, 112, 119
fear, 2, 17, 58, 78, 84, 85, 90, 92, 102, 188, 210, 221
feature, 90
feedback, 90, 164, 213, 214
feeling, 25
femininity, 4, 63–65, 71–73, 75, 76, 196, 197
feminization, 60, 71, 153, 154
feminizing, 5, 58, 64, 195, 204
fertility, 154, 204
fiber, 1, 25, 33, 34, 36, 37, 116, 119, 200, 201, 203, 204
fiction, 35, 175
field, 40, 120, 148
finding, 17, 19, 77, 101, 161, 162, 164, 200
fish, 25, 26, 29, 33, 35, 36, 38, 165
fitness, 10, 61, 63, 64, 79, 88, 205, 207, 208
fix, 175
flexibility, 12, 49, 99, 125
flow, 119, 120, 123
fluid, 28, 73

focus, 34, 42, 53, 56, 71, 72, 79, 85, 86, 88, 103, 144, 164, 183, 191, 207, 211–213
folate, 76, 201
food, 2, 6, 7, 26, 30–35, 37–40, 55, 65, 74–78, 127, 141, 148, 154, 157, 161, 163, 164, 167, 169, 170, 173–180, 203, 205, 207
footprint, 38, 167, 168
force, 90, 92
form, 4, 13, 18, 21, 84, 89, 126, 142, 149, 212
formation, 26, 119, 125, 129, 131, 132, 134, 139, 145, 202
Foster, 171
foster, 2, 3, 5–7, 17, 46, 53, 55, 56, 65, 71, 74, 83, 91, 95, 97–99, 103, 104, 106, 135, 169, 170, 176, 179, 189, 197, 208, 210, 213, 216, 217, 221
foundation, 97, 107
fracture, 131
fragility, 3, 4, 84–86, 131
framework, 19, 32, 48
frequency, 31, 67, 134, 151, 204
fruit, 25
frying, 30
fuel, 25, 207
fulfillment, 19, 20, 192, 198
fullness, 25, 77, 164, 175, 207
function, 9, 25, 26, 28–30, 36, 66, 112, 114, 118, 120, 124, 125, 153, 154, 160, 179, 201, 202, 209
functionality, 70
functioning, 27–29, 36, 111, 186, 207

funding, 95, 175
future, 54, 84, 89, 106, 161, 170, 206

gain, 6, 26, 31, 33, 50, 72, 90, 164, 171, 174, 213
gap, 98
gardening, 21, 209
gas, 168
gender, 64, 65, 68–70, 73–77, 96, 122, 196, 214, 217, 221
genderqueer, 75
gene, 149
generalization, 96
generation, 3, 6, 83–88, 93, 95–98, 102, 197–200
genetic, 13, 33, 136, 139, 143
genistein, 59, 60, 116, 118, 121, 133, 134, 136, 149
geography, 55
gland, 138, 139, 196
glass, 128
globe, 164
glucose, 25, 111
gluten, 174
goal, 6, 30, 103, 198
good, 13, 15, 17, 30, 32, 35, 54, 62, 91, 112, 127, 158, 181, 182, 191, 192, 201, 208
government, 175
grain, 29, 37, 178
gratification, 197
gratitude, 72, 191, 192
greenhouse, 168
grocery, 79
ground, 104, 200, 205
group, 2, 3, 6, 81, 98, 102, 105, 118, 133, 134, 148, 149, 205, 208, 214

growth, 3, 4, 7, 22, 25, 28, 36, 46, 53, 58, 61–64, 69, 71, 72, 75, 76, 83, 86, 91, 92, 95, 97, 98, 101, 103, 105–109, 112, 120, 136, 139, 143, 145, 153, 154, 188, 189, 203, 205, 212–214, 216, 217, 220–222
guest, 105
guidance, 7, 26, 31, 75, 88, 93, 99, 125, 141, 142, 150, 179, 180, 186
guide, 30, 43, 46, 169, 170, 173
guilt, 188
gut, 126, 141, 149, 150
gym, 72

habit, 207
habitat, 168
hair, 148
hand, 25, 26, 33, 73, 87, 111, 126, 149, 151, 209, 213, 214
happiness, 17, 22, 198, 206, 209
harassment, 85, 92, 216
harmony, 46, 209
healing, 43, 44, 46, 53–56
health, 1–3, 5–7, 9–33, 35, 36, 38–40, 43, 45–49, 51, 53–59, 61, 63–68, 71–80, 82–89, 91–95, 97, 98, 100–103, 111–116, 118–132, 134, 135, 138–142, 145, 148, 150, 153–155, 157–159, 161, 163, 164, 167, 169–171, 174–176, 180–192, 195–198, 200–211
healthcare, 13, 15, 26, 40, 42, 43, 45, 46, 49, 50, 53–56, 79, 82,

86–89, 101, 113, 117, 118, 123, 125, 135, 138, 141, 142, 150, 153, 179, 188
healthiness, 176
heart, 26, 31, 33, 38, 65, 66, 76, 112, 117–121, 123–125, 164, 174, 196, 201, 202
heat, 30, 134
helicopter, 84
help, 3, 14, 18, 19, 21, 25, 26, 28, 30, 32–36, 39, 57, 58, 60, 64–67, 71–76, 78, 79, 85, 91–95, 97, 99, 100, 102, 103, 105–107, 111, 112, 116–120, 122, 126, 129, 133, 135, 139, 145, 150–152, 163, 168, 172–175, 179, 180, 185, 186, 188–191, 196, 199, 201–205, 208, 210, 212, 213, 215, 216
heritage, 74, 167
hike, 209
hiring, 216
history, 135, 139, 141, 143
home, 24, 87
honey, 25
hope, 7
hormone, 1, 2, 4, 5, 28, 57–59, 61, 67, 71, 131, 135, 136, 139, 149, 153, 195, 204
host, 208
hostility, 188
hunger, 34, 77, 164, 175, 207
hydration, 32
hygiene, 208
hypersensitivity, 96
hypertension, 119, 121–125
hypertrophy, 61

idea, 2, 4, 58, 78
ideal, 36, 76
identity, 64, 65, 74, 75, 77, 92, 164, 189, 196
illness, 50, 54–56
illusion, 91
image, 70–72, 74–78, 90
imbalance, 20, 54, 117, 133, 158
immigrant, 87
immigration, 199
impact, 5, 6, 17, 19, 20, 22, 24, 33, 38, 46, 54–56, 58–62, 64, 65, 67, 69, 71, 72, 78, 85, 87, 89–91, 100, 101, 116, 117, 122, 124–128, 130, 133–135, 138, 148–150, 153, 154, 159, 161, 167–170, 180, 189, 190, 195, 197, 199, 201–204, 206, 207, 215, 220, 222
implement, 95
importance, 6, 9, 12, 16, 19, 30, 31, 36, 45, 50, 53–55, 61, 65, 70, 72, 76–79, 88, 91, 92, 94, 96, 97, 103, 117, 141, 144, 159, 169, 171, 172, 188, 199, 205, 210, 214, 217, 220
improvement, 108, 120, 213, 216, 221
in, 1–7, 9–11, 13, 16–22, 24–41, 43, 46–48, 51–82, 84–107, 111, 112, 114–143, 145, 147–155, 157–161, 164–169, 171–177, 179–181, 183–186, 188–190, 192, 195–217, 220–222
inadequacy, 85

incidence, 140
inclusion, 65, 77, 117, 213–215
inclusivity, 3, 7, 17, 46, 53, 54, 74, 75, 77, 86, 97, 98, 103, 106, 120, 135, 197, 200, 209, 214, 216–222
income, 101
incorporating, 2, 6, 11, 27, 32, 45, 46, 56, 67, 74, 109, 112, 117–120, 122, 124, 127, 128, 130, 131, 144, 145, 147, 148, 152, 155, 157–160, 171, 173, 182, 184, 190, 196, 200, 203, 204, 206, 207, 209, 213
increase, 18, 22, 26, 29, 34, 39, 57, 61, 63, 64, 66, 95, 112, 116, 119, 125–127, 136, 149, 195, 197, 205
independence, 73
indicator, 90, 121
individual, 14, 19, 21, 39, 46, 48, 49, 65, 67, 69, 74, 75, 77, 91, 93, 95, 99, 122, 130, 135, 138, 141, 150, 153, 163, 172, 180, 184, 187, 189, 196, 199, 206, 220, 221
individuality, 72, 81, 90, 92
indulgence, 31
industry, 168
inequality, 214, 216
infant, 76
inflammation, 26, 112, 119, 139, 201–203
influence, 5, 16, 24, 33, 54, 55, 60, 66, 69, 72, 74–78, 86, 89, 99, 116, 117, 126, 130, 132, 135, 140, 141, 149, 153, 210, 215

information, 6, 30, 35, 39, 78, 79, 82, 88–91, 94, 102, 105, 133, 135, 141, 153, 169, 171–176, 180, 204, 205, 212, 220
ingredient, 178, 179
injustice, 96
input, 213
insecurity, 84, 198
insight, 164
insomnia, 16, 134
inspiration, 20, 37, 158
instance, 28, 34, 55, 60, 76, 87, 124, 126–128, 151, 199
insurance, 53, 95
intake, 25–27, 29–31, 33–37, 57, 58, 61–63, 67, 76, 112, 116, 117, 119, 121–124, 127, 132, 134, 135, 140, 149, 151, 154, 157–159, 161, 163, 164
integration, 45, 46, 50, 53, 205
integrity, 28
intelligence, 67–70, 102, 103
intensity, 134, 207
interaction, 134
interconnectedness, 20, 45, 46, 181, 205, 206
interest, 136, 142, 151, 200
internet, 85, 86, 88
interplay, 59, 60
interpreting, 56, 141, 179
interrupting, 211
intersection, 69, 75, 77
intersectionality, 188
intervention, 59, 135
intestine, 126
introduction, 173
introspection, 216

iodine, 28
iron, 28, 29, 76, 201
irrigation, 168
irritability, 16, 134
isoflavone, 59, 120, 122, 125, 130, 134, 149, 154
isolation, 25, 94, 188
issue, 3, 70, 86, 121, 148

Japan, 60, 119
job, 16, 84, 198
jogging, 207
journal, 151
journaling, 94, 213
journey, 19, 21, 39, 54, 72, 106, 108, 109, 153, 167, 184, 211, 220–222
joy, 20, 72, 94
judgment, 65, 77, 78, 90, 92, 102, 188, 210, 221
justice, 96, 197, 198, 220, 222
justification, 214

key, 9, 13, 14, 28, 30, 36, 43, 46, 50, 58, 63, 65, 68, 74, 84, 86, 88, 91, 102, 116, 118, 120, 121, 123, 132, 133, 135, 140, 145, 155, 159, 161, 165, 167, 169, 174–176, 182, 183, 188, 190, 204, 211, 215, 220, 221
kindness, 20, 21, 92
kitchen, 37
knowledge, 7, 37, 55, 79, 86, 120, 138, 169, 171, 175, 178, 213, 216

label, 2, 4, 68, 70, 96, 177, 195, 198
labeling, 4, 68, 189
labor, 55, 168–170

lack, 3–5, 53, 57, 85, 91, 96, 102, 121, 174, 188, 198, 205
lactation, 76
land, 167–169
landscape, 53, 84, 86
language, 4, 56, 189, 212
learning, 22, 83, 100, 103, 108, 171–173, 179, 180, 211–214, 221
legume, 1, 59
level, 21, 28, 39, 99, 106, 163, 181, 217
libido, 59
life, 9, 11, 13, 16–20, 22, 24, 25, 33, 35, 40, 55, 66, 70, 84, 85, 88, 90, 92, 94, 95, 99, 100, 109, 131–135, 182, 185, 186, 192, 197, 199, 202–204, 208, 209, 221
lifestyle, 11, 27, 33, 49, 53, 55, 60, 61, 67, 79, 80, 84, 94, 103, 107, 117, 118, 120, 123, 125, 127, 129, 131, 132, 135, 138–140, 142, 143, 145, 148, 164, 175, 179, 206–209
light, 1, 61, 84, 96, 150, 195
like, 2, 13, 25, 26, 28–30, 32, 36–38, 70, 72, 73, 76, 87, 90, 93, 114, 116, 126–128, 132, 134, 135, 149, 158, 164, 165, 173, 174, 179, 180, 190, 199, 202
limit, 26, 73, 159, 174, 205, 207, 214
Linda Elder, 173
lining, 120, 143
link, 78, 142, 203
lipid, 201
list, 178

Index

listen, 34, 105, 164, 175, 211
listener, 208
listening, 56, 92, 98, 104, 106, 189, 210, 211, 214
literacy, 91, 216
literature, 62, 67, 214
liver, 27, 116, 124, 174
living, 13, 84, 131, 189
loneliness, 92
longevity, 12, 22, 38, 165, 208
look, 11, 88, 114, 161, 200
loss, 26, 30, 32, 131, 134, 169, 172, 174
love, 17, 20
low, 31, 32, 34, 36, 38, 66, 76, 90, 112, 131

macronutrient, 12, 25, 36, 74, 111–113, 158, 159, 161, 163, 164, 179
magnesium, 28, 29, 201
mainstream, 1
maintenance, 25, 36, 58, 112, 154
majority, 58
making, 3, 11, 24, 30, 33–36, 56, 76, 78, 111, 112, 117, 121, 135, 141, 167, 168, 170, 172, 175, 176, 179, 188, 196, 204, 206
male, 2, 58, 71, 75, 78, 153–155, 195, 204
man, 1, 72, 80
management, 12, 34, 45, 68, 95, 103, 117–119, 121–123, 125, 135–137, 153, 208
manganese, 28
manner, 2, 4, 17, 81, 102, 171, 185, 211
marginalization, 188

marker, 124
market, 84, 198
marketing, 35, 76–78
masculinity, 1, 2, 4, 6, 64, 65, 68, 70, 72–76, 78, 79, 155, 195–197
mass, 5, 58, 61–64, 71, 76, 112, 131, 196, 197, 201, 207
matter, 171
meal, 39, 79, 163, 179, 180
mean, 127
meaning, 19–21, 112, 200
means, 69, 73, 74, 79, 80, 209, 211
measure, 120
meat, 25, 26, 73, 78
mechanism, 60, 119, 139
media, 1, 3–6, 79, 85, 86, 88–92, 94, 105, 171, 172, 174, 189, 199, 210, 216, 217
medication, 187
medicine, 6, 33, 40–47, 50–56, 87
meditation, 19–21, 88, 103, 182, 208, 221
Mediterranean, 35, 37, 38, 161, 164
memory, 29
men, 1, 2, 4, 5, 57–60, 62, 64, 65, 67, 68, 70–74, 76, 78–80, 131, 138, 140, 148, 153–155, 195–197, 203, 204
menopause, 58, 67, 76, 131, 133–135, 148, 151–153, 204
menstruation, 76
message, 211
meta, 58, 64, 119, 122, 124, 125, 154
metabolism, 116, 141, 149
method, 105, 179, 180
microbiota, 141, 149, 150

micronutrient, 29, 30, 36
milk, 1, 37, 57, 59, 112, 117, 127, 128, 140, 148, 201
millennial, 3
mind, 20, 21, 46, 50, 53, 54, 152, 166, 167, 177, 181, 197, 221
mindedness, 2, 6, 53, 212, 214, 221
mindful, 26, 31, 34, 77, 148, 159, 164, 179, 207
mindfulness, 7, 19–21, 49, 72, 88, 94, 103, 109, 164, 181, 182, 184, 190–192, 209, 221
mindset, 6, 18, 35, 75, 101, 107, 109, 174, 191, 204, 205, 210, 216
mineral, 28, 64, 66, 125, 126, 128–130, 132, 134, 202
miracle, 175
misconception, 1, 3, 5, 59, 62–64, 71, 96, 173, 195, 202
misinformation, 2, 5, 171, 174, 206, 212, 220
misinterpretation, 174
miso, 127, 165
mix, 26, 27, 160
moderation, 31, 58, 175
modulation, 60
molecule, 120
molybdenum, 28
moment, 167, 182, 190
monitoring, 117
monotony, 39
mood, 29, 30, 59, 133–135, 150, 202, 204, 209
morphology, 154
mortality, 35, 137
motility, 154

movement, 1
muscle, 5, 28, 58, 61–64, 71, 72, 76, 112, 153–155, 164, 196, 197, 201, 207
muscularity, 74
music, 20, 183
myth, 57, 58, 174, 195, 196

narrowing, 124
native, 59
nature, 5, 19–21, 91, 205, 209, 220
need, 3, 7, 17, 22, 36, 54–56, 79, 81, 88, 90, 93, 97, 102, 141, 161, 179, 189, 200, 210
nerve, 28, 201
network, 22, 94
news, 105
night, 58, 67, 133–135, 150, 202, 204, 207, 208
nitric, 120, 121
noise, 38
note, 4, 19, 28, 32, 58, 59, 64, 67, 69, 75, 87, 112, 116, 117, 120, 125, 126, 132, 135, 140, 142, 147, 149, 151, 154, 198
notice, 135, 192
notion, 68, 71, 79
number, 90
nurture, 164, 181, 184, 207
nutrient, 2, 25, 26, 29–31, 33–35, 37, 67, 73, 74, 76, 77, 79, 80, 113, 117, 123, 127, 129, 155, 157–159, 174, 175, 179, 180, 205, 207
nutrition, 2, 6, 7, 27, 30, 35–40, 58, 65, 67, 77–79, 127, 131, 141, 142, 150, 155, 164, 167, 171–173, 175, 176,

179, 180, 200, 204, 207, 211
obesity, 31, 33, 34, 121, 165
observation, 40, 42, 140
occurrence, 33
off, 28, 175
offensive, 85
offer, 37, 67, 85, 92–94, 112, 135, 159, 160, 173, 180, 183, 190, 208
oil, 29, 35, 38, 161, 164, 174
olive, 29, 35, 38, 161, 164, 174
one, 2, 6, 19, 21, 39, 61, 68, 69, 73, 98, 102, 105, 107, 118, 127, 135, 136, 138, 163, 172, 175, 182, 196, 199, 203, 205, 210, 214, 220
onset, 9, 100
openness, 85, 205
opportunity, 98, 206, 213
optimism, 99
option, 111, 112, 159, 201
order, 7, 25, 30, 33, 36, 79, 102, 104, 107, 111, 197, 206, 212, 213
orientation, 214, 217
osteoporosis, 28, 58, 59, 66, 76, 125, 128, 131, 132, 134, 202
other, 18, 19, 25, 26, 32–34, 37, 63, 66, 67, 70, 73, 75, 79, 87, 103, 104, 106, 111, 115–121, 125–127, 131, 132, 135, 139, 141–145, 147–149, 151, 153, 155, 157–159, 161, 172, 174, 185, 187, 196, 199, 204, 205, 209, 214, 216, 217
outlook, 84, 185

Overcooking, 30
overeating, 34, 37, 39
overinvolvement, 84
overprotection, 84
Overreliance, 157
overreliance, 42, 157–159
oversimplification, 97
overview, 175
oxide, 120, 121

pain, 49
painting, 183
palate, 160
pandemic, 101
pantry, 38
parenting, 3, 84, 86
park, 209
part, 1, 2, 19, 58, 65, 89, 117, 122, 125, 128, 131, 132, 135, 137, 138, 140, 142, 144, 147, 150, 159, 161, 199, 204, 209, 210, 221
participation, 104
pasta, 29
path, 40
pathway, 139
patient, 45, 46, 53, 55, 56
pattern, 35, 74, 164
peer, 24, 95, 171, 173
people, 3, 5, 6, 81, 84, 86, 89–92, 98, 101, 105, 174, 188, 203, 206, 212, 220
peptide, 122
percentage, 76
perception, 4, 70, 76, 79, 81, 85, 86, 89, 92, 97, 186, 189, 197–199
perfection, 90, 91

performance, 16, 60, 61, 63, 78, 79, 112
period, 87
perpetuate, 2, 4, 5, 73, 78, 95, 188, 214, 216
perpetuation, 90
perseverance, 198
person, 2, 12, 13, 19, 21, 45, 46, 49, 50, 53, 81, 93, 104, 106, 175, 181, 189, 210, 213
personality, 99
perspective, 58, 60, 155, 164, 184, 204–206, 210–213
phase, 133, 135, 150
phenomenon, 3–6, 81, 83–86
philosophy, 205
phone, 208
phosphorus, 28, 201
photo, 90
phrase, 81
physique, 61, 72
phytate, 126
phytochemical, 147, 148
phytoestrogen, 64, 116, 136
picture, 49, 92
place, 78, 90, 97
placebo, 120, 122, 134
plan, 7, 46, 49, 172, 180
planet, 161, 170, 180, 206
planning, 39, 79, 163, 179, 180, 207
plant, 1, 4, 5, 25, 26, 34–38, 57, 58, 63–67, 69, 71, 77, 112, 116, 121, 124, 126–129, 135, 136, 139–141, 144, 147, 150, 153, 155, 157–161, 164, 196, 200–202, 204
plaque, 123–125, 202
plate, 179, 180

platform, 3, 80, 90, 91, 189, 199, 213
play, 13, 17, 26, 28, 32, 33, 36, 48, 61, 73, 74, 76, 82, 86, 87, 94, 99, 100, 103, 112, 114, 117, 119, 121, 123, 125, 128, 131, 135, 139, 169, 174, 179, 201, 203, 209, 214, 215
playing, 30, 102, 210
pleasure, 77
plenty, 157, 179, 207
point, 87, 141
policy, 95, 222
popularity, 1, 4, 52, 53, 70, 81, 90, 96, 174, 195
population, 149
portion, 26, 31, 32, 34, 37, 164, 175, 179
portrayal, 189, 199
positivity, 71, 72, 74, 77
post, 88, 90
posture, 49
potassium, 28, 119, 201
potency, 149, 154
potential, 6, 45, 50, 53, 56, 58, 59, 61, 63, 66, 67, 77, 98, 106, 109, 116, 118, 120, 121, 124, 127–140, 142–146, 148, 150, 151, 153–155, 188, 203–205, 216, 219
poultry, 25, 35, 36
power, 19, 30, 40, 54, 101, 175, 189, 206
powerhouse, 200
practice, 19, 40, 42, 46, 51, 53, 69, 99, 104, 107, 164, 172, 173, 179, 190, 207, 211, 213, 214, 217, 221
prayer, 20

Index 241

precision, 168, 169
predisposition, 33
pregnancy, 76
prehypertension, 122
prejudice, 7, 17, 53, 70, 120, 214–217, 220–222
prepping, 39, 180
presence, 28, 29, 54, 57, 60, 119, 134, 153, 197, 202
present, 57, 60, 85, 88, 90, 92, 114, 124–126, 142, 149, 164, 172, 173, 182, 190, 192, 201, 209–211
pressure, 20, 31, 34, 66, 70, 72–74, 76, 84, 92, 103, 119–125, 196, 201, 202
prevalence, 3, 84
preventing, 32, 33, 35, 55, 59, 60, 118, 120, 122, 124, 125, 128, 138, 143, 145, 202
prevention, 29, 48, 53, 55, 67, 88, 120, 125, 127, 132, 136–138, 140, 142, 145, 147, 148, 159, 197, 203
print, 88
priority, 184
problem, 85, 99, 100, 103, 172
process, 11, 41, 61, 109, 128, 131, 139, 150, 171, 173, 185, 204, 210, 216, 221
processing, 126, 168
produce, 29, 128
product, 176
production, 28–30, 38, 59, 112, 116, 120–122, 124, 133, 161, 167–169, 201
productivity, 16
profession, 101
professional, 19, 26, 93, 103, 113, 117, 118, 150, 153, 180, 186, 188
profile, 6, 111, 112, 116–118, 141, 145, 158
progesterone, 133, 150
program, 10, 63
progress, 97, 98, 197, 220
progression, 140
prominence, 199
promise, 53, 135, 147, 174
promotion, 55, 216
propensity, 84
prosperity, 87, 88
prostate, 58, 67, 138–142, 154, 155, 195–197, 203
protease, 143
protection, 28, 148, 155
protein, 1, 4, 5, 25–27, 29, 36, 37, 57–59, 61–67, 69, 71–73, 76, 79, 112, 114, 116, 118, 119, 121, 122, 124, 126, 129, 132, 141, 149, 154, 155, 157–161, 179, 196, 197, 200, 201, 204
provider, 55, 135
pseudoscience, 171, 172, 206
public, 131, 174, 189
purpose, 6, 19–21, 221
pursuit, 61, 181, 198

quality, 9, 12, 18, 21, 34–39, 53, 58, 64, 71, 112, 131–134, 138, 144, 154, 155, 175, 179, 186, 196, 204, 207, 208, 212–214
quest, 90
question, 4, 77, 91, 171, 172, 212
questioning, 171
quinoa, 29, 37, 158, 161

quo, 97

race, 96, 214, 217, 221
rainbow, 36
rainwater, 168
range, 1, 13, 18, 28–32, 34, 36, 38, 43, 45, 47, 51, 55, 58, 63, 64, 67, 77, 79, 89, 91, 93, 113, 127, 128, 133, 141, 150, 153, 157–161, 179, 205
rapport, 46
ratio, 74
reading, 49, 175, 212
reality, 69–71, 197, 198
realm, 46, 92, 206
reason, 57, 174
reasoning, 105, 171, 172
recognition, 45, 85
recovery, 5, 61, 72, 112, 189, 196
rectum, 142, 143
recurrence, 137, 140
reduction, 88, 95, 122, 123, 125, 134, 151, 182
reductionism, 42
reflection, 21, 69, 99, 103, 105, 108, 164, 172, 197, 199, 213, 215, 216, 221
regimen, 205
region, 142
regulation, 17, 29, 30, 53, 57, 59, 61, 67, 85, 99, 119, 121, 148, 182, 185, 188, 202
reinforcement, 173
relation, 97, 142, 171
relationship, 26, 39, 57, 59, 61, 63, 65, 67–70, 75, 77, 120, 121, 126, 128, 129, 137, 138, 140, 142, 148, 153, 196, 203
relaxation, 91, 94
release, 111, 112
reliability, 39, 171, 205, 212, 220
reliance, 85, 90, 92
relief, 67
religion, 221
reluctance, 90
remedy, 151
remodeling, 128, 131, 132
repair, 25, 28, 36, 61, 76, 112
replacement, 135
representation, 216
reputation, 174
research, 2, 5–7, 30, 33, 39, 57–59, 62, 63, 67, 99, 118, 120–122, 124, 130, 134, 136–142, 145, 149, 150, 154, 171–173, 175, 196, 203, 204, 206
resilience, 2–5, 13, 17, 18, 81, 83–86, 91, 92, 96, 98–103, 106, 185, 189, 190, 192, 198
resistance, 61, 63
resorption, 131, 132, 134
resource, 168, 206
respect, 46, 55, 56, 71, 75, 83, 92, 106, 167, 180
response, 17, 117, 135, 185, 211
responsibility, 15, 97, 216, 217, 220, 222
rest, 12, 91, 94
restriction, 174
restructuring, 186, 188
result, 4, 54, 85, 90, 157, 188, 205, 206
retention, 171

review, 59, 62, 64, 151, 154
rice, 29, 37, 38, 158, 165
Richard Paul, 173
richness, 220
ridicule, 102
right, 1, 161, 162, 164
rise, 88
risk, 5, 17, 20, 22, 26, 28, 33–35, 38, 58, 64–67, 76, 101, 111, 112, 118–121, 124, 125, 128, 131, 132, 134, 136–142, 144, 145, 148, 150, 154, 164, 174, 195–197, 201–205, 208
role, 3, 6, 9, 11, 13, 17, 21, 25–28, 32, 33, 36, 48, 53, 54, 57–59, 61, 68, 72, 74, 76, 79, 82, 85–87, 94, 98–100, 102–105, 107, 111, 112, 117, 119–125, 128, 131, 133–136, 138–140, 145, 148, 149, 153, 161, 167, 169, 174, 179, 181, 184, 203, 209, 210, 213–216
root, 42, 50
routine, 172, 182, 191, 192, 207, 209

sadness, 17
sample, 141, 175
Sarah, 16, 117, 127, 128
satiety, 34
satisfaction, 16, 18, 21, 22, 55, 68, 176, 185
sauce, 165
scale, 37, 124, 137, 169, 222
scarcity, 168
scenario, 127, 199
schedule, 208
schizophrenia, 13, 93

school, 210
science, 5, 6, 155
screen, 94
sea, 141, 173
seafood, 38
section, 1, 5, 9, 12, 19, 27, 30, 33, 36, 53, 54, 61, 63, 65, 67, 70, 72, 78, 84, 89, 93, 96, 102, 104, 106, 114, 118, 121, 126, 128, 133, 138, 145, 148, 153, 157, 159, 164, 167, 171, 173, 176, 181, 185, 190, 195, 197, 200, 204, 209, 211, 214, 217, 220
seeking, 18, 20, 54, 85, 88, 93, 94, 101, 104, 105, 112, 148, 180, 188, 189, 199, 212, 213, 215, 220, 221
seitan, 161
selenium, 28, 29
self, 3, 7, 13, 19, 21, 22, 67, 69–72, 74, 75, 77, 85, 89–92, 94, 96, 98, 101, 103, 105–109, 181–186, 190–192, 197, 205, 208, 213, 215, 216, 221
semen, 138, 154
sensationalism, 189
sense, 19–23, 25, 75, 84, 92, 94, 95, 97, 99, 104, 182, 184, 190, 192, 197, 198, 209, 215, 221, 222
sensitivity, 3–5, 56, 73, 85, 86, 102, 174, 197, 216
series, 116
serotonin, 134
service, 208, 222
set, 30, 69

setting, 24, 91, 94, 103, 104, 109, 221
severity, 67, 100, 134, 151, 204
sex, 4, 39, 58, 73, 75, 153, 163, 195
sexism, 196
sexuality, 221
shame, 188
shape, 56, 75, 77
shift, 79, 84–86, 88, 191
shopping, 79
show, 18, 117, 122, 130, 135, 147, 208
sign, 68, 188
significance, 10, 20, 150, 164, 204
situation, 99
size, 39, 61, 73, 77, 141, 163, 175, 196
skill, 69, 98, 101, 102, 171, 179, 210, 212
skin, 26, 148
sleep, 94, 103, 133–135, 150, 176, 207–209
smoothness, 125
snowflake, 2–6, 81, 84–86, 93, 95–98, 197–200
society, 2–7, 13, 17, 33, 54, 65, 70–73, 75, 78, 84, 86, 95, 96, 98, 101, 104–106, 167, 169, 173, 188, 189, 197, 199, 200, 205, 209–211, 216, 217, 220–222
sodium, 28, 31, 33, 34, 121, 123, 180
soil, 168, 169
solubility, 126
solution, 49, 117, 125, 140
solving, 85, 99, 100, 103
soul, 221

source, 1, 4, 20, 25, 26, 36, 37, 59, 62, 65, 69, 71, 111, 112, 114, 116, 121, 124, 126, 129, 136, 157–159, 164, 171, 174, 200, 201, 204
sourcing, 168
Soy, 126, 200
soy, 1, 2, 4–7, 37, 46, 57–72, 111–145, 148–155, 157–159, 161, 165, 167–170, 195–197, 200–205
soybean, 168
space, 7, 74, 104, 185, 211, 220
speaker, 211
specific, 3, 10, 37, 39, 54, 55, 57, 61, 62, 65, 75, 76, 81, 85, 86, 93, 99, 113, 122, 138, 145, 149, 150, 172, 174, 175, 180, 198, 201, 205, 213
spectrum, 65, 93, 179
speculation, 151
sperm, 58, 154, 204
spirit, 20, 50, 54, 181
spirituality, 19–21
spread, 3, 85, 139, 140, 143, 145, 174
staff, 56, 95
stage, 122, 202
standard, 142
staple, 60, 119, 151
stargazing, 20
starting, 87, 117, 135
state, 9, 182
status, 89, 97, 122, 214
step, 192
stereotype, 3–5, 97, 102, 188, 197–199
stiffness, 120

Index 245

stigma, 5, 17, 93, 95, 187–189
stigmatization, 93, 206
stir, 30
stomach, 126
storytelling, 189, 190
strain, 119, 168
strategy, 78, 105, 120, 132, 168, 179, 215
stream, 85, 90
street, 208
strength, 1, 5, 12, 61, 63, 71–73, 79, 101, 128, 131, 132, 196, 207
stress, 12, 16–18, 20, 22, 28, 49, 68, 88, 92–95, 98, 100–103, 119, 123, 135, 139, 175, 182, 185, 202, 208, 209
stroke, 33, 121, 196
structure, 5, 26, 59, 66, 151, 195, 202
struggle, 84
student, 84, 95, 198
study, 16, 39, 57–59, 64, 72, 95, 119, 120, 122, 124, 129, 130, 132, 134, 137, 141, 149, 151, 154, 172, 175
style, 140
subject, 126, 171
substance, 126, 202
substitute, 49, 112, 133
success, 90, 95, 101, 106
sugar, 25, 32, 34, 111, 112, 164, 178, 201
summary, 2, 58, 60, 118, 135, 138, 154, 206
supplement, 172
supplementation, 71, 120, 122, 125, 129, 130, 135, 149
supply, 139, 140, 168, 169

support, 7, 12, 13, 16–18, 20–22, 26–31, 64, 70, 75, 76, 79, 83–86, 92–95, 98, 99, 101–103, 112, 117, 131, 134, 135, 142, 145, 153, 154, 158, 159, 162, 164, 169, 172, 174, 176, 179, 185, 186, 188, 189, 198, 200, 202, 205, 207–210, 214, 221
surgery, 40, 42
susceptibility, 131
sustainability, 6, 38, 159, 161, 167–170, 180
sustenance, 164
sweating, 134
symptom, 45
synthesis, 5, 28, 29, 61–63, 71, 116, 126, 196
system, 20, 28, 35, 40, 42, 43, 46, 53, 56, 57, 85, 98, 133, 148, 169, 170, 179, 201

table, 25, 83
tapestry, 167
tasking, 88
teaching, 101, 171, 173, 188, 210
technique, 105, 106, 186
technology, 3, 88, 94
television, 88
tempeh, 1, 38, 59, 117, 127, 128, 140, 161
tendency, 105, 214
term, 1–5, 67, 69, 70, 78, 81, 96, 107, 169, 175, 180, 188, 195
testosterone, 2, 5, 6, 58–62, 64, 153, 154, 195–197, 204
the Mediterranean Sea, 164

the United States, 119
therapy, 53, 88, 93, 95, 135, 184, 186, 205, 209, 221
thiamine, 201
thinking, 3, 7, 38, 40, 53, 75, 77, 91, 92, 99, 105, 106, 171–173, 180, 205, 206, 212, 214, 216, 220
thought, 57, 90, 116, 118, 119, 183, 186, 215
tillage, 168
time, 16, 20, 21, 33, 39, 63, 72, 81, 94, 95, 98, 102, 133, 143, 180, 207–209, 213, 221
timing, 62, 153
tissue, 61, 128, 131
tobacco, 148
today, 2, 3, 33, 38, 70, 75, 78, 104, 164, 167, 173, 190, 204, 205, 212, 217, 220
tofu, 1, 29, 36, 38, 57, 59, 112, 117, 127, 140, 148, 161, 201
tokenism, 216
tomorrow, 222
tone, 212
tool, 21, 91, 135, 213
topic, 60, 65, 141, 142, 148, 150, 153, 167, 200
touch, 2
trace, 28
traction, 1, 5
trade, 168–170
training, 56, 61, 63, 95, 102, 103, 207, 215, 216
trait, 3, 98, 197, 198
tranquility, 209
transcendence, 19, 20
transgender, 75
transition, 24, 169

transport, 126
transportation, 38, 168
trauma, 17, 100
treat, 42
treatment, 4, 40, 41, 44–46, 49, 54–56, 97, 138, 140, 147, 187–189, 220
tree, 168
trial, 134
trick, 164
trigger, 97
triglyceride, 66
trust, 46, 55
truth, 212
tumor, 139, 203
turn, 88, 104, 210
turnover, 132
type, 33, 34, 57, 64, 117, 136

uncertainty, 84, 98, 101, 198
understanding, 2–7, 12, 17, 19, 21, 46, 50, 56, 65, 69, 73, 74, 80, 83, 86, 91–93, 95, 97, 98, 103–106, 120, 138, 142, 145, 150, 155, 164, 167, 170, 171, 178, 180, 188, 189, 199, 200, 205, 206, 209–217, 220, 221
unease, 198
uniqueness, 81
unity, 20, 21
universe, 19, 20
unwillingness, 198
up, 25, 84, 87, 88, 90, 96, 117, 141, 172, 178, 190, 208
upbringing, 198
usage, 91, 92, 167, 168
use, 32, 38, 42, 85, 90, 92, 94, 151, 158, 167–169, 179, 199,

211

validate, 185
validation, 22, 81, 90, 92, 199
validity, 98, 171, 172, 205, 212, 220
value, 54, 55, 70, 72, 78, 88, 207, 209, 212, 216
variety, 12, 26, 27, 29, 31, 33, 36–39, 44, 58, 63, 65, 74, 105, 113, 116, 117, 120, 123, 126, 127, 135, 144, 147, 148, 150, 155, 158–161, 175, 176, 179, 198, 204, 207
version, 85, 90
vessel, 66, 202
view, 88, 99, 171, 213
vision, 27
vitality, 73, 78, 135, 201
vitamin, 28, 29, 37, 76, 126, 128, 129, 131, 132
volunteer, 97
volunteering, 20, 208, 222
vulnerability, 3, 85

walk, 209
warning, 92
waste, 38, 180
water, 27, 32, 167, 168
watering, 168
way, 17, 21, 30, 37, 70, 79, 84, 88, 89, 99, 103, 105, 112, 141, 155, 158, 199, 205, 208, 210–212, 221, 222
weakness, 68, 188
wealth, 37, 160, 167
week, 37, 39, 59, 172, 207
weight, 26, 27, 31–34, 123, 141, 163, 172, 174, 202, 207

welfare, 161, 206
well, 3, 5–7, 9–14, 16–22, 24, 26, 27, 29–31, 33, 35, 37–40, 43, 45, 46, 49, 51, 53, 54, 56, 58, 60, 61, 63–65, 68–71, 74, 75, 77, 78, 80, 82–86, 88, 92–96, 98, 99, 101–103, 105, 109, 112–115, 118, 121, 125–128, 130–133, 135, 138, 139, 142, 144, 148, 150, 153, 155, 158, 159, 161, 164, 168, 169, 176, 179–186, 188, 190, 192, 200–211, 214, 220–222
wellbeing, 106, 176
wellness, 6, 7, 33, 46, 48–50, 53–55, 86, 88, 89, 120, 135, 161, 164, 176, 204–206, 211
wheat, 29, 37
whole, 13, 17, 25, 29, 31, 33–39, 46, 49, 50, 53, 59, 74, 77, 118, 123, 125, 141, 158, 160, 161, 164, 174, 175, 178, 179, 188, 206, 207, 217
wildlife, 168
willingness, 6, 46, 53, 221
window, 164
wisdom, 20
woman, 117, 127, 133, 134, 202
wonder, 20, 21
work, 10, 16, 49, 54, 55, 86, 88, 89, 95, 97, 141, 147, 175, 208, 217, 220, 222
working, 16, 28, 46, 101, 168, 217, 221
workplace, 16, 85, 86
world, 6, 7, 21, 38, 43, 49, 60, 91, 96, 97, 141, 160, 164, 167,

170, 172, 190, 204, 209, 220, 222
worldview, 46
worry, 154
worth, 60, 72, 90, 92, 122, 130, 135, 141, 180
writing, 21, 102, 183

Xavier, 72

year, 117, 127
yoga, 19, 49, 88, 208
yogurt, 37, 127

zinc, 28, 29, 201